MONOGRAPH SERIES
UNITED STATES CATHOLIC HISTORICAL SOCIETY

UNITED STATES CATHOLIC HISTORICAL SOCIETY

MONOGRAPH SERIES
XXXIV

THE NEW YORK REVIEW
(1905-1908)

by

The Reverend Michael J. DeVito, Ph.D.

NEW YORK
UNITED STATES CATHOLIC
HISTORICAL SOCIETY
1977

Library of Congress Card Number: 77–75637
ISBN 0–930060–14–8

Office of the Secretary
St. Joseph's Seminary, Dunwoodie, Yonkers, New York 10704

TABLE OF CONTENTS

i

TABLE OF CONTENTS
(continued)

ABBREVIATIONS

AAB   - Archives of Archdiocese of Boston.

AANY - Archives of Archdioces of New York.

AAP   - Archives of Archdiocese of Philadelphia.

ABC   - Archives of Baltimore Cathedral.

ACUA - Archives of Catholic University of America.

ACPF - Archives of Congregation of the Propaganda of the Faith.

ADR   - Archives of Diocese of Rochester.

ASMB - Archives of St. Mary's Seminary, Baltimore.

BM   - British Museum.

BN   - Bibliotheque Nationale.

WFP   - Ward Family Papers.

PREFACE

The New York Review (1905-1908) was a short lived
theological journal published by the professors of St. Joseph's
Seminary, Dunwoodie, New York during the first decade of
this century. It was founded in the peak years of modernism
and silently but mysteriously ceased publication immediately
after the promulgation of Pope Pius X's encyclical Pascendi
Dominici gregis, 1907, which condemned modernism. This
sudden cessation of The Review caused serious repercussions
not only in the life of the American Catholic Church, but
also in the life of the Catholic seminary system in the United
States, and the lives of its scholarly editors. Compared with
American Catholic religious magazines which were previous
to and contemporary with The New York Review, this
publication witnessed to be the first American Catholic
scientific theological journal.

The advances and discoveries made in scientific and
historical research during the last half of the nineteenth century forced religion at the beginning of the twentieth century
to consider new problems and render necessary the restatement of many theological positions. The New York Review
addressed itself specifically to this religious and scientific
condition of the day. But, it did so with an apologetic purpose

by aiming to be a journal of the ancient Faith and modern knowledge. This publication examined in its articles and editorials
the relation that such new sciences as the historico-critical
method, archeology, Assyriology, Egyptology, philology, and
the "New Apologetics" (which was then known as the method of
immanence) had with the Faith, and demonstrated how these
sciences could be reconciled with the ancient faith. The New
York magazine also considered topics such as biblical
inspiration, patrology, Christology, comparative religions,
divorce and the New Testament, and modern philosophy.

Because of this journal's aim to reconcile new knowledge
with Church tradition (and thus endeavor to update theology
and the Church's approach to the world) as well as the theological caliber of its articles and their authors, who were
such eminent and popular scholars of the day as George
Tyrrell, Baron von Hugel, Maude Petre, Joseph Turmel,
and Wilfrid Ward, etc., I consider that a work
along the line of "Principle of Ecclesial Reform according to
The New York Review (1905-1908)" is feasible. I believe that
not only the conclusions of this work will be a
contribution to the field of theology, but the work as
a whole will open up an area of American Catholic thought
which up to now has not been seriously developed: namely, the
American Catholic Church and modernism. My work, I hope,
will also dispel the thesis that the American Church and its

priests in the last decade of the nineteenth century and the first decade of the twentieth century were not intellectually oriented, nor participated in the great theological movements of the day. It will also give us a good idea of the state of American Catholic theology at the turn of the century.

I want to express my deepest gratitude to those members of the theology department at Fordham University, New York, who have assisted me in this work. I am especially grateful to my mentor, Rev. Sabbas J. Kilian, O. F. M. , for the encouragement, confidence, and guidance he afforded me throughout the research and writing of my dissertation. No adequate amount of gratitude can be expressed for all he has taught me during my years at Fordham. Next, I am appreciative of Rev. Gerald Fogarty, S. J. who has taught me the significant value that history has for theology, and who has taken the time to read this dissertation and to offer suggestions. Also, I owe thanks to Professor John Heaney for inspiring me in this endeavor and for reading the manuscript of it.

I wish to thank all those who made archival materials available to me: Msgr. George Tiffany and Rev. Terrence O'Donnell of the Archdiocese of New York. Mrs. Frank Sheed (Maisie Ward), Rev. Robert McNamara of the Diocese of Rochester, Mr. Richard Pachella of Union Theological Seminary, New York, Rev. Edmund Halsey, O. S. B. , of the Archdiocese of Philadelphia, Rev. George Gaffey of Santa Rosa, California,

Mr. Robert Matthews of St. Mary's Seminary, Baltimore and Mr. Alan Seabury of Harvard Divinity School.

I am indebted to Very Reverend Thomas J. Gradilone, president of Cathedral College and my superior, for the enormous amount of support and understanding he gave me during the time that I wrote my dissertation. And finally, I want to thank all my colleagues on the faculty of Cathedral College, especially Revs. James McMahon, Conrad Dietz, and Donald Hendricks, for extending to me help and encouragement throughout this endeavor.

Vol. 1.   JUNE-JULY, 1905.   No. 1.

THE
NEW YORK
REVIEW.

Published Every Two Months.

St. Joseph's Seminary, Yonkers,

A Year: 3 Dollars.   NEW YORK.   Single Copy:
(Foreign: 12s 6d).   50 cts.

Registered at Yonkers Post Office as Second-Class Matter.

CHAPTER I

THE INCEPTION OF THE NEW YORK REVIEW

A new journal is the result of several evolutionary stages. First, it emerges from and because of the conditions of the day. Secondly, the background and character of the founders enable it to be gracefully culled from these conditions, as well as influence the direction, approach, and scope that the journal will take. Finally, the editors, contributors, and benefactors give shape, substance, and support to a journal before it makes its debut to contemporaries and subscribers.

These stages are part of any journal's emergence, and they were very much part of The New York Review's in 1905. A consideration of these different stages comprise the inception of The New York Review.

Conditions of the Day

The conditions of religion and science at the turn of the century were in an acute state of transition from fast-dying medieval institutions to a modern technological world. Medievalism in science and absolute monarchial concepts in government were giving way to modernity and relativity because of the rapid urbanization of society, industrialization, tech-

nological research and innovations, and the emergence of socialism. [1]

In religion, the foundations of time-honored beliefs and institutions were experiencing tremors, if not debacles, because the

scholarship of the last half of the nineteenth century was coming

to fruition. Archeological discoveries in the Middle East, the

evolutionary theories of Charles Darwin, and the historico-

critical method, all shed new light on the understanding of sacred

scripture. From these new discoveries and advances in know-

ledge resulted new and different interpretations of the recorded

data of revelation. [2]

Theologians' regard of philosophy was also changing radi-

cally during this time. In the course of twenty years, from 1879

to 1900, Catholic seminary and university professors moved from

the dusty, rigid scholastic philosophy of the Middle Ages through

---

[1]
    In the last decade of the nineteenth century and the first
decade of the twentieth the American people witnessed the rise
of the city due to the effects of the Industrial Revolution and
enormous numbers of immigrants from central and southern
Europe. They saw mechanical inventions culminate in the motor
car and airplane. And due to these radical changes and innovations, to name a few, in their life they began to look upon their
relation to society as organic, Cf. David W. Noble, The Progressive Mind, 1890-1917, Chicago: Rand McNally and Company,
1970; and Charles H. Cooley, Human Nature and the Social
Order, New York: Charles Scribners and Sons, 1902.

[2]
    Jean Levie, S. J. , The Bible, Word of God in Words of
Men, London: Geoffrey Chapman, 1961, 6.

the creative elastic teaching of Thomism, and in some cases, to

the relative subjectivism of Immanuel Kant. [3] This 180° turn cer-

tainly affected man's reflection of himself, his world, and his god.

At the turn of the century the Roman Catholic Church, spec-

ifically, was also reaping the harvest not only of the times but

also of Pope Leo XIII's overtures to modern knowledge and the

modern world. During his pontificate he evisaged the Church's

mission to be one of making every effort in leading the modern

world back to the Church, and to reconcile the new with the old.

The motto of his reign was perficere vetera novis. [4]

Far from isolating herself from the world, the Church, he

believed, must enter it in a spirit of conquest. Right from the

beginning of his pontificate, therefore, he proposed to accomplish

this mission by re-establishing the Church's influence in the in-

tellectual life, by promoting among the clergy an idea of true

---

[3]
    Pope Leo XIII's encyclical letter Aeterni Patris, August 4,
1879. In this encyclical Leo showed his admiration for and recommendation of the study of St. Thomas Aquinas's philosophy,
Thomism, because it made adequate preparation, he believed,
for approaching the questions prominent at the time. By Aeterni
Patris Leo hoped to lead priests and seminarians to a more
liberal spirit of Catholic theology. Although Thomism was considered the philosophy of the Church, some ecclesiastical thinkers such as Charles Denis, and Marcel Hebert subscribed to
Kantianism.

[4]
    Levie, 40. Cf. also E. Hocedez, S.J., Histoire de la
théologie au XIXe siècle, Vol. III, Le règne de Léon XIII,
Brussels: Edition Universelle, 1947.

culture, and by restoring a high level of ecclesiastical studies.[5]

The means that Leo took to achieve these goals were, first, the recommendation of the revival of Thomism in Catholic seminaries and universities. He considered Christian philosophy "a bridge" for joining together secular concerns and religious beliefs.[6] Secondly, the pope opened the Vatican archives in 1883 to all research workers, both Catholic and non-Catholic, in order to encourage historial studies and their pursuit in the most absolutely candid and critical spirit.[7] Thirdly, he urged the foundation of Catholic universities and the work of faculties of already established universities.[8] The Catholic University of America, the Higher Institute of Philosophy at Louvain, and the permission for Catholics to attend Oxford and Cambridge Universities resulted from this.[9]

---

[5]
Ibid.

[6]
Pope Leo XIII, Aeterni Patris, encyclical on scholastic philosophy, August 4, 1879, printed and translated by Paulist Press, New York.

[7]
Pope Leo XIII's encyclical letter Saepenumero Considerantes, August 18, 1883. Cf. Acta Sanctae Sedis, Vol. XVI, Romae: Typis Polyglottae Officinal S.C. De Propaganda Fide, 1883, pp. 49-57.

[8]
Cf. Leo XIII's encyclical Longinqua Oceani, printed in Documents of American Catholic History, Vol. II, ed. by John Tracy Ellis, Chicago: Regnery Co., 1961, 503.

[9]
Pope Leo XIII's encyclical letter Ad Anglos Regnum Christi,

Many of Leo's encyclicals, expressed the importance for
Catholics to be open to modern knowledge in order to become
leaders in the world. But one, in particular, was most representative of the expressions as well as the spirit of many of Leo's
actions which effected this openness to knowledge. This
encyclical was Longinqua Oceani (1895), and it portrayed the
pope's praise of modern knowledge:

> An education cannot be deemed complete which
> takes no notice of modern sciences. It is obvious
> that in the existing keen competition of talents
> and the widespread and, in itself, noble and
> praiseworthy passion for knowledge, Catholics
> ought to be not followers but leaders. It is
> necessary, therefore, that they should cultivate
> every refinement of learning and zealously
> train their minds to be discovery of truth and
> the investigation, so far as it is possible, of
> the entire domain of nature. This in every age
> has been the desire of the Church. [10]

If Pope Leo was attempting to turn the universal Church
toward modern knowledge and the modern world, some churchmen in the American Church, most specifically, became caught
up with the pope's attempts and opened themselves to the spirit
of the age and of their country. The American episcopacy en-
thusiastically led the clergy and laity into this vibrant participation in the pope's program and the world's movement toward

April 14, 1895. Cf. Acta Sanctae Sedis, XXVII, Romae, 1894-95,
pp. 583-593.

[10]
Ellis, 503.

modernity. Bishop John L. Spalding (1840-1916) of Peoria,
Illinois believed that to have an effective participation, the clergy
must inspire the laity to take their place in modern knowledge
and the modern world. Therefore, he strongly recommended that
the Church abandon the idea that the sole purpose of seminaries
was to impart basic professional skills for the ministry and not
necessarily to inculcate in the young clerics the best of intellectual culture. The eventual upshot of his thinking was the founding
of the Catholic University of America in 1889 which was to provide
the clergy with the opportunity to pass beyond the required skills
for the ordinary exercise of ministry and to develop in them a
fine intellectual culture. [11]

Archbishop John Ireland (1838-1918) of St. Paul, Minnesota
was another proponent of the American Church's participation
in Leo XIII's program for reconciling the Church with the modern
world. In 1889, in a sermon on the occasion of the hundreth
anniversary of the American Hierarchy, he said, "This is an intellectual age, it worships intellect. The age will not take
kindly to religious knowledge separated from secular knowledge". [12] In 1893 on another occasion the Archbishop said, "Men

[11]
Michael V. Gannon, "Before and After Modernism: The
Intellectual Isolation of the American Priest", The Catholic
Priest in the United States, ed. by John Tracy Ellis, Collegeville:
St. John's University Press, 1971, 322.

[12]
"The Mission of Catholics in America", a sermon preached

must be taught that the Church and the age are not hopelessly

separated... I preach the new, the most glorious crusade. Church

and age! Unite them in the name of humanity, in the name of

God".[13] In this crusade many American bishops, notably Cardinal

John Gibbons, Bishop Keane and Denis O'Connell, joined him.[14]

Because of the American Church's incipient interest in matters

intellectual at that time, there naturally arose a number of reli-

gious journals which were an important means of continually

educating the clergy and informing the laity. The theological re-

views were The American Catholic Quarterly Review, published

by the Archdiocese of Philadelphia. It printed articles by such

thinkers as Thomas Shahan, Walter Elliot, C. S. P. and John

Kerby on mostly scripture, evolution, and history. The Catholic

University Bulletin was another of this caliber, but it limited

itself to writers from the faculty of Catholic University and in-

---

on November 10, 1889 in the Cathedral of Baltimore on the occasion of the 100th anniversary of the establishment of the American
hierarchy; published in John Ireland, The Church and Modern
Society, New York: D. H. McBride and Co. 1896, 74.

13
    "The Church and the Age", a sermon preached in the
Cathedral of Baltimore on the occasion of the silver jubilee of
Cardinal Gibbons' episcopal consecration; published in Ibid.,
97.

14
    For an exposition of the events in this crusade by these
American bishops confer Thomas T. McAvoy, The Americanist
Heresy in Roman Catholicism (1895-1900), Notre Dame: Uni-
versity Press, 1963, pp. 1-109.

8

cluded the other branches of knowledge besides theology. The
American Ecclesiastical Review, edited by Rev. Hermann Heuser
of St. Charles Borromeo Seminary, Philadelphia, presented
articles by such advanced thinkers as Alfred Loisy (1857-1940),
George Tyrrell (1861-1909), and Maurice Blondel (1861-1949)
until they fell into the Church's disfavor.[15] Other magazines such
as The Dolphin, The Homiletic and Catechist, The Catholic World,
and the Sacred Heart Messenger were devoted more to literary
and popular cultural tastes.[16] It was not until the emergence of

---

[15]
    Alfred Loisy began to fall into the Church's disfavor in
1893 but Rome put his works on the Index of Forbidden Books in
1903. George Tyrrell was suspended a divinis in 1906 when the
Jesuits expelled him. Maurice Blondel, although his thought
was suspected during the reign of Pope Leo XIII, was never
censured.
    The Ecclesiastical Review, even though it published some
articles by Loisy, Tyrrell and Blondel, was never a scholarly
journal like The New York Review. An examination of this
Philadelphia magazine will immediately strike the examiner
that it was much more pastoral than scientific. It published
such titles as "Protonotaries - Their Rank and Privileleges",
"The Care of Our Churches and Sacristies", "The Training of
the Voice for Public Speaking", and "The Sacred Vessels and
their Appurtenances".
    In the twelve issues for the year 1904 - when Duffy and
Brady were planning the first scientific theological journal in
America - this writer only found two articles in The
Ecclesiastical Review on the par with those of The New York
Review; viz., "The Term 'Immaculate' in the Early Greek
Fathers", and "The Doctrine of the Immaculate Conception and
St. Thomas Aquinas".

[16]
    The Dolphin was a monthly, and the "sister magazine" of
The American Ecclesiastical Review. Geared for educated
Catholics, it began publishing in 1901 and ceased in 1906 due to
lack of funds.
    The Homiletic and Catechist was started in New York in 1901

The New York Review in 1905 that the American Church had its

first scientific theological journal on the par with such European

scholarly journals as Revue du Clergé Français, Revue Biblique,

and Theologische Revue.[17]

The Catholic Church's participation in the apparent liberal

program of Leo XIII, therefore, encouraged scholars and church-

men to hope that it was worth attempting a synthesis of Catholic

theology with modern science and the modern world. However,

these attempts toward syntheses were not without dangers. Some-

times thinkers went beyond syntheses and fell into heresy.

One ideology resulting from these synthesizing attempts was

Americanism. According to Bishop Denis O'Connell (1849-1927),

one of its proponents, it was nothing else than the loyal devotion

---

by John F. Brady who was its first editor. Brady eventually
assumed the post as managing editor of The New York Review.
The Homiletic and Catechist merely presented sermon outlines
for the parochial clergy.
    The Catholic World was a Paulist publication out of New York;
and the Sacred Heart Messenger was put out by New York
Jesuits.

   17
    Revue du Clerge Français began publishing in 1895 in Paris
(Letouzey). This journal was very scholarly, contained many
articles on biblical exegesis, and was concerned with the controversies of the day. It ceased publication in 1921.
    Revue Biblique was another scholarly journal intimately in-
volved in the scientific discoveries of the day and their influence
on the Bible. It was begun in 1892 by M. F. Langrange and
published from Jerusalem.
    Theologische Revue was founded by Professor Diekamp of
Munster in 1902. Like The New York Review, it was a faculty
effort (University of Munster) and extremely scientific.
    The New York Review was similar to these and other Euro-
pean journals in its scholarship and wide range of contributors.

that Catholics in America gave to the principles on which their
government is founded, and the conviction that these principles
afforded favorable opportunities for propagating the glory of God,
the growth of the Church, and the salvation of souls in the United
States. This, however, was one form of Americanism, and the
American bishops supporting it, believed that this was in line with
the thinking of Pope Leo XIII. The other form, according to its
proponent, Rev. Isaac Hecker (1819-1888), not only urged the
compatibility of American political institutions with the Church,
and stressed the adaptation of the Church to modern conditions,
but also advocated individualism and a greater devotion to the Holy
Spirit. This form aimed particularly at winning American
Protestants to Catholicism.[18]

When Hecker's biography was translated into French, the
editors aimed to adopt it to the French audience.[19] They emphasized some ideas in his life to the detriment of others. What resulted in the French edition was a distortion of Hecker's idea of

---

18
McAvoy, pp. 110-132.

19
Ibid., 120-122. Walter Elliott, The Life of Father Hecker,
New York: Columbus Press, 1891. The French edition was Le Père
Hecker, Fondateur des "Paulistes" Americains, 1819-1888, traduit
et adapté de L'anglais avec autorization de L'auteur. Introduction par Mgr. John Ireland. Preface par l'Abbé Felix Klein,
Paris: Lacoffre, 1897. There is a controversy concerning the
translator but for our purposes, it does not concern this dissertation. Cf. McAvoy, pp. 119-120.

Americanism and it appeared as a false irenicism of the Deposit of Faith. There arose then a caricature of Americanism, distinct from its reality.

This caricature consisted of the following tenets. First, it emphasized the importance of not stressing unpopular Catholic doctrines and of not adverting to defined dogmas in order to create a harmony between the Church and the world. Secondly, the Holy Spirit was more active then than in past ages within the individual who should live a spiritual life in accordance with his own aspirations. Thirdly, the natural (and, therefore, active virtues) were more important than the supernatural ones (the passive virtues). Active virtues met the needs of modern Catholics. Fourthly, the vows of Religious Life, were antiquated and were to be diminished because they destroyed the freedom of the Christian. And, finally, the convert methods of the past were considered impotent in converting non-Catholics.[20]

Pope Leo XIII spoke out against these tenets in his encyclical Testem Benevolentiae (1898). The American bishops, to whom this encyclical was addressed, although many of them acknowledged that no such thinking existed in the American Church, nevertheless, avowed their fidelity to the pope's letter.[21] In

---

[20]
Gustave Weigel, "Americanism", Sacramentum Mundi, Vol. I, 19-21.

[21]
McAvoy, 247; and Jean Riviere, Le Modernisme dans

the years following the Pope's condemnation of Americanism,
these same bishops often insisted that Americanism was in no
way concerned with doctrine. They said it was merely a practical
approach for the Church in the United States. [22]

Scholars such as McAvoy and Rivière, believe that this
caricature of Americanism which was condemned played a significant role in the history of the Church. Its significance lies in
the facts that it attempted to up-date the Church to the modern
world by a false irenicism of dogma; it put forth a concept of
Christian spirituality which had no essential relation to Christian
dogma; and it called for the diminishment of Religious Life, the
vows, and the supernatural virtues because they did not meet the
needs of the modern world. In this way, then, the Americanism which came to be condemned was a sort of practical preface
to the second ideology resulting from Leo XIII's synthesizing

l'Eglise, Paris: Librairie Letouzey et Ané, 1929, 113. Archbishops Michael A. Corrigan of New York and Frederick X.
Katzer of Milwaukee admitted the existence of the Americanist
heresy.

[22]
The New York Herald, August 17, 1908, p. 9. Cf. also
Rivière, 114. George Tyrrell in a letter to Baron Friedrich
von Hügel, quoted Archbishop Ireland who said: "The Pope [Leo
XIII] told me to forget that letter on Americanism which has no
application except in a few dioceses in France". Tyrrell to von
Hügel, September 7, 1900, von Hügel-Tyrrell Correspondence,
Vol. I, presented by Maude D. M. Petre, British Museum
Additional Manuscripts, 44, 927. Hereinafter this source will
be abbreviated B M Addit. Mss.

program, modernism. [23] Briefly, because it will be fully treated later, this ideology aimed to reconcile science with faith by radically changing the Deposit of Faith, sometimes to the point of denying it. [24]

Extreme tendencies are the result of any transitional era. In such conditions of thought there are always the excessively hasty and rash radicals that seize upon the newest and often un-verified findings or inadequately based inferences and inter-pretations in order to substitute them for the essential content, thus, throwing out the baby with the bath. And, also, these same conditions of thought provoke the extreme intransigent tendency that sees no room for progress and so hold stubbornly to tradition, not distinguishing in it the substance and the divine elements from the accidental and the human.

Wilfrid Ward, editor of The Dublin Review, offered an explan-ation for these extreme tendencies and believed that theological journals could reconcile them when he said:

> One reason at least for these extreme attitudes is the fact of actual demands may probably be found in the fact that both fail to interpret, or rather to understand, the implications or relations of their respective positions. The ultra-conservative, the intransigeant, having come by heredity and ed-

23
    Riviere, 114.

24
    Cf. Chapter V of this dissertation for a full treatment of modernism.

ucation to reduce the content of faith to a formula,
and its practice to the use of the sensible sign,
has lost sight of the inner life and hence progres-
siveness of both theory and conduct: while the too
eager innovator, the rashly transigeant, fails to
notice that the new conquests of the mind, in so
far as they are proven to be true, must be
implied or connected with the older deposit of
truth.   Mediating between these two extremes,
there have always been - nor are they wholly
wanting now - men of larger mould, minds that
see farther and deeper and are steadier and surer
in their methods.   These are the providential
leaders who carry over without destroying the old
to the new.   To seize this mediating spirit, to
organize, and effectuate it, should obviously be
the aim and programme of our reviews. [25]

Another editorial, this time of The Catholic World, singled

out The New York Review as a journal which could effect what

Ward believed was the aim of reviews during a transitional era.

It said:

It has become almost a truism among us that the
Church's greatest need, today, is a genius who
would do for our age what St. Thomas did for his,
which was to bring our theological system in
harmony with the advancing gains in secular knowledge.   But no commanding intellect like that of
the great Dominican has been vouchsafed to the
Church in these later days.   Indeed, the vast growth
of the sciences forbids the possibility that, ever
again, one single mind within the compass of a life-
time, should be equal to forming the synthesis of
science and theology.   The task must be achieved
by many men working under one co-ordinating
principle, along many distinct lines. [26]

25
    The New York Review, II, No. 1 (July-August, 1906), 111.

26
    The Catholic World, September, 1905, Vol. LXXXI, No.
486, p. 842.

This editorial then went on to state that The New York Review was one such coordinating principle. Its contributors from America, England, and France afforded consoling evidence, it said, that everywhere there was a strong movement in progress towards this desired end. It continued to say that the English speaking world was in need of such a journal as The Review because of the theological and scientific conditions of the day. Such conditions, then, warranted the emergence on the American theological scene a journal like The New York Review which would attempt, in a scholarly way, to reconcile the ancient Faith with modern science.

The Review's Founders

The men who brought forth The Review were American Catholic scholars of their day. About American Catholic scholarship at the turn of the century Tyrrell once wrote to Baron Friedrich von Hügel that it was "crude", "instinctive", "lacked culture and learning;" and that, although there were some first rate thinkers in America, they "know not of what spirit they are" and they are "full of contradictions". [27]

But, this opinion of Tyrrell lacks validity because the men who founded The New York Review were American Catholic

---

[27] Letter, Tyrrell to von Hügel, October 7, 1902, von Hügel-Tyrrell Correspondence, B M Addit. Mss. 44, 928.

scholars in their own right, who were definitely <u>au courant</u>
with the times. A consideration of the lines of these men's life
not only dispels Tyrrell's claims of American Catholic thinkers
but, more importantly, discloses that their lives were con-
verging on such a scholarly enterprise as <u>The New York
Review.</u>

James Francis Driscoll

A man who was very much indicative of these exciting intellectual times was James Driscoll (1859-1922), the editor of
<u>The New York Review.</u> George Tyrrell considered him to be
the best theological thinker in the United States at that time. [28]

Born in Vermont, Driscoll studied at the Grand Seminaire in
Montreal, St. Sulpice, <u>Institute Catholique</u> in Paris, and in Rome
where he was ordained a priest in 1887 for his home diocese of
Burlington, Vermont. [29] However, soon after he arrived home
he entered the Society of St. Sulpice, whose sole purpose was the
education of young men for the diocesan priesthood.

28
     Letter, Same to Same, February 19, 1905, B M Addit.
Mss., 44, 929.

29
     The following information about Driscoll's life was gath-
ered from Arthur J. Scanlon, <u>St. Joseph's Seminary, Dunwoodie,
New York, 1896-1921,</u> The United States Catholic Historical
Society, Monograph Series, 1922, Vol. VII, pp. 92-117, <u>passim.</u>
Also, cf. obituaries in <u>The Catholic News,</u> July 15, 1922, p.
2:1-2; <u>New York Herald,</u> July 6, 1922, p. 9:7; <u>The New York</u>

VERY REV. JAMES F. DRISCOLL, S.S., D.D.

As a Sulpician, Driscoll taught almost the entire spectrum of theological courses. In his first teaching assignment at the Grand Séminaire in Montreal (1889-1896), he taught dogmatic theology and Hebrew; at St. Joseph's Seminary, Dunwoodie (1896-1901), dogma, music, moral theology, scripture, and semitic languages, and at St. Augustine's (the Sulpician scholasticate near Catholic University in Washington), and St. Mary's Baltimore (1901-1902), sacred scripture in semitic languages. In 1902, he returned to Dunwoodie and became president until 1909. Besides being president, he also taught during this time, moral theology, edited The New York Review, and lectured at Columbia University and Union Theological Seminary.

Driscoll was always an excellent student. As a professor he often attended courses at John Hopkins University and Catholic University, Washington. His prime interest was semitic languages and biblical literature which he first came to learn under Ignazio Guidi and Henri Hyvernat. [30] Early in his teaching

Times, July 6, 1922, p. 19:5; and The New York Tribune, July 7, 1922, p. 9:7.

[30]
Dr. Ignazio Guidi (1844-1935) was one of the most competent Orientalists of modern times. He was professor of Hebrew and Semitic languages at the University of Rome from 1876-1919.
Eugene Xavier Louis Henri Hyvernat (1858-1941) was one of this country's formost Oriental scholars. After teaching in Rome from 1885 to 1889, he came to Catholic University of America, becoming at different times head of the Department of Semitic and Egyptian literature, and professor of Oriental languages and archeology. The field to which he contributed most, and in which he was most proficient, was Coptic.

career he became very good friends of both and with them
carried on an extensive correspondence. [31]

This correspondence reveals the man of deep scholarship
that Driscoll was. As early as 1889 he wrote to Hyvernat about
his ambition: to teach for a while in the seminary, work with
Hyvernat at Catholic University and together advance Oriental
studies, maybe study in Rome. [32] In other letters, Driscoll
disclosed his scholarly activity; e. g. , the excitement he received deciphering letters off a rock from the Middle East. [33]
He also mentioned to Hyvernat that he was made a member of the
New York Oriental Club, "a rather select and exclusive group of
scholars here - about twelve in number"[34] - among whom at that
time (1900) were Dr. Charles A. Briggs and Wilfrid Ward. His
correspondence to Hyvernat showed his deep love for semitic

---

[31]
Hyvernat's papers at the archives of the Catholic University of America (hereinafter abbreviated as ACUA) contain a
great deal of correspondence from 1885-1902. However, after
1902 there is no letter available from Driscoll. Hyvernat's
papers also disclose that Driscoll wrote to Guidi.

[32]
Letter, Driscoll to Hyvernat, Solitude, Issy-sur-Seine,
March 4, 1889, ACUA.

[33]
Letter, Same to Same, New York. Holy Thursday, 1901,
ACUA.

[34]
Letter, Same to Same, New York, December 21, 1900,
ACUA.

languages and biblical literature so much so that he switched

courses with Rev. Joseph Bruneau at Dunwoodie so that he could

teach scripture. [35] Also, he prepared students in Oriental lan-

guages to teach with Hyvernat at Catholic University. [36]

But Driscoll was by no means any "closet scholar". He main-

tained extensive correspondence with deep friendships with many

of the advanced theological thinkers of the time, and he also

believed that scholarly ideas should be disseminated in public-

ations.

As will be indicated later on more fully and in depth,

Driscoll was friendly with progressive thinkers of the day and in

sympathy with their ideas. [37] He knew Alfred Loisy very well

but this relationship seemed to have been, at least in its early

stages, more filial than equal. About his relation to Loisy, his

contemporaries referred to him as "Loisy's good New York

Driscoll" and "the much beloved pupil of Loisy". [38] He was, how-

ever, very friendly with George Tyrrell and both carried on a

---

[35]
    Scanlon, 122.

[36]
    Letter, Driscoll to Hyvernat, Montreal, April 20, 1893,
ACUA.

[37]
    Cf. Chapter V of this dissertation.

[38]
    These claims were made in a letter by von Hügel to
Tyrrell, January 24, 1905, B M Addit. Mss., 44, 929. Cf
also John R. Slattery, "The Workings of Modernism", The

very extensive personal and professional correspondence until

Tyrrell's death in 1909. About this relationship more will be

said later. [39] Driscoll corresponded also with Albert Houtin,

Wilfrid Ward, his good friend Dr. Charles A. Briggs of Union

Theological Seminary, Bishop Denis O'Connell, and of course,

with Baron von Hügel, who is considered to be the "coordinator"

of the modernist movement. About Driscoll, von Hügel once

wrote to Ward:

> I have never myself met him. But he has a
> fine and considerable reputation; his sympathies,
> interests, and abilities are evidently remarkable
> and most promising; and he is in a position to
> give and get a hearing and a public for Catholic
> work of the most modern sort. Hildegarde [von
> Hügel's daughter] has now seen him twice, each
> time for a good long while - and though she is,
> no doubt a direct judge of such matters, her vivid
> description of his talk and tone was very interest-
> ing and satisfactory. [40]

Besides sharing ideas with the most advanced thinkers of the

day, Driscoll believed that these ideas should be set down in print

for the sake of other minds as well. As early as 1893, twelve

years before The New York Review was founded, Driscoll ex-

American Journal of Theology, XIII, 4 (October, 1909), 571.

[39]
Cf. Chapter V of this dissertation.

[40]
Letter, von Hügel to Wilfrid Ward, January 19, 1905, The
Wilfrid Ward Family Papers. This writer is grateful to Mrs.
Frank Sheed (Maisie Ward) for permission to examine these
papers. The Ward Family Papers are in the custody of Mrs.
Sheed's daughter, Mrs. Neil Middleton of London, England.

pressed his thoughts about founding a review to Hyvernat who was
planning a scriptural journal. He considered his friend's idea to
be excellent "for surely something in that line must be done before
long unless we consent to remain entirely behind our age regarding a branch of study so intimately and vitally connected with the
foundations of Christian religion". However, he had some mis-
givings about the project. Money and the great difficulty of
managing a standard publication were some. The review's
orthodoxy was the greatest:

> Nevertheless, here is a thought which preoccu-
> pies me a little. Being given the animus of a
> certain very orthodox and professedly anti-liberal
> religious society towards the University, I feel
> that the new publication would meet with a very
> determined opposition not to say a passionate one.
> (Of course it goes without saying that the passion
> would belong to the department called "Holy
> Indignation", based exclusively on zeal for
> orthodoxy and the greater glory of God). It is
> natural to suppose that the review as you con-
> ceive it must be pretty well up to the times and
> consequently accept a certain amount of the con-
> clusions arrived at by modern Biblical criticism,
> conclusive, which (If I can in any way judge the
> state of affairs) are every day becoming more
> definite, more alarming to certain ultra-orthodox
> defenders of Christian doctrine who under the
> cover of great names and exaggerated principles
> would all along the line, from Beyrouth to Woodstock
> [Maryland], open fire on the new publication. . . [41]

It is in this letter that we get Driscoll's sense of the times
and the effect it would have on a new theological journal. He con-

---

[41]
 Letter, Driscoll to Hyvernat, Montreal, April 20, 1893,
ACUA.

tinued to relate to Hyvernat how necessary extraordinary pre-
caution was for a review, and his fear that it would meet with
little success because of the meager interest excited by the
results of modern scientific investigations and because it would
have to be in English.

In addition to advising and encouraging the foundation of
Hyvernat's publication, Driscoll also took a direct hand in
attempting to disseminate scholarly ideas in print. He wrote to
Albert Houtin in 1902 asking him for the permission to translate
into English his recent book, La Question Biblique chez les
Catholiques de France which, he said, pleased him very much. [42]
Houtin must have evidently agreed because further correspondence
indicated that he sent his notes to Driscoll who was just about
to begin translating when he was made president of Dunwoodie. [43]
Driscoll wrote Houtin that the duties of his office were so press-
ing that he could not do the translation but recommended that someone else surely should do it.

Driscoll's correspondence to Houtin not only disclosed his

42
    Letter, Driscoll to Albert Houtin, March 31, 1902,
Bibliothèque Nationale de Paris, Cabinet des Manuscripts,
Nouvelles Acquisitions Françaises, No. 15699, fol. 436-437.
Houtin's book La Question Biblique chez les Catholiques de
France was published in Paris by Picard et Fils, 1902.

43
    Letter, Same to Same, December 10, 1902, Bibliothèque
Nationale, No. 15699, fol. 436-437.

desire to translate French scholarly thought into English but also
revealed his own thoughts at the time. In these letters Driscoll
indicated that he was a classmate of Felix Klein, a great devotee
of biblical criticism; and a firm opponent of the Sulpician strictures on publishing liberal ideas which the Society considered
"protestant infiltrations". Driscoll finally revealed his optimism
for a new, freer and more scientific era for Catholic exegetes.

Although Driscoll expressed to Houtin that the pressures of
his new office as president of Dunwoodie did not allow him to
translate his work, a year later, in 1903, he wrote to Alfred
Loisy asking for permission to translate into English his
L'Evangile et L'Eglise and its supplementary volume, Autour
d'un petit livre. Driscoll indicated that his general motive for
translating these works was the importance of putting them in
contact with English readers. His specific reason was that,
since Catholic and protestant English journals had reproduced
only the "radical" parts of his work, L'Evangile et L'Eglise it
would be well to translate the entire work so that people would
see these parts in context. He then mentioned that he would use
a pseudonym and have the translation published by a protestant
library, e. g. Longmans. [44]

---

[44]
    Letter, Driscoll to Alfred Loisy, December 11, 1903,
Bibliothèque Nationale, No. 15652, fol. 189-191. L'Evangile et
L'Eglise, Paris: Alphonse Picard et fils, 1902; Autour d'un petit
livre, Paris: Alphonse Picard et fils, 1903. L'Evangile et
L'Eglise was translated into English in 1904 under the title The

After a while Driscoll went beyond translating other people's
ideas into English. He began to put his own ideas into print,
especially on biblical criticism, in such scholarly publications
as The Catholic Encyclopedia, The Schaft-Herzog Encyclopedia,
The American Ecclesiastical Review, as well as his own journal.[45]

In addition to writing, Driscoll also had another medium to
present scholarly ideas. (This medium would have far deeper
and extensive effects than his writing would ever have). He was
president of St. Joseph's Seminary, and in charge of training
future priests from 1901-1909.

As president of the seminary, he believed that he and his
faculty should not only produce holy priests but also intelligent
ones.[46] (In this he had a view of a seminary similar to Bishop
Spalding's). He wished that his future priests would effectively

---

Gospel and the Church by a Christopher Home and published by
Charles Scribner and Sons. This writer investigated Home and
it seems that he wrote several articles for the Catholic Truth
Society in London around 1902. It is this writer's conclusion that
Home is not a pseudonym of Driscoll.

45
 Driscoll wrote for the Catholic Encyclopedia in 1908; for
the Ecclesiastical Review in 1912; and from 1908 to 1912 he wrote
twenty-one articles for the Schaft-Herzog Encyclopedia. Farley
also put him in charge of a project in 1908 to translate the
Catechism of Modernism from French into English for the exclusive use of the Archdiocese of New York.

46
 This is evident by a perusal of the Regulator's Diary for
St. Joseph's Seminary, Dunwoodie, for the period of Driscoll's
rectorship, 1902-1909. Archives of the Archdiocese of New
York (hereinafter abbreviated AANY).

REV. FRANCIS P. DUFFY

participate in the modern thought of the day. His aim was not that they be protected from the world but made to relate to it for that would be the locus of their future work.

To make these desires realities he changed the subject matter of the cultural committee's weekly evening presentations. The course of these presentations went from such innocuous subjects as "Songs of the Sunny Faith", "The Melodies and Music of Ireland," and "Dry Rot in Current Literature" by such provincial lecturers as J. Talbot Smith and Thomas McLaughlin, to more exciting and timely topics as "Theological Needs", "Catholic Church in the Twentieth Century," "Anglican Controversy," "Auricular Confession," "The Progress of the Church," "Ecumenism" and "Socialism" by such notable thinkers as Charles A. Briggs, Père Giovanni Genocchi, William L. Sullivan, Abbot Gasquet, Cornilius Clifford, and Joseph McSorley. [47]

With such a scholarly and contemporary background it was not any wonder that Driscoll became the editor of The New York Review.

Francis Patrick Duffy

If Driscoll was the most lettered man connected with The New

---

[47]
Ibid. It is interesting to note that after the condemnation of Modernism by the papal encyclical Pascendi dominici Gregis (September 8, 1907) these lectures again became innocuous.

York Review, associate editor Francis P. Duffy (1871-1932) was
the one most responsible for it. It was he and John F. Brady
(1871-1940) who originally thought of founding a theological
journal. [48] As with Driscoll, considering the flow of Duffy's life,
it is not any wonder that such an idea would originate with him.

Duffy, whom Americans will remember and honor as the
most popular and heroic military chaplain in United States history,
was born in Coburg, Canada, to a mining family. [49] Having
attended St. Michael's College, Toronto and St. Joseph's Seminary, Troy, New York, he was a member of the class that would
have been ordained from Dunwoodie in 1897. However, Archbishop Michael A. Corrigan ordained Francis Duffy a priest in
September, 1896 to allow him to pursue graduate studies at
Catholic University, Washington. Because of reasons of ill
health Duffy did not complete his studies but returned to New
York in 1897 and served as an assistant curate to auxiliary bishop,
John M. Farley, then pastor of St. Gabriel's Church in New Rochelle,

---

[48]
Letter, Driscoll to Very Rev. Edward R. Dyer, S. S. Vicar
General of Sulpicians in the United States, January 11, 1905,
Archives of St. Mary's Seminary, Baltimore (hereinafter abbre-
viated ASMB). A copy of this letter is also in Dyer's Letters on
the N. Y. Seminary Secession, 1906, for private circulation, p. 11.

[49]
The following facts of Duffy's life came from some of his
letters in AANY which are available up until 1903 and then begin
again with 1912; and from The Golden Jubilee Bulletin of Church
of Our Savior (1962), Bronx, New York, Duffy's first pastorate,
passim.

New York. A year later he became professor of philosophy at St. Joseph's Seminary, Dunwoodie and spent his next fourteen years there.

Father Duffy was a man of wide interests. [50] He taught philosophy, theology, biology, and history. He often extended his scholarly talents by doing editorial work for several reviews, writing articles for numerous ones, and accepted every opportunity of lending the results of his studies to the work of the Catholic University, its summer school in New York, the Colleges of St. Angela and Mt. St. Vincent, as well as various parochial courses especially concerned with the movements of Catholic education and anti-socialism.

Duffy was also active in ecumenism, an interest which many a churchman did not hold in esteem at that time, and one to which the Catholic Church would not officially address itself until Vatican Council II.

When he left Dunwoodie in 1912 he founded Our Saviour's parish in the Bronx, built it up, and then wrote to the Ordinary, now John M. Farley, for another challenge because he "didn't want to get rusty". In this request he demonstrated the depth of his character. He expressed to Farley that it did not matter

---

[50]
Duffy's wide interests are disclosed by himself in a letter to Farley, petitioning for a parish which was vacant in 1916; Letter, Duffy to Archbishop John M. Farley, January 12, 1916, AANY.

whether he sent him to people who were rich or poor, educated or the reverse. All Duffy wanted was a "man's" job - one big enough to tax his energies to the full.

When World War I broke out and America entered into the fighting, Duffy served heroically as chaplain in France with the 69th Regiment - the same outfit with which he once served briefly during the Spanish-American War.

As a seminary professor in Dunwoodie, he was so interested in this apostolate that he became the ideal seminary man. His manliness, intellectual ability, and spiritual depth combined with a warm and outgoing personality enabled him to relate well to the seminarians and train them effectively for the ministry. [51]

He was such an all around success in the seminary apostolate that his former rector, Very Rev. Edward J. Dyer, S.S., then rector of St. Mary's Seminary, Baltimore, recommended him in 1903 for an honorary doctorate in theology. Having been informed of this honor, Duffy expressed his gratitude to Dyer by writing:

"No man is ever another - nor ought he to be - but there will be always a bit of your liberal - conservative self in my views and actions."[52]

---

[51]
This information about Duffy's career as a seminary professor comes from a letter of Dyer to Driscoll, January 18, 1905, ASMB; and Dyer, p. 15.

[52]
Letter, Duffy to Dyer, June 12, 1903, ASMB.

Duffy's sentiment expressed in this letter would become a reality in The New York Review's editorial policy and in the spirit of its editorials that Duffy himself wrote. It seems that this honorary doctorate was a vote of confidence for Duffy to take writing more seriously for he continued in the same letter to Dyer:

> [This honorary doctorate] will be of service to me in my work as teacher, editor and writer. It will be a stimulus to me to live up to your expectations and exhortations, by devoting myself more to the work of writing. I hope that my work will bring no discredit on my new alma mater nor on you.

Duffy's interest in writing grew stronger over the years. In a letter to his very good friend at the time, Patrick J. Hayes (1867-1938), later Cardinal-Archbishop of New York, Duffy gave indication that his literary interests were becoming crystalized. The letter was a response to Hayes who had written to praise Duffy for a letter he wrote to the editor of The New York Sun protesting its handling of a sacerdotal controversy. Duffy mentioned to Hayes that the reason why he had written the protest was because he felt the Catholic mind would be perturbed by The Sun's report and it would be beneficial "to print something with a hopeful and faith-ful [sic] tone concerning the position of the old Church" [53] He then said to Hayes:

---

[53] Letter, Duffy to Rev. Patrick Hayes, April 30, 1904, AANY.

> I tried to write so as to encourage the weaklings,
> and at the same time to hint a warning to the
> wise. The intellectual air is full of future
> trouble - I am not afraid for the Church ulti-
> mately but we must be ready for a time of trial
> and what I say of the fate of many theological
> opinions is eminently true. God grant me
> ready to meet the issues as they come.

This portion of Duffy's letter reveals his sensitivity not only

to the times but also to "the little ones", the common folk who

were bewildered by rash journalism. It also shows his balance,

as well as his great sense of the Church and his willingness to

come to grips with the problems of the day. Duffy then made a

personal predication at the end of this letter:

> You suggest that I write more. I feel it a duty
> but I go slow purposely. My mind is still grow-
> ing - in health and clearness, I think, and I am
> reluctant to turn out stuff to bad magazines
> withal. If God gives me life, you will hear
> from me when I can speak with authority. Mean-
> while I shall be grateful for a friendly prod
> from you to push me in this direction.

Duffy did eventually speak with authority when The New York

Review was founded. The lines of Duffy's life did converge on

this journal and much of his personality was expressed in the

spirit of The Review's editorial policy and editorials. They

certainly exhibited his scholarship, sense of the times, belief in

the Church, balance of liberal and conservative tendencies, his

clarity of expression, concern for the uneducated, and even a

militancy towards the over-wise. Much of The New York Review

was Duffy, from beginning to end.

Others Connected With The Review

There were three other Dunwoodie professors connected with The New York Review but who figured less prominently in its history than Driscoll and Duffy. They were John F. Brady, The Review's managing editor, Francis E. Gigot, professor of sacred scripture, and Joseph Bruneau, professor of dogmatic theology. All were of the same scholarly caliber as Driscoll and Duffy.

John F. Brady (1871-1940) was a New Yorker and his life was in some respects similar to that of Duffy. [54] Born on the lower east side of Manhattan, he attended St. Francis Xavier College in New York City. After graduation in 1892, he went on to study medicine for two years and received his doctorate in medicine (M. D.). Feeling called to the priesthood, he entered St. Joseph's seminary in 1895 which at that time was located in Troy, New York. He was ordained a priest three years later in the chapel at Dunwoodie and was immediately sent to Catholic University in Washington to study philosophy for a year. Returning to Dunwoodie in 1899, he taught science, philosophy, sacraments, dogma, and liturgy and served as vice-president of St. Joseph's Seminary.

_____

[54] The facts of Brady's life are from the obituary of his twin brother Rev. James Aloysius Brady, who died as pastor of St. Augustine's Parish, Larchmont, New York (The Catholic News, January 18, 1936, p. 3); Scanlon, opcit., p. 141; and The Catholic Directory for the years 1898 to 1940.

During the early years of his seminary assignment Brady founded and was the first editor of The Homiletic Monthly (now The Homiletic and Pastoral Review). This review was a theologically conservative magazine mainly for parish priests. It offered sermon outlines to help the parochial clergy prepare for their Sunday preaching, as well as catechetical hints and pastoral directives from the latest decisions and decrees of the Roman congregations.

Such an interest in writing and editing which was similar to Duffy's led him and Duffy to consider seriously the founding of The New York Review; and he became its managing editor. Very little is known about his role in this position on The Review's staff. He never wrote for it nor figured prominently in its scholarly endeavor. The probable reason for this was that during this time Brady, besides his duties as a professor at Dunwoodie, also edited The Homiletic and wrote numerous sermons for it. All we can say about his relation to The Review was that he read its galley sheets and dealt with the printer. [55]

After The Review's demise in 1908 he remained on the seminary faculty and also acted in the capacity of vice president of Mt. St. Vincent's College, a woman's institution in Riverdale

---

[55] Letter, Brady to Diomede Falconio, January 17, 1908, AANY. Brady mentioned his duties on the staff of The Review to the Apostolic Delegate.

(Bronx), New York until 1916, when he left to become pastor of St. Francis de Sales Church in New York City. When the United States entered World War I in 1917 he served as a marine chaplain on the front and was awarded the Distinguished Service Cross. He returned to St. Francis after the War and again managed several other jobs besides that of pastor. He was Director of the Health Division of Catholic Charities and founder of the hospital apostolate as well as teacher of religion at Mt. St. Vincent's College. He served the Church so well in many and simultaneous positions that the Archdiocese of New York honored him with the ecclesial ranks of Papal Chamberlain and Domestic Prelate. Monsignor Brady, the only Dunwoodie professor connected with The Review who was so honored, died in 1940.

Francis Ernest Charles Gigot (1859-1920) was another priest of exceptional talent associated with The Review. [56] Born in France, he studied under the Christian Brothers and attended the University of France, Theological Seminary of Limoges, and the Institute Catholique (Paris) where he was ordained in 1883.

A member of the Society of St. Sulpice, Gigot's first teaching assignment was at St. John's Seminary, Brighton, Massa-

---

[56] For general biographical information on Gigot cf. The New York Review, I, (June-July, 1905), p. 130; Scanlon, op. cit., pp. 105-158, passim; Georgina Pell Curtis, The American Catholic Who's Who (St. Louis: B. Herder), 1911, 241-242; The Catholic Encyclopedia and Its Makers, New York: The Encyclopedia Press, 1917, p. 65; and obituaries in The New York Times, June 16, 1920, 11:3; New York Herald, June 15, 1920, 9:5; and The Catholic News, June 19, 1920, 16: 2-3.

chusetts as professor of dogma, and then as professor of sacred scripture.   Biblical studies was the field he was most interested in and he wrote voluminously on it.   Some of his works became the actual textbooks used in most seminaries in the United States and a standard authority in every institute of higher learning in the English-speaking world. [57]   Though liberal in tendency, he was wise to see that in the long run a cautious approach would do most to advance the cause of Catholic scientific investigations. [58]

Besides teaching at St. John's Seminary, Brighton, Gigot also taught at St. Mary's Seminary, Baltimore and St. Joseph's Dunwoodie.   It was at Dunwoodie that he encountered difficulties with the Sulpician regulations for censorship concerning his two volume work, Special Introduction to the Study of the Old Testa-

---

[57]
The New York Tribune (January 25, 1906, 1:4) said of his works: "His works are the standard authority on the Bible and Biblical criticism in every Catholic Institution of higher learning and the English speaking world."   John E. Sexton and Arthur J. Riley, History of St. John's Seminary, Brighton (Boston: Roman Catholic Archdiocese of Boston), p. 67, in speaking of his textbooks said: "As a pioneer author of these scriptural manuals, he put the American Church under deep obligation."   Gigot's books were certainly in use at Dunwoodie, Brighton, Seton Hall, and St. Mary's, Baltimore.   There is indication of their use in England when T. B. Scannell, in his The Priests' Studies (London: Longmans, Green and Co. , 1908, p. 31.) said "Gigot's General Introduction should be in every English-speaking priest's hands".   Scannell also recommended Gigot's Special Introduction to the Study of the Old Testament, Ibid. , p. 29.

[58]
Cf. Letter, Driscoll to Houtin, March 31, 1902, op. cit.

ment and New Testament. [59] These difficulties eventually led to

the sucession of the Sulpician members of Dunwoodie's faculty

from the Society of St. Sulpice and their incardination into the

Archdiocese of New York.

In addition to writing books, Gigot wrote numberable articles

for The Catholic Encyclopedia, The American Ecclesiastical

Review, The Irish Theological Quarterly, and The New York

Review. He taught at Dunwoodie for twenty years until his death

in 1920. His connection with The Review was that he wrote twenty-

one articles for it plus just as many book reviews during the three

years that it published.

Joseph Bruneau (1866-1933) was another member of St.

Joseph's faculty who was deeply involved in the work of The New

York Review. [60] Like Gigot, he too was born in France (Lyons)

and took courses at the Institute Catholique de Paris where he

studied under such notables as Paulin Martin, Fulcran Vigouroux,

S. S. and Alfred Loisy. [61] As a student he was excellent, as a

---

59
Dyer, pp. 4-58, passim. Gigot's two volume work was
published by Benziger Brothers, New York; Volume I in 1901
and Volume II in 1906.

60
For this biographical sketch of Bruneau the following information came from The New York Review I, No. 4 (December,
1905-January, 1906), p. 540; John E. Sexton and Arthur J.
Riley, pp. 127-128; Scanlan, pp. 92-11, passim; and the
obituary in The New York Times, August 28, 1933, 13:4.

61
Paulin Martin (1840-1890) was professor of Scripture,
Hebrew, and Syrian at the Institute Catholique from 1878 until

teacher, brilliant, scintillating, and restless, not to say im-

patient with the slow, dull and average student. He organized

groups of students to discuss a special theological problem, as

well as groups to translate books from French into English. [62]

He himself did a good deal of translating theology also into French

which, as will be discussed, later brought him into difficulty with

Rome. [63] He was very friendly with Marie Joseph Lagrange and

Alfred Loisy. In fact, available correspondence indicates that

for a number of years Bruneau acted as Loisy's literary agent in

---

his death. Owing to his poor state of health, Martin had his
confrère, the Abbé Loisy, take one part of his teaching assign-
ments.

Fulcran Vigouroux S. S. (1837-1915) was professor of Scripture and Hebrew at the Grand Séminaire de Saint Sulpice. He
eventually was appointed professor of Scripture at the Institute
Cathlique de Paris in 1890 in preference to Loisy. Later he
went to Rome to become Secretary of the Biblical Commission.

Alfred Firmin Loisy (1857-1940) was undoubtedly the most
well known of all the modernist. Ordained in 1879 he came to
the Institute Catholique de Paris as a student in 1881. His
brilliance won him a lectureship in Hebrew before a year passed;
1883 saw him teach Old Testament exegesis and in 1886,
Assyriology. His "advanced" views were the direct cause of his
dismissal from the Institute in 1893. From 1900 to 1904 he
taught at the Ecole des Hautes Etudes, Excommunicated,
Vitandus, by the Holy Office in 1908, he thereafter held the chair
of church history at the College of France from 1909-1932.

62
Sexton and Riley, pp. 127-128.

63
Bruneau translated Bishop John Cuthbert Hedley's Retreat
into French (Paris; Lethielleux, 1905); and also into French,
Henry Nutcombe Oxenham's History of the Dogma of Atonement
(Paris: Bloud, 1909), and The Principle of Theological Develop-
ment, (Paris: Bloud, 1909).

the United States, sending his articles to different reviews and returning the financial remunerations to Loisy. [64]

Bruneau taught theology at Autun, France; was one of the original faculty members of Dunwoodie when it opened in 1896 and remained there until 1906 when five Sulpicians on the faculty left the Congregation and remained at Dunwoodie. A Sulpician himself, Bruneau chose to stay with St. Sulpice and went to Brighton for three years, then returned to St. Mary's where he taught theology and became its director until his death in 1933. [65]

His association with The Review seems to have been something more than being merely a contributor. Duffy, in a letter to Bruneau indicated that it was Bruneau who acquired for The Review articles from the pens of famous thinkers. [66] For this Duffy thanked him but also expressed his envy of Bruneau's entry into such notable intellectual circles.

64
Letter, Bruneau to Herman Heuser, (editor of the Ecclesiastical), June 8, 1897, and March 14, 1898, Archives of the Archdiocese of Philadelphia, St. Charles Boromeo Seminary, Overbrook. Hereinafter this source will be abbreviated AAP. There is a very extensive collection of Bruneau's correspondence at ASMB but not a letter from Loisy is found among them.

65
Scanlon, op. cit., 92-111, passim.

66
Letter, Duffy to Bruneau, undated. ASMB. In this letter Duffy indicated that Bruneau acquired articles for The Review from Henri Bremond, Ernest Dimnet, and a Père Pourrat from Lyons, France who contributed two unsigned articles on the Eucharist. The Review, for some reason, did not print Dimnet's article.

38

Inception of The New York Review

It is out of this context of the times and the lives of its founders that The New York Review came to be. William L. Sullivan,
(1872-1935) who seemed to have spoken of himself as one of the
Review's founders, described in his autobiography the immediate context which led to founding The Review.

> It occurred to some of us who were watching the
> battle abroad that we should try, however modestly,
> to prove that American Catholics were not bar-
> barously indifferent to the great problems of ex-
> panding knowledge which were agitating the Church
> in Europe. We know that American priests are little
> given to study, and that the American laity were
> almost wholly innocent of intellectual activity.
> Nevertheless, we saw a chance to light a little
> candle which might recapture a tiny area from the
> darkness around about. After awhile there came
> from I know not where, a bit of money to serve as
> a bushel in which our candle might be set, and we
> found a bi-monthly which, in its brief life, was
> called The New York Review. [67]

Sullivan then proceeded to state the general purpose of the
journal. It was not to be destructive but rather to awaken intelligent priests and lay folk to some of the critical and philosophical questions which, as he said, they would have to face
anyhow. It would attempt to give solutions to those questions
that liberal Catholic scholarship could discover.

---

[67]
    Under Orders: The Autobiography of William Laurence
Sullivan, Boston: Beacon Press, copyright 1944 by Richard R.
Smith (reprinted in 1966 by arrangement with the Smith Co.
Inc.), pp. 105-106.

ST. JOSEPH'S SEMINARY, DUNWOODIE, YONKERS,
NEW YORK

Actually, according to Driscoll, this whole idea of a
contemporary theological magazine originated with Duffy and
Brady. [68] For a long time, previous to the Review's emergence,
they were contemplating such an idea and shared their reflections
with their colleagues at Dunwoodie. Duffy, in a letter to Hanna,
disclosed the lines of these reflections which eventually led to
the decision to embark on such venture as that of The Review.
He wrote:

> Some of us have long felt that there is room for
> a review in English devoted mainly or altogether
> to presenting the views of Catholic scholars on
> religious questions of present interest. Scattered
> articles bearing on these questions do appear in
> secular or Catholic publications, but they are
> scattered too much, and an objection is made
> against mooting difficult problems in magazines
> for the laity. Probably the [Catholic] University
> Bulletin best fills the bill, but not entirely. It
> is somewhat local in its nature, and it concerns
> the whole field of University studies. We believe
> there is room for a review which would treat of
> religious questions alone and which would have
> for contributors Catholic scholars, not only in
> America, but in England and France. [69]

The only drawbacks the originators had, Duffy continued in

68
     Letter, Driscoll to Dyer, January 11, 1905, ASMB; copy
of letter in Dyer, op. cit., p. 11.

69
     Letter, Francis P. Duffy to Edward J. Hanna, January 8,
1905, copy, Archives of Diocese of Rochester, St. Bernard's
Seminary. Hereinafter this source will be abbreviated ADR. The
original is at ACUA, Rector's Office Correspondence 1903-1909
(Box-3, H-L) because Hanna enclosed this letter with one of his
own to Denis O'Connell.

the letter, were doubts as to the attitude of Church authority and the probable scarcity of subscribers, which would present financial problems. However, he said that they believed so deeply in the importance of such a review that the latter drawback would not present that much of a problem because some of them resolved to stand the deficit, if there would be one.

Although Duffy and Brady believed that the conditions of the times warranted a review along the lines that Duffy mentioned to Hanna, they nevertheless were sensitive to contemporary periodicals and wished to avoid rivalry by infringing on their scope and subscribers. They, therefore, consulted several Catholic editors in America who were already doing good work, at least incidently, along the lines the Dunwoodie editors had chosen. The response they received was overwhelmingly favorable. [70]

They first laid their plans before Dr. Herman Heuser, editor of the Ecclesiastical Review and (at that time) of the Dolphin. They chose to consult Heuser first because they said it was eminently proper to do so, due to his length of service and efficiency, which merited him the title of "Dean of the (Publishing) Corps." Their plans having met with his approval, they next contacted Dr. Thomas Shahan of The Catholic University Bulletin,

[70] The New York Review, I, No. 6 (April-May, 1906), 801.

who responded: "A new venture like this does no harm to those already in the field; it only stirs up wider interest and all are benefited by it; and what matter it after all if we do lose a few subscribers, so long as the good work is done?" He and his colleague, Dr. Edward Pace, devoted many long hours of their time in advising the Dunwoodie professors about publishing a journal. The Review's editors also spoke of their plans to Father John J. Wynne of The [Sacred Heart] Messenger. They found him most willing and helpful in suggesting contributors. The Review also planned to present an article from Wynne's eminent colleague, Father Anthony J. Maas, S. J. Father John Burke of the Catholic World was from the outset of The Review its generous and helpful friend and The Review's opening number contained articles by two of Burke's most valued contributors, Dr. James J. Fox, and Father Joseph McSorley.

The Review's reception by editors of foreign periodicals was no less encouraging. The first article in its opening number was by Wilfrid Ward who was no doubt then considering his own future editorship. An even more striking proof of Ward's good will and generosity toward The Review, was when Ward did become editor of The Dublin Review. In spite of the exacting duties of his new position, he found time to write another article which opened The Review's second volume. The Dunwoodie editors also communicated their plans to Dr. Walter McDonald of Maynooth. He

posal was far more than favorable. It was a hearty and enthu-

siastic approval, and he strongly endorsed their plans. About

Farley's enthusiastic response Driscoll once wrote:

> It was just what he wanted. He expressed his deep,
> long standing regrets at the backwardness of Cath-
> olic writers in matters of modern scientific interest,
> and gave as his opinion that it was due in great mea-
> sure to the exaggerated restrictive policy of the
> ecclesiastical authorities who, through their un-
> reasonably stringent methods of censorship (Index,
> etc), only succeed in stifling all initiative on the
> part of the ablest and best disposed Catholic
> scholars. He had said as much, he added, when
> in Rome to Cardinal Satolli and to Cardinal
> Martinelli. [76]

Farley then was simply delighted with their idea for a review.

He told them to go ahead with it "by all means", and that even if

through any unforseen contingency the project were to fall through,

they would have, at any rate, rendered a service to the good

cause by having started it.

A few months after he gave his strong endorsement to the

projected magazine, Farley spent a few days at Dunwoodie. While

he was there, he addressed the seminarians and spoke enthu-

siastically about the coming review saying that he wanted it at

Dunwoodie and that it had to be "first class". [77] As time went

on, Farley was very proud of the plans for The New York Review.

---

[76]
Ibid.

[77]
Letter, Driscoll to Dyer, January 26, 1905, ASMB; and
Dyer, p. 17.

He regarded the future journal as a fine witness to the scholar-ship of his seminary. [78] Because of this more than sympathetic attitude taken by Farley to the proposed review, Driscoll and Duffy were convinced more than ever of their proposal. They worked at founding their review "with an alacrity stimulated and strengthened" by the moral support of Archbishop Farley. [79]

The first item of business in their task now was to contact people to contribute articles for their journal. In this regard, they solicited Catholic scholars from among the clergy, the laity, and the Religious, and from such countries as England, France, the United States, Italy, Ireland, Germany, Austria and Belgium. Among those thinkers they first asked or planned to ask were Wilfrid Ward, Baron Friedrich von Hügel, George Tyrrell, Albert Condamin, S. S., François Prat, S. J., M. J. Lagrange, O. P., Archbishop Eudoxe-Irenee Mignot of Albi, France, M. Ferdinand Brunetière, Francis E. Gigot, Joseph Bruneau, James Fox, Edward Hanna, Joseph McSorley, Bishop John L. Spalding, Edward Pace, Thomas Shields, etc. [80] Although not all of these

---

[78]
   Under Orders, p. 107.

[79]
   Letter, Driscoll to Dyer, January 11, 1905, ASMB and Dyer, p. 11.

[80]
   Cf. Announcement Sheet of The New York Review; Driscoll to Dyer, January 11, 1905; Duffy to Hanna, January 8, 1905; Driscoll to Dyer, February 16, 1905, ASMB and Dyer, op. cit., p. 34.

proposed contributors wrote for The Review, those who did responded to the appeal were enthusiastic about the projected journal.
Many expressed their sentiments about the real need for Catholic
scholars to concentrate their efforts. Up to then these efforts
seem to have carried little weight because they were scattered
through a number of reviews. [81] About this enthusiastic response
from these projected contributors Driscoll wrote:

> The projected periodical is receiving an unexpect-
> ed amount of enthusiastic encouragement. Every
> answer received so far from contributors has
> been favorable beyond our expectations. Among
> those who have written stating their willingness to
> contribute and their very hearty approval of the
> scheme are Tyrrell, Wilfrid Ward, Baron von
> Hügel, Fonsegrive, Brunetière, Archbishop
> Mignot (He however will not write at least for
> the present) to say nothing of the many enthu-
> siastic adherents on this side. [82]

However, one solicited contributor, Edward J. Hanna of St.

Bernard's Seminary, Rochester, even though he expressed to

Father Duffy his interest and desire to cooperate in the New York

magazine, feared that it would hurt the Catholic University

Bulletin's subscription. [83] He wrote of this fear to Bishop Denis

---

81
    Letter, Driscoll to Dyer, January 11, 1905, ASMB.

82
    Letter, Driscoll to Dyer, February 16, 1905, ASMB and
Dyer, p. 34.

83
    Letter, Edward J. Hanna to Bishop Denis O'Connell, Janu-
ary 10, 1905, ACUA, Rector's Office Correspondence 1903-1909,
(Box 3, H-L).

O'Connell, rector of Catholic University. O'Connell must have
dispelled Hanna's fear almost immediately because the professor
of dogma from Rochester wrote three articles for the second,
third, and fourth issues of The Review's first volume. [84]

In time, The Review would add to its original list of contrib-
utors other notable clerical scholars of the day, such as Joseph
Turmel, Vincent McNabb, Hugh Pope, Pierre Batiffol, Cornelius
Clifford, Aurelio Palmieri, Ernesto Buonaiuti, Henri Bremond,
and William L. Sullivan. The laymen that would participate in
The Review's task would be Wilfrid Ward, Miss Maude Petre,
Mr. Albert Reynaud, Justice Frank Mcgloin.

The Review's Announcement

Having secured the commitment and cooperation of many
notable thinkers to contribute articles to their magazine, the
editors then sent out to Catholics and non-Catholics, 25,000
flyers announcing the date of appearance and purpose of The
Review. [85] This announcement sheet formally introduced the
new journal as The New York Review, "A Journal of the Ancient

---

[84]
    These articles became a cause célèbre in the American
Church in 1908. Cf. Chapter VI of this dissertation for a full
consideration of these articles and the effect they had on The
New York Review.

[85]
    Letter, Driscoll to Dyer, April 13, 1905, ASMB, gives
the figure of 25,000 copies. Also, the Announcement Sheet

Faith and Modern Thought" and indicated that its first number
would be issued in June (1905). [86] It stated clearly that the new
publication had the approval of Archbishop Farley and also that
it would appear every two months, edited by the professors of
the diocesan seminary at Yonkers. The four page flyer then gave
The Review's purpose as apologetic with special reference to
present day religious and scientific conditions and its method
as positive and constructive. The reasons that it listed for
founding The Review were:

> (1) To treat in a scholarly fashion, yet in a
> manner intelligible to the ordinary cultured mind,
> topics of interest bearing on theology, Scripture,
> Philosophy and the corporate sciences.
> (2) To draw attention to the needs of the pre-
> sent intellectual situation in matters of religious
> belief.
> (3) To secure the united effort of the most
> eminent Catholic Scholars, lay and clerical,
> throughout the world, for the discussion and
> solution of problems and difficulties connected
> with Religion.
> (4) To treat by means of shorter studies,
> minor topics in Sacred Scripture and Archeology,
> etc.
> (5) To keep the readers informed on most
> recent developments of religious questions by
> careful reviews or summaries of important
> books and publications.

It then acknowledged the present need for such a publication
in English by thoughtful and informed persons. The editor ex-

---

itself stated that subscriptions went out to Catholics and non-
Catholics.

[86]
    Cf. "Announcement Sheet" in appendix A.

plicated this need by saying on the flyer:

> The studies made by scientific and historical
> research during the past half century have
> forced upon us consideration of new problems
> and have rendered necessary the restatement
> of many theological problems.
> The new issues thus raised cannot without
> ever increasing harm continue to be ignored
> by Catholics as has too generally been the case
> in the past. They are currently discussed in
> reviews and newspapers by writers of every
> shade of religious opinion and only too often the
> solution proposed is irreconcilable with any
> sane interpretation of historic Christianity.

It then affirmed that many Catholic scholars, especially in

Europe, were doing excellent work along the lines indicated above.

But, because their productions, were, for the most part, scatter-

ed through various journals, many of which were not available

to the average English speaking public, it would be advantageous

to bring in one specific periodical the combined results of these

scholars' scientific labors.

The flyer then ended with a list of the names of twenty six

scholars, mentioned above, as contributors and with an announce-

ment of the annual subscription rate of $3.00.

Reaction to the Emerging Journal

As was already indicated, the reaction of other journals to

the announcement of the forth-coming review was very favorable.

Now with its formal announcement by means of a circular the

reaction was almost just as favorable. Bishop Thomas F. Cusack,

Auxiliary Bishop of New York, announced his strong approval of the review and his willingness to help the cause with his own money. Also, quite a number of priests, without any solicitation on the editor's part, offered to contribute a hundred dollars or more to subsidize the Dunwoodie journal. [87]

However, private correspondence disclosed that some people did take exception to the new journal mainly because of their vested interest in their own periodicals and in one case, because they considered the Review would be another factor for breaking the Sulpician professors at Dunwoodie away from the Society of St. Sulpice.

The people who took exception to the announcement of The New York Review for personal reasons were close associates of Herman Heuser of The Ecclesiastical Review. Bishop William F. Stang of Fall River, Massachusetts, as soon as he received notice of the new journal, wrote to Heuser:

> Now I consider the appearance of such a maga-
> zine a serious mistake. The "Review"
> [The Ecclesiastical] does all which these men
> intend to do. We need concentration, not
> expansion. It is a surprise to me that the
> Sulpicians undertake such a job.
>   I intend to write to the Archbishop of
> N. Y. and tell him of my apprehension of the
> fatal consequences. [88]

_____

87
    Letter, Driscoll to Dyer, February 16, 1905, ASMB.

88
    Letter, Bishop William F. Stang to Herman Heuser,
March 25, 1905, AAP, Overbrook.

Another close associate of Heuser, John Gabally, the New

York publisher of The Ecclesiastical Review was much more

positive toward the Dunwoodie journal at the beginning of a letter

to Heuser but then exhibited vested interest. In doing so, he

presented some ideas about publications at the time.

> I am much interested in the projected New
> York Magazine and for one I heartily welcome
> it. From what I can learn it will be a Dunwoodie
> venture with the Archbishop of New York's en-
> couragement. How much this latter is worth,
> I would not care to guess. At any rate, now
> perhaps there will be more warmth - absit verbo
> invidia - in the smile of our own great Arch-
> bishop when he contemplates the Philadelphia
> Review and The Dolphin.
> Another reason for my gratitude is that the
> prospective of the newcomer promises learned
> treatises on philosophy and scripture à la
> apologetics. Very Good. It may be heresy but that
> way faces apathy in America, yet. Theoretically,
> a magazine that is meant to aim high should start
> high; but perhaps practice requires that you get
> your readers first, before you lead them up the
> heights. In Europe where many are already up
> the sacred mount of learning and many others are
> today after, such a magazine as I fancy to be the
> N. Y. projection would find supporters. Here
> popularity serves better and then raise the stand-
> ard. Shout or whisper from the heights and you
> will be left alone to shout or whisper - and die.

Then Gabally revealed another reason, one based on vested

interest, for his welcome of The Review's appearance.

> I even have a third reason for gratitude in this
> regard, although it is a melancholy sort of
> self-defense. For before discouragement and
> an empty bin overtakes the new charger [The
> New York Review] it may run to death the
> A C Q R [American Catholic Quarterly Review],
> The University Bulletin and perhaps the Cath-
> olic World. It is admitted that these poor

steeds are barely limping. Well, if these or
any of them are removed and the New Yorker
too drops, that leaves the way clear to The
Review and the Dolphin. [89]

The negative reaction to the announcement of The New York

Review's coming was not all that mild. In one case it became

indignant, bitter, and most probably influential in effecting the

secession of the Sulpician professors at Dunwoodie from the So-

ciety of St. Sulpice. When Driscoll first wrote to his Sulpician

Superior, Rev. Edward Dyer, the Vicar General of the Sulpicians

in the United States, announcing the founding of The New York

Review, he was not aware that the projected journal would cause

a great furor in the Sulpician headquarters at Baltimore, Upon

receiving the news that Dunwoodie professors, many of whom

were Sulpicians, were founding a theological review, Dyer noted

that this came as "quite a surprise" to him. [90] He immediately

wrote back to Driscoll trying to discourage the projected enter-

prise no doubt because he feared that such a New York venture

would be another reason among many - perhaps even a very

significant one for the young Sulpicians in America to execute

the then much discussed and contemplated secession from the

Society of St. Sulpice. He affirmed the need for such a publica-

---

[89]
    Letter, Edward J. Gabally to Heuser, undated, AAP,
Overbrook.

[90]
    Dyer, p. 14.

tion and acknowledged his delight with the proposed contributors.
But then he asked Driscoll whether it was necessary or important
that the review be published at Dunwoodie; whether the work be too
much on Father Duffy who already was involved in many other
interests; and what would Farley's attitude be when criticism
came from Rome. He also expressed his indignation that, as
Superior, he was not consulted about the journal and not allowed
any say in it.

> Is it the right thing that a man who has the duty
> and consequent right to speak, to give a decision,
> be set over in a corner to look on at the perform-
> ance, and told to approve if he feels like it, but
> that he is not expected to manifest any disapproval
> should such be his judgement, for if he does,
> what is he going to do about it?

Dyer continued in his letter to say that at a recent general
meeting of the Society in Baltimore one desire expressed which
every one present accepted (including Driscoll) was that no noteworthy departure from the accepted working of any of the Sulpician
houses be decided upon without the approval of the Vicar with the
ordinary council. He concluded his letter by expressing his fear
that the good work of St. Sulpice in America would be marred by
such a project and that the Generalate in Paris would be aroused
by Driscoll's action. [91]

Driscoll responded to Dyer's letter first by stating that the

---

[91]
    Letter, Dyer to Driscoll, January 18, 1905, ASMB; and
Dyer, pp. 14-17.

reasons Dyer proferred for the journal not to be officially
connected with St. Joseph's Seminary were not very cogent. [92]
He then proceeded to dismiss each of those reasons with his perception of the situation. In this letter, Driscoll also hinted to
Dyer that Farley would very much like to have had the Seminary
in the hands of the diocesan clergy. This was already a long-
standing fear of Dyer. [93]

After considering Driscoll's arguments that the new journal
be connected with Dunwoodie, Dyer resigned himself to this fact. [94]
The one condition he put on the resolution of the matter was that
Farley sign a statement, which would read something like this:

> My dear Father Driscoll:
> You may inform your superior that I wish
> this review to be started, and conducted in
> connection with my seminary; and the Fathers
> there may consider themselves as responsible
> to me alone in all that concerns it. [95]

The reason why Dyer wanted Farley to sign such a statement
was that, since The New York Review created great tension

92
   Letter, Driscoll to Dyer, January 26, 1905, ASMB, and
Dyer, pp. 17-19.

93
   Dyer, p. 21.

94
   Letter, Dyer to Driscoll, January 28, 1905, ASMB, and
Dyer, p. 20.

95
   Ibid.

among the Sulpicians, it would smooth things out with the community. Superiors could show it to confreres, some of whom Dyer considered influential and worthy of such consideration. He was anticipating the fact that these men might be disposed to call into question the attitude of the Dunwoodie Sulpicians who took up such a project. But then because of such a signed statement of Farley they could say nothing about the project once they knew that it was the expressed desire of the Archbishop. [96]

In his response to Dyer, Driscoll never alluded to the matter of the signed statement but rather reported the great amount of enthusiastic encouragement the contributors have been giving the projected journal. [97] He then addressed himself to Dyer's anxiety over the review by saying:

> It may perhaps help to allay your misgivings relative to the attitude of the authorities in Paris, to know that Brunetière was secured (as a contributor) through the very kind and prompt negotiations of Father de Fovillo to whom Father Bruneau wrote explaining the object of the review, etc.
> Father de Fovillo's answer is quite long and without the shadow of preoccupation regarding censorships or anything of the kind. We are convinced that the folks in Paris will trouble

---

96
   Dyer to Driscoll, March 21, 1905, ASMB, Dyer, p. 51.

97
   Letter, Driscoll to Dyer, February 16, 1905, ASMB. Dyer op. cit., pp. 34-35.

themselves about the publication only in so far
as we choose to trouble them about it. [98]

This letter evidently did not satisfy Dyer's anxiety over the

signed statement because he sent off a note to Driscoll again

reminding him of the matter.   Driscoll responded by informing

Dyer that Farley was away in the Bahamas but as soon as he

returned he would get his signature on the statement. [99] He also

expressed in this letter his timidity about asking Farley to sign

such a statement.   One reason Driscoll gave for this was that

Farley had been widely quoted by Catholic periodicals and news-

papers about confiding the management of the review to the sem-

inary faculty.   He believed, Farley would consider this a sufficient

statement for the Sulpicians as well as for the public at large.

Another reason was that he may have felt that those who require

it were unwarrantably exigent since he was not obliged to render to

them an account of his doings or intentions.   A final reason was

that Driscoll did not see this statement as a safeguard for the

Sulpicians in case of a change of attitude.   This was because,

-----

98
    In the Archives of the Company of St. Sulpice (6, rue du
Regard, Paris) M. Noyé, S.S., archivist, informs me that there
exists: a dossier concerning the founding of The New York Review;
a dossier on the Sulpician secession from Dunwoodie in 1906; and
a statement by Driscoll on this secession (Cf. p. 150 of Dyer's
book) - all of which is present in ASMB.

99
    Letter, Driscoll to Dyer, March 12, 1905, ASMB; and Dyer,
p. 47 indicates that a note was sent.

according to Driscoll, if Farley ever wanted to discontinue or suppress the review, it would have been much easier for him to go back on such a private statement than on the statements he made that had appeared in the leading Catholic and other periodicals.[100]

A month later, however, Archbishop Farley, apparently on his own initiative, stopped and lunched with Dyer at St. Mary's Seminary, Baltimore, as he was returning from his journey to the Bahamas.[101] Both men discussed the projected review at this luncheon, and Dyer found the Archbishop to be very gracious. Farley agreed to sign the statement of responsibility and directed Dyer to mail it to him in New York. This Dyer did and within the month he received the statement signifying that Farley would accept full responsibility for The New York Review.[102] This

---

[100]
There was not too much printed in the Catholic and secular press about the forthcoming review and Farley's confidence in its Editors. Dyer indicates this to Driscoll in a letter (March 21, 1905) after he asked many of his Sulpician confreres at Baltimore about this matter. At this time the only periodicals that mentioned the projected journal was The Catholic News (XIX, 23, March 25, 1906), p. 4 editorial) and The Ecclesiastical Review, March, 1905, Vol. II, No. 3, (XXXII), p. 333.

[101]
Dyer, p. 52.

[102]
Letter, Archbishop John M. Farley to Dyer, March, 1905, "Statement" ASMB and Dyer, p. 54. Dyer states that he received this proposed statement from Farley "about a month later" from the date of March 23, 1905 when Dyer sent it to Farley in New York. Dyer, p. 53.

statement would also resolve any problems that Dyer had with the censorship of Review articles. [103]

Censorship was a thorny issue with the Sulpicians in America at this time. Concurrent with the genesis of The New York Review was a crisis between Francis E. Gigot and the Sulpician Generalate over granting an Imprimatur for his two volume work A Special Introduction to the Old Testament and New Testament. Volume one was acceptable to the two appointed Sulpician censors, one of whom was Driscoll. But, when the time came to examine volume two, the other censor no longer cared to act in that capacity. So Driscoll, who was then Gigot's superior at St. Austin's College, Washington, D. C. , gave the permission to have the second volume printed because he believed that as Superior he had the power to grant such permission. However, the Superior General did not agree with Driscoll about this power of a superior. He examined Volume II and rejected it not only because it was not in accord with the recently promulgated directions from the Superior General on censorship but also the General believed the spirit and opinion of this work were not in accord with the writings of Catholic scholars. This judgement by the Superior General of the Sulpicians, John Lebas, inaugurated a long drawn out hassle between Gigot, Driscoll, and

---

[103]
Dyer, p. 54.

the Sulpician Generalate.

Lebas' examination of volume two then caused him to call
for an examination of volume one. He personally appointed new
censors to review it. They rejected it even though it was widely
accepted in the United States and acclaimed by the American
bishops.

When a new superior general was elected shortly after
Lebas' death, he wrote to Dyer to appoint two new censors to
reexamine volume two. They judged the work to be acceptable
and sent their report to the general. The Generalate, however,
wanted Gigot to make some changes in this volume with which
he complied. However, after he did so, they left him waiting
for the final decision. [104]

This was the immediate background for Dyer's request that
Farley sign a statement of responsibility for the new review.
Among his letters dealing with this statement, Dyer left a notation
indicating that Father Garriguet, the new superior General,
thought that Driscoll should have written him expressing regret
that the circumstances in which The Review started did not allow
him to consult with Garriguet beforehand about it. [105] Garriguet

---

[104]
    Dyer, pp. 5-9; Dyer states here that the printed sheets
of Volume II were shown by Gigot to another professor at St.
Mary's who had no appointment to act as censor and even as
it was, never gave his approbation.

[105]
    Ibid., p. 55 and also Letter, Dyer to Driscoll, May 15,
1905 ASMB.

also thought that the Sulpicians should not appear too conspic-
uously in the journal, that their articles for it be submitted to the
Sulpician censors and that they were not to be financially engaged
in it. He finally recalled to Dyer that according to the regulations
of the Index each member of the review should have episcopal
Imprimatur. [106]

These desires of Garriguet on censorship communicated to
Driscoll and Gigot's fight with the Generalate over his book
were becoming too much for the young Sulpicians to take. More
and more the decision to secede from St. Sulpice and be in-
cardinated into Archdiocese of New York seemed very tempting.
But this would not happen for another year. [107]

---

[106]
No issue of The Review bore an Imprimatur except the final
one (III, May-June, 1908) which stated "cum permissu superiorum".
This caused The Ecclesiastical and its sister-journal The Dolphin
to remark "We note that there is no censor mentioned in connection with the magazine, such as the Index rules demand, and as
is customarily noted upon the cover of European magazines,
issued under ecclesiastical auspices. This means probably that
the Archbishop of New York confides in the orthodoxy and
propriety of the utterance of the publication under the editorship
of the rector of St. Joseph's Seminary. St. Sulpice stands for a
high scholarship." The Dolphin, VIII, (August, 1905), p. 241,
and The Ecclesiastical Review, III, September 1905, p. 318.

[107]
On January 9th, 1906 Revs. James F. Driscoll, R. K.
Wakeham, Francis E. Gigot, John R. Mahoney and Timothy P.
Holland seceded from the Society of St. Sulpice and were in-
cardinated into Archdiocese of New York. They remained on
the faculty of St. Joseph's Seminary. Rev. Joseph Bruneau, the
only other Sulpician at Dunwoodie at this time, did not secede
from the Society, and he returned to St. Mary's, Baltimore in
January, 1906. For full treatment of the secession, cf. Dyer's
book, pp. 58-160. Although a consideration of this secession

Debut

In the meantime the editors were hard at work to get out the
first number of The Review. They aimed for it to appear on May
15, 1905, but it was not until the week of June 21st that The New
York Review made its debut. [108]

For the next three years (1905-1908) The New York Review
would address itself to the theological and scientific conditions
of its day and attempt by means of its articles, editorials, and
book reviews to reconcile modern thought with the ancient Faith.

---

is beyond the scope of our present purpose here, suffice it to say
that these young Sulpicians no longer saw a future for St. Sulpice
in America since many bishops then wanted complete control of
their own seminaries. This secession merits mention here only
because some believed that the founding of The New York Review
had a bearing on it; viz., Sulpician theological conservatism (cf.
Boston Evening Transcript, February 3, 1906, II, 2:4). Driscoll,
however, adamantly discounted any connection between the
secession and The Review. In this regard he wrote to the Boston
Evening Transcript stating: "The action recently taken by certain Sulpician professors employed in the theological seminary
of New York was not the outcome of any controversy concerning
their orthodoxy or that of the Review, but was due to a con-
currence of circumstances quite foreign to that matter." Cited
in Dyer's op. cit. p. 104 (dated February 13, 1906).

[108]
Letter, Duffy to Hanna, January 8, 1908, ADR and Duffy
to Pace, June 16, 1905, ACUA, B23-7. In Duffy's letter to Pace
he said that Farley read the entire first issue before it went to
print, "a fact which we wish to be known for obvious reasons."

CHAPTER II

EDITORIAL POLICY OF THE NEW YORK REVIEW

The purpose of the new theological journal, as its annouce-
ment sheet indicated, was mainly apologetic with special reference to the religious and scientific conditions of the day. The
editors disclosed the particular sense of apologetics that they
had in mind on The Review's cover in the form of its sub-title:
"A Journal of Ancient Faith and Modern Knowledge". They said
that this sub-title, which Duffy revealed later to be suggested by
William S. Lilley's book, Ancient Religion and Modern Thought,
expressed their magazine's intention. [1] Since the intention of
The New York Review, as will be seen, was to reconcile tradition with modern knowledge, the sub-title soon became one of
its two hallmarks.

The second hallmark of The Review was also on the cover
of every issue. It was the scriptural quote:

---

[1]
Cf. Announcement Sheet (Appendix A). Duffy made this
disclosure in a review of William Samuel Lilley's book, Many
Mansions, London: Chapman and Hall, 1907. In this review he
referred to Lilley's earlier work, Ancient Religion and Modern
Thought, London: Chapman and Hall, 1886. See The New York
Review, III, Nos. 4 & 5 (January-February: March-April,
1908), 590.

> Every scribe who is instructed in the kingdom
> of heaven, is like unto a man that is a house-
> holder, who bringeth forth out of his treasure,
> things new and old. (Mt. 13, 52)

This quote revealed the positive and constructive method
that the editors said would be employed in their magazine.[2] It
was a method that affirmed that there was value in the old knowledge as well as the new. The method, then, respected tradition
and was open to new discoveries. In this way, it attempted to
come to the fullness of truth and reconcile science with the Faith.
Thus, these two hallmarks on the cover of The New York Review
gave the reader a good idea of what lay inside its pages as well
as the policy along which the new journal would conduct itself.

But, besides The Review's hallmarks which disclosed the
intention and method of the editors, there was also correspondence which gives one a good indication of what these men had
in mind for their theological journal. This thinking would eventually constitute their editorial policy.

Driscoll in a letter to Dyer, informing him that Duffy and
Brady intended to found The Review, presented how his associates
had conceived the new magazine. He wrote:

> The object of the publication (which would be
> brought out every two months) would be to dis-
> cuss in a scholarly way, yet in a manner in-
> telligible to ordinarily cultured persons, lay
> or cleric, the various questions with which the
> modern Christian apologist has to deal - mainly

---

[2] Cf. Announcement Sheet (Appendix A).

> those pertaining to Scripture and Philosophy.
> Though apologetic in purpose, it would not be
> polemical, i. e. , apologetical along the lines
> of such publication as the [Sacred Heart]
> Messenger. The idea is to publish careful
> studies on scriptural topics, the field of which
> is at present so exceedingly extensive, but
> which to the vast majority of even educated
> Catholics is still an unknown and unexplored
> region; - also on philosophical subjects, es-
> pecially on those bearing on religious beliefs.

Most of what Driscoll said here in this letter was similar
to what appeared on The Review's announcement sheet. The
new journal was to be scholarly and apologetic with the expressed
purpose of introducing Catholics to the new knowledge of the day.
It was to demonstrate the positive and negative
influence that this knowledge had on the Faith. In this way, it
would endeavor to arrive at an honest and balanced reconciliation
of science with the Faith.

Driscoll also disclosed how the editors of the new journal
were to carry out their apologetic purpose.

> Our intention is to enlist as contributors the
> foremost Catholic scholars of the United
> States, England and France - men who are
> really in touch with modern thought and its
> problem, and who are both able and willing
> to discuss them from the modern point of view.

Here, Driscoll expressed that the contributors that would be
solicited for The Review would be Catholics; i. e. , men steeped
in the Church's tradition. And, also, they would be people who
wrote from a modern point of view; i. e. , men well versed in the
scientific methods of the day. Only contributors with such a

positive regard for tradition and science, the editors believed,

could fulfill The Review's aim of being a journal of ancient

faith and modern knowledge. As will be seen, the editors did have

only this caliber of writer contribute to their magazine.

Then, the editor intimated in the letter the name and form

of his journal. This intimation revealed more of the incipient

thinking regarding The Review's policy. About its name and

form, he said:

> The name will be "The Apologist" or "The
> Apologetic Review" and in tone will be
> positive and constructive (better "recon-
> structive") rather than controversial. In
> form it will resemble the "Expositor".[3]

Although this name and form was later changed by the

editors, they did manifest the basic direction the journal was

to take.[4] It would be apologetic in the sense that the above-

mentioned hallmarks indicated it would be; viz., apologetic in

---

3

Letter, James F. Driscoll to Edward R. Dyer, January 11,
1905, ASMB. A copy of this letter is also found in Edward R.
Dyer's edition of Letters in the New York Seminary Secession,
Baltimore: private circulation, 1906, 11-14.
The magazine, The Messenger, to which this letter
referred was the monthly Jesuit publication which addressed
itself to apologetics. Rev. John J. Wynne was its editor.

4

Later the editors dismissed this tentative title because as
Duffy wrote to Rev. Edward J. Hanna of Rochester, New York
about the title, "The Apologist": "It has its advantages but it
could be improved on." See, Letter, Francis P. Duffy to
Edward J. Hanna, January 8, 1905 copy. ADR.
The editors' choice for the title, The New York Review,
could most likely have been in compliance with Archbishop
Farley's wish and suggestion that the new journal be "a

the sense of "reconstructive" by binding the ancient Faith with
modern knowledge. And, it would pattern itself somewhat after
the "Expositor", a London theological magazine which published
every month six or seven articles dealing with the higher criticism
of the Bible.

Another letter during The Review's genesis, this time by
associate editor Duffy, also presented the lines of thought that
the editors had in mind for their publication. With the same
enthusiastic spirit that Driscoll manifested in his letter to Dyer,
Duffy wrote to Rev. Edward J. Hanna of St. Bernard's Seminary,
Rochester, asking him to prepare an article for the first number
of The Review. Duffy said:

> ... and yesterday Dr. Driscoll and I submitted
> the scheme to Archbishop Farley. He gave it
> his enthusiastic approval. He feels the need
> of something such as we propose, and endorsed
> our action heartily. He was given clearly to
> understand that it was not to be a magazine of
> popular apologetics, but a serious work, to be
> conducted on modern lines. This is precisely
> the feature which meets with his commenda-
> tion... [5]

He continued:

> We have almost decided to call it (The Review)
> "The Apologist", a title which has its advantages
> but which might be improved on. You might
> suggest something else. Of course, the sort of

New York project". Cf. Chapter I of this dissertation.

[5]
Duffy to Hanna, Ibid.

apologetics we aim at is not polemical but of
that constructive (or "reconstructive") sort
that you know is most necessary.

Duffy's mentioning to Hanna that The Review would be "a
serious work", "conducted on modern lines", and "of the reconstructive type of apologetics" demonstrates again the lines
of the editors' thinking as regards the policy of The New York
Review. Their publication would not take lightly the value of
the past; it would employ new methods, and attempt a reconstruction or synthesis between tradition and science. Later
on when a newspaper, The Boston Transcript, erroneously reviewed The New York Review and made it appear disrespectful
to Church tradition, Driscoll wrote a very strong letter to its
editor correcting certain inaccuracies.[6] This letter is another
very good exposition of the aims and objectives of The Review.
He wrote:

> Two editorial articles published recently in
> the Transcript (January 13 and February 3)
> and referring to what is called the 'New liberal
> Catholicism' have been brought to my notice.
> In both of them frequent reference is made to
> the New York Review and to various persons
> connected with it, and though we are grateful
> for the friendly appreciation and the broad-
> minded fairness which the articles express,
> I feel it my duty to correct certain inaccuracies
> in the statement of facts as well as some
> erroneous impressions especially noticeable
> in the inferences.

---

[6]
"Editorial", The Boston Transcript, January 13, 1906, part
II, p. 2; and February 3, 1906, part II, p. 2.

In the first place, it is hardly necessary to say that there is not the least intention on the part of the founder and promoter of the <u>Review</u> to inaugurate a movement that could in any sense be termed 'a new Catholicism'. To entertain such an idea would be absurd - there could be no surer means of defeating the real purpose we had in view. The purpose, as implied in the sub-title: "A Journal of Ancient <u>Faith and Modern Thought"</u> is not to abandon <u>the old in favor of the new, but rather to in-</u> <u>terpret with becoming care and reverence the</u> <u>old truths in the light of the new science.</u> The <u>task, as it appears to us, is not one involving</u> <u>doctrinal change but restatement and readjust-</u> <u>ment - in other words, the preservation and</u> <u>not the rupture of continuity.</u> To this end, <u>viz.</u>, the gradual assimilation by theology of what is sound in the results of modern scholarship, we hope to contribute our mite, and I am glad to say that our efforts thus far have met nothing but encouragement. Reports to the contrary not-withstanding, there has been no question of censure being passed upon <u>The New York Review</u> or its contributors, either by Sulpician superiors, or any ecclesiastical authority whatsoever.[7]
(Italics mine)

This long letter indicated very clearly the reconstructive purpose of <u>The Review</u> as was disclosed by its sub-title, and it did define the sense of apologetics that <u>The New York Review</u> purported to present in order to achieve its purpose.

Driscoll continued in this letter to drive home to the editor

---

[7] Letter, Driscoll to the editor of <u>The Boston Transcript,</u> February 13, 1906, p. 8. This letter also appeared in "Statement from Rev. Dr. Driscoll", <u>The Catholic News,</u> XXI, 19, February 24, 1906, p. 5; and in the <u>Catholic Times and Standard,</u> March 3, 1906. Copies of this letter are at ASMB and in Dyer; pp. 103-106.

of the Transcript the fact of The Review's allegiance to Church

tradition.

> We desire, moreover, to affirm most emphat-
> ically that the New York Seminary (and the
> same is equally true of the New York Review)
> will stand for nothing that can be taken as
> a departure from strict Catholic orthodoxy.
> It has no ambition but that of standing in
> the front rank in the education of those who
> are to be enlightened exponents of the faith
> once delivered to the saints. Those who know
> the Archbishop of New York need not be
> assured that anything deviating ever so little
> from the standard would not be tolerated by
> him either in the seminary or in the Review
> which has been established under his auspices.
> (Italics mine)

This excerpt from Driscoll's letter emphasized the line of

respect for Church tradition that The Review's editors would

follow in their policy. According to its editor, The Review had

no purpose whatsoever to depart from tradition as it attempted

to synthesize that tradition with the finds of modern science

while using the new scientific methods.

In these letters, then, there is present the genesis of the

editors' thought in regard to their review. They disclosed very

well, as did The Review's hallmarks, what the editors' per-

ception of their journal would be, and they presented the lines

according to which the editors would conduct it.

The perception of The New York Review was that it would

be a journal of ancient faith and modern knowledge. Its approach

would not be polemical but rather positive and constructive in

order to reconcile the findings of modern science with Church tradition. In this approach it would be open to modern scientific methods while at the same time very respectful of Church tradition in order to interpret with becoming care and reverence the old truths in the light of modern science. It would also reject the anti-Christian claims of modern science. Only by such a serious and scholarly approach would The New York Review fulfill its purpose of reconciliation between science and the ancient Faith and effect a preservation, and not a rupture, of continuity between the past and the present.

Since the lines according to which The Review would be conducted were so clearly present in The Review's hallmarks and its editors' correspondence, the editors sincerely believed that they did not need to write out a formal editorial policy for their journal. [8] Instead, finding their thinking expressed in The Review's introductory article, "The Spirit of Newman's Apologetics" by the prominent lay-theologian, writer, and future editor of The Dublin Review, Wilfrid Ward, they chose that article to state their review's editorial policy. [9]

---

[8]
The New York Review, I, No. 1 (June-July, 1905), 129.

[9]
I, No. 1 (June-July, 1905), 3-14. Since there will be numerous references to articles in The New York Review throughout this dissertation, hereinafter only the volume number, issue, and pages will be cited. Unless it is not evident that the writer is referring to a Review article, the full title of this journal will then be cited in the footnote.

About this highly significant choice, the editors said:

> ...that for their purpose it would be difficult
> to find a more representative writer or a
> better subject... Happily his [Ward's] choice
> fell upon a theme which in his handling of it
> is admirably suited to our needs, not only
> as an appreciation of the greatest modern
> leader in English Catholic thought but also
> and mainly, as outlining better than we our-
> selves could do the temper and spirit in
> which we purpose conducting this Review.
> There was no need of formal editorial state-
> ment of aims and intentions when we could
> offer as an introduction Mr. Ward's article
> on "the Spirit of Newman's Apologetics."[10]
> (Italics mine)

This clear and unequivocal statement of The Review's

editors demonstrated the relation between Wilfrid Ward's article

and the editorial policy of The New York Review. It showed that

the editors chose this well-known theologian's article because

it fell in line with their thinking concerning the purpose of their

magazine.

The Article as Statement of the Editorial Policy

This article concerned John Henry Cardinal Newman's approach

to the Christian Church as a religion, as a theology, and as a

polity. The approach was the via media, Newman's famous bal-

ancing of opposing poles in the three areas of religion, theology,

and ecclesiastical polity. In the article Ward analyzed this

10
 Ibid., 129.

approach to the three areas and concluded with what he considered to be Newman's contribution to the religious thought of the twentieth century: a synthesis between the two sets of opposing poles
in tradition - science, and reformers - authority.

To Newman's approach to the Church as religion, the article
gave very little consideration because Ward believed that the
world at large was well acquainted with Newman's writings in
this area.

But, in the areas of the Church as theology and the Church
as polity Ward demonstrated fully and clearly Newman's spirit
of apologetics which aimed to bridge these areas' respective
poles.

In the area of theology proper Ward showed how Newman
desired to combine the two opposing poles of Church tradition
and the findings of modern science. Newman, like St. Thomas,
believed that both poles could be combined into a synthesis only
by first respecting tradition and then by adopting the methods
of history and science to theology without taking these methods'
anti-Christian claims.

Ward's article then logically considered the setting where
this combination takes place and the people who can effect it.
Here, Ward presented Newman's approach to ecclesiastical
polity.

He said that this combination takes place in the Church as
people who because of their prejudices, feelings, and sympathies

can easily be led to dissension, disloyalty, and rebellion because of new thought. Therefore, for Newman, the people who can prevent such a chaotic situation and effect a reconciliation between tradition and science are the reformers who are open to the findings of science, and authority who respect tradition and by tradition check the anti-Christian conclusions of these new methods. Only a synthesis of this second set of opposing poles, reformers and people in authority, can effect the reconciliation of tradition with science.

In view of this, Ward then presented Newman's lines for reconciling the two poles of reformers and authority. According to the article, Newman believed that reformers must respect the constitution of the Church; be practical in the expression of their views; not advocate abstract theory (no matter how important) as to cause present disruption; and respect the claims of existing government and order in the Church. On the other hand, authority must have the zeal for those liberties which are essential to life, growth, and necessary reform. It should always grant reformers the freedom to research; never act tyrannical, and never neglect being informed.

Ward concluded the article with what he believed was Newman's contribution to twentieth century religious thought; the ideal constitution of the Church. Newman, the article stated, attempted to combine in the long run tradition with science by the

ideal constitution of the Church; i. e. , the <u>ecclesia</u> of saint,
thinker, and ruler (the Church as the great body of which every
baptized Christian is a member) working together. However,
the ruler would keep the balance and prevent the thinker and
saint from predominating over one another.

From this summary of Ward's article, it is evident how
much the lines of the article run similar to <u>The New York Review's</u>
editors' thinking for their journal which its hallmarks and editorial correspondence disclosed. They therefore simply chose
Ward's article to express the editorial policy of their review.
That the journal would be apologetic in the sense which the
article used that word; i. e. , to reconcile the new findings of
science with the tradition of the Church, constituted in essence
its editorial policy.

The Review's Editors and Wilfrid Ward

In addition to this article, there is other evidence which
demonstrates how much the editors' thinking was similar to Ward's
and how much they respected him as a theologian. In a biographical sketch of Ward the editors said that throughout all his
apologetical works they could trace one main purpose - "the
endeavor to reconcile Catholic teaching with all that is best in
the science of the day."[11] Ward's purpose in writing was then

---

11
Ibid.

obviously the same as that of The New York Review.

When Ward became editor of The Dublin Review, the Dunwoodie editors applauded this fact in one of their journal's
editorials. Their tribute again disclosed the similarity in their
thinking.

> Mr. Ward is eminently fitted for his new
> position. He is personally acquainted with
> a large number of the leaders of thought in
> England and elsewhere; he is equally at
> home in Catholic theology and in the general
> task of reconciling old beliefs with new dis-
> coveries, he takes a liberal-conservative
> attitude which makes him a model for Cath-
> olic apologists. [12]

Besides having similarity of purpose with Ward, the editors
also had a great respect for him. Their respect becomes evident
in Driscoll's correspondence with him.

When the editors were first lining up contributors for their

---

[12]
I, No. 4 (December-January, 1905-1906), 514. Wilfrid
Ward (1856-1916) editor of The Dublin Review. Upon assuming
this position, the new editor decided to lay different tracks for
his inherited journal in order to fulfill a different objective
from that of his father's editorship. The English Catholic
Who's Who described these tracks and objective as: "To bring
into combination the work of those Catholic thinkers and men
of learning who know the intellectual language of the day, who
accept what is true in modern research, science and criticism,
while still reverencing the authority and ancient tradition of
the Church - that is to pave the way for a synthesis between
Faith and learning which any age of intellectual activity of a
new kind demands". This quote, cited from III, Nos. 4 & 5
(January-February: March-April, 1908), 587-588, described
Ward's editorial policy as approximately the same as that of
The New York Review.

publication, Driscoll wrote Baron Friedrich von Hügel requesting him to ask Ward for an article for the first number of The Review.[13] At that time, Driscoll did not know Ward personally, as the correspondence attests, but he no doubt wanted this famous lay-theologian among The Review's first contributors in order to insure its immediate success. The article that Ward wrote for the first number of The Review was, of course, "The Spirit of Newman's Apologetics" which, as we saw, fell happily in line with the editors' thinking that they chose it to state their review's editorial policy.

A year later, Ward wrote a second article for The Review, "The Function of Intransigeance".[14] Driscoll wrote to him acknowledging receipt of this second article. In his letter we have another expression of these editors respect for Ward. Driscoll wrote Ward saying how much the Review's editors "prize an article from your pen that we preferred to use it as a leader in our next issue and, thus, you will open our second volume as

---

13
    Letter, Baron Friedrich von Hügel to Wilfrid Ward, January 19, 1905, The Wilfrid Ward Family Papers. In this letter von Hügel evidently enclosed Driscoll's letter to Ward for it read "... I want to do my duty and at once post this letter to you, which Dr. Driscoll has asked me to read, add a line of introduction, and to post to you".

14
    II, No. 1 (July-August, 1906), 3-18.

you did the first. "[15]

Besides revealing personally to Ward their esteem for him, the editors did not hesitate also to make this respect known to others, for the same letter continued:

> ...and to repeat what Dr. Duffy and myself have often said to others, viz., that among all our neo-apologists there is no one whose work is so efficient for the interests of the good cause as is your own. It is so moderate, and well-balanced that it is eminently well-fitted to meet the intellectual exigencies of these rather troublous times.

Obviously, Driscoll's letter shows that the editors of The New York Review considered Ward's writings to be balanced, timely, and similar to their own views.

Driscoll warmly concluded this letter to Ward with the words:

> Please consider the invitation to contribute articles to The New York Review as always open and most cordial... Both interest and elevation of tone and scholarship would be happily balanced if the majority of our articles were like the "Function of Intransigeance."

It is no doubt, then, that because of the similarity in thinking between Ward and the editors of The New York Review as well as their esteem for him, as those editorial tributes and correspondence indicated, one of Ward's articles would be chosen to state formally the editorial policy of The Review.

15
  Letter, Driscoll to Ward, April 27, 1906, The Wilfrid Ward Family Papers.

Acknowledgement from Contemporary Periodicals

This editorial policy made The New York Review a theological
journal which was then unique to the English-speaking world. Before The Review's emergence, no Catholic theological journal
had the apologetic objective and scholarly approach that this new
magazine had. As was indicated earlier, because of its uniqueness in objective and approach contemporary periodicals responded favorably to the editors' plans for founding The Review. We
also saw that when its first issue appeared, these same periodicals heartily welcomed it in their reviews. But also, in their
reviews they gave particular applause to The Review's editorial
policy.

The Catholic World in its review of this new journal paid a
superlative tribute to its editorial policy. In enthusiastic
language it said:

> The most striking and encouraging feature
> of The Review is that the entire contents,
> articles, book reviews, editorial notes,
> scriptural studies, breathe one and the same
> spirit. This fact is all the more remarkable
> because, as we have learned, this unanimity
> is not the result of any previous understand-
> ing, consultation, or editorial direction. The
> intellectual attitude unmistakably manifested
> throughout the number is a cheerful willing-
> ness to welcome the legitimate claims of the
> modern mind, and regard it as a potential
> ally to the cause of Catholic truth.[16]

---

[16] The Catholic World, LXXXI, 486 (September, 1905), 842.

This intellectual attitude that the Catholic World identified as reconciling science with faith and acknowledged as pervading the whole first number of the new journal was, of course, The Review's editorial policy. This positive critique continued to extoll this policy by stating how important it was to the contemporary theological scene and how The Review was the first organ in the English language with this all-important policy. The review ended with praise for Archbishop Farley for bestowing on the English-speaking world The Review which it so badly needed because of its apologetic caliber.

Another of The New York Review's contemporaries, The Ecclesiastical Review, also reacted positively to its appearance. In a three page critique it said:

> The special aim of the New York magazine is ... to bring into prominence the true achievements of modern scientific thought, and to show how far they are in accord with the unchanging principles of the Christian faith. The purpose is well expressed in the sub-title, - "a journal of the ancient faith and modern thought", and readers who happen to study The Dolphin will there find an article - the beginning of a series of studies on the same subject - which shows how carefully we must steer in this matter, and how zealous it behooves us to be in its pursuit at the same time. It may be argued that a new magazine of this kind simply reasserts a programme already established by such high-class periodicals as the American Catholic Quarterly Review, or The Catholic University Bulletin, which does in particular and necessarily cultivate this same field of the theological and philosophical discipline ... Yet even if this were true, the establishment of a periodical such as The New York Review

promises to be, would be amply justified in
its appeal to the scholarly or educated reader in English-speaking countries. [17]

Although this review was not as enthusiastic as that of the

Catholic World's, it did express how timely the editorial policy

of The Review was to theology. The review also presupposed the

objections that the Dunwoodie journal would suplicate the efforts

of already existing theological periodicals. Its answer was that

the objections were in a way unfounded and even underlined The

Review's uniqueness in policy. Some of these objections, as we

have already seen, came from friends and supporters of The

Ecclesiastical Review. In the exact three page critique, The

Dolphin, which was the sister-magazine of The Ecclesiastical

Review, praised the New York journal a month earlier. [18]

The Boston Evening Transcript, which was referred to earl-

ier, also acknowledged the aims and objectives of The New York

Review. In two editorials it stated that it welcomed The Review's

intention to meet the conditions and needs of the day. [19] One

editorial read as follows:

17
    The Ecclesiastical Review, fourth series, III (XXXIII),
No. 3 (September, 1905), 315-316. The critique ran from pp.
315-318.

18
    The Dolphin, VIII, No. 2 (August, 1905), 239-241.

19
    "Editorial", The Boston Evening Transcript, January 13,
1906, part II, p. 2; and February 3, 1906, part II, p. 2.

> We called attention a while ago to the liberal
> utterances of The New York Review, "a
> journal of the ancient faith and modern
> thought," published at Yonkers, N. Y. ,
> under the auspices of Archbishop Farley,
> four numbers of which had appeared, and
> we expressed gratification at the evidence
> found in the editorials and in the contributions
> published that the clergy and educated laity
> of the Church had a journal which would
> fearlessly face the problems of apologetics
> which present-day conditions in the world
> at large require. [20]

As was already mentioned, these editorials exaggerated

The Review's openness to the methods of modern science stating

that it accepted the anti-Christian claims of these methods.

Driscoll, as we saw, wrote to The Transcript's editor correct-

ing these inaccuracies. However, in the quote above from its

second editorial on The Review, the Boston paper did capture

the basic spirit of the editors' thinking, and it welcomed their

editorial policy.

Having paid tribute to the balanced scholarship of Rev.

Francis E. Gigot's articles in The Review, this editorial con-

tinued by speaking of Driscoll:

> Collaborating with Dr. Gigot. . . has been Rev.
> James F. Driscoll D. D. , who in the first
> number of the review under the title "Recent
> Views on Biblical Inspiration", set forth very
> ironically but very frankly the motives which
> led to the founding of a journal in which Amer-
> ican Catholic scholarship could speak as freely

20
"Editorial", Ibid. , February 3, 1906, part II, p. 2.

> on issues of the hour as progressive French
> and English Catholics are speaking.
>   The inclusive point of view, ironic temper
> and expert handling of the delicate problems
> involved which Dr. Driscoll showed in his
> article, in which he set forth his aims and
> those of his collaborators, were admirable;
> and subsequent issues of the review have
> justified the hopes of those who saw in it the
> herald of a new day. [21]

There is no corroborative evidence available for this re-

ference to Driscoll's article as setting forth the motives for

founding The Review. The same is true about its claim that

his article's style was "ironic". Nevertheless, upon examination

of the article, there is present a good estimation of the problems

of the day, the confusion in theological circles, people's

desire for authority to settle controversies between science

and faith, and the need for guidance. These reasons would

warrant a theological journal with the aim and policy of The New

York Review. Later on in the article Driscoll spelled out the

steps to be taken to remedy this controversial theological sit-

uation - steps which were very similar to those in The Review's

editorial policy and at times a further explication of them. How-

ever, it is only academic that an article written by the editors of

a journal would contain thoughts similar to and consistent with

those of his editorial policy.

----

[21]
    Driscoll's article which is mentioned here appeared in
The Review, I, No. 1 (June-July, 1905), 81-88.

Across the Atlantic came more accolades of The New York

Review. The English Catholic Weekly was also a friendly

welcomer and critic of this Dunwoodie jouranl. In a belated

review it remarked:

> When it [The New York Review] started three
> years ago, its promoters realized that the
> strides made in historical and scientific
> research during the past half century de-
> manded the consideration of new problems.
> But they also realized that those problems
> could not be adequately dealt with except
> by working in sympathy with the Holy See.
> The journal, issuing from the diocesan
> seminary of New York was under the re-
> sponsibility of Archbishop Farley, whose
> intimate friendship with and devotion to
> Pius X were sufficient guarantee of the
> utmost loyalty. Working then in this spirit
> of progress under authoritative guidance,
> the editors have been able to produce in one
> special periodical some of the best work of
> Catholic scholars both at home and abroad.

This review praised the New York editors for being au

courant with the theological conditions of the day as well as

for bringing forth some fine scholarly results. In regard to the

editorial policy specifically The Catholic Weekly stated:

> The first place [of The New York Review] is
> naturally given to the apologetic questions
> of the hour. They are treated however in a
> positive and constructive manner rather than
> a controversial or destructive manner. Thus,
> Mr. Wilfrid Ward, in an article entitled,
> "The Spirit of Newman's Apologetics" outlines
> the temper and spirit of the review.
> (Italics mine)

This quote revealed how cognizant this English paper was

of The Review's statement regarding Ward's article expressing its editorial policy. It made Ward's article the natural and

logical expression of a positive, constructive apologetic.

The Catholic Weekly then went on to give a critique of

The Review's articles, contributors, and format. It praised

the fact that the editors published articles dealing with

scripture, patrology, and archeology by writers of the first

rank as Joseph Turmel, Gabriel Oussani, and Francis Gigot.

Finally, this review considered the section in The Review

entitled "Notes" and its book reviews. Of the reviews, it said

that their value rested in the fact that they are all signed by the

reviewer - "a most desirable feature in these days of the

writing of many books, and when so much depended on the review-

er. " Of the "Notes" it stated:

> ". . . it ought to be said that they are worthy
> of a better name. They are unsigned. We
> suggest to the writer that his work is of an
> importance which should justify him in
> coming to the front with his name. Practically
> every recent event worth speaking about which
> has happened in the world of religious thought
> is recorded with suitable, and sometimes
> very vigorous comment. It is largely through
> "notes" of this kind that general opinion is
> formed. It is particularly here that those
> expressions of loyalty to the Holy See find
> vent. It is here than an attitude is taken
> towards orthodoxy and unorthodoxy. It is
> here that we find an indication of that spirit
> of true progress which pays due regard to
> the guidance of authority and to the choice
> of the most distinguished thinkers and
> writers.
> Those of our readers who desire to be
> kept up to date and at the same time to be
> kept within the safety limits, cannot do better

than add The New York Review to their list
of periodicals. We commend it especially to
the hard-worked parochial clergy. [22]

This critique's belief that this section of The Review should
have been carried a better title is valid. "Notes" was more than
just a mere chronicle of events. It was in reality, editorials.
It commented on scholarly projects and endeavors in the light
of The Review's aim to reconcile science with faith.

The writer of "Notes" was most likely Duffy. Although there
is no available corroborative evidence for this identification, one
just simply has to compare its literary style and theological tone
with those from some of Duffy's articles to realize that he composed these editorials. It is for this tone primarily that the
Catholic Weekly praised "Notes" for its balance.

From this consideration, then, of the editorial policy of
The New York Review as it was disclosed in its hallmarks and
editorial correspondence, as it was formally stated by Wilfrid
Ward's article "The Spirit of Newman's Apologetics"; and as it
was heartily welcomed and encouragingly endorsed by contemporaries periodicals, one may form a good estimate of how
The New York Review in its articles, book reviews, and
editorials would approach theology, the Church, and the theological controversy of the day, modernism.

---

[22] "Editorial", The Catholic Weekly, November 15, 1905, p. 8.

CHAPTER III

THE NEW YORK REVIEW'S APPROACH TO THEOLOGY

The primary objective of The New York Review was, as its
editorial policy stated, to be apologetic in the sense of bringing
into prominence the true achievements of modern scientific
thought and to demonstrate how far they were in accord with the
essential teachings of Church tradition. As has already been
indicated, The Review's sub-title: "A Journal of Ancient Faith
and Modern Knowledge" and its scriptural slogan well expressed
this apologetic's objective and method; the editors' correspondence articulated the importance of such an apologetic; the
introductory article formally defined it; and contemporary periodicals heartily endorsed it because of its timeliness of the religious and scientific conditions of the day.

However, it was the articles, editorials, and book reviews
of The New York Review that realized this objective. All of
them unmistakably and consistently manifested throughout all
The Review's numbers a serious attempt to reconcile modern
knowledge with Church tradition. To effect such a reconciliation
they portrayed a scholarly openness to the legitimate claims of
modern scientific methods and a deep respect for Church tradition. This openness to the scientific methods of the day and ,

respect for tradition for the purpose of reconciling both con-

stituted The New York Review's approach to theology.

Respect for Tradition

Beyond the shadow of a doubt, The Review presented in its

pages the first aspect of this approach to theology; viz. , a

reverential respect for the truths and value of Christian tradition

in order for theology to take its rightful and necessary place in

the modern world. Although one clearly senses this respect

pervading all of The Review's articles, editorials, and book

reviews, there were, however, certain ones that specifically

addressed themselves to it. These underlined the importance

of respecting tradition in order to effect a reconciliation of

science with the ancient faith.

The two articles that the editor himself, James F. Driscoll,

wrote for his journal were among the ones that accented this

importance. In them he primarily discussed the recent views

of biblical inspiration at that time. But, one can easily cull from

his scholarly discussion specific references to the importance for

a positive regard for tradition in theological enterprises.

In his first article Driscoll made his first reference to this

respect for tradition in an extremely long but necessary intro-

duction to his subject when he clearly asserted that modern

scientific investigations into sacred scripture respected Chris-

tian Tradition by leaving intact its substantial beliefs and

doctrines.[1] These investigations, he went on to say, only
addressed themselves to the traditional opinions concerning
matters peripheral to doctrine as the authorship of Isaias
XL-LXVI, the literary genre of the Book of Jonas, and the mode
of biblical inspiration, not its fact. If these investigations produce results contrary to these traditional opinions, then adjustment, he said, must be made by apologists and scripture scholars.

In speaking of this group of thinkers involved in the task of
adjustment, Driscoll made a second reference to the respect
for tradition. He praised them by saying:

> Ever deferential to authority and maintain-
> ing firmly the just claims of the faith once
> delivered to the saints, they at the same time
> accept, without misgiving or arrière pensée,
> albeit in a spirit of keen scholarly determin-
> ation, the facts and inferences of modern
> criticism on their scientific face value.
> Thoroughly alive to the need of an adjustment

---

[1]
James F. Driscoll, "Recent Views on Biblical Inspiration
(I)", I, No. L (June-July, 1905), 82. This article, as well as
the ones that will be cited, speaks of tradition in two senses:
the essential truths of the Christian faith and the time-honored
forms or vehicles of these truths. The former, the authors
held, could never be changed without doing away with the Faith
itself; while the latter can be improved or replaced. However,
these writers' call for the respect for both senses of tradition
constituted the first aspect of The Review's approach to theology.
Hereafter, to avoid ambiguity as to which sense of tradition is
being used, I will write Tradition with a capital "T" to denote
the sense of essential, unchangeable Christian truths, and
tradition with a small "t", sometimes in the plural, to indicate
the time-honored forms of essential truths, as well as the
generic concept of tradition.

between these facts and certain traditional
views, they are earnestly seeking to
establish the basis of a more uniform solution of biblical difficulties on principles in
harmony alike with the data of revealed
truth and scientific progress of the age. [2]

It is evident from this quote that this task of adjustment

would not touch the basic Christian Tradition at all. But, slowly

and deliberately would these men seek principles that would not

only solve long-standing biblical questions but also ones that

would respect the data of revelation and promote scientific pro-

gress. These thinkers, Driscoll was confident to say, could

carry out this tedious task of adjustment because of their respect

for tradition and openness to science.

In the second article which concerned exclusively Father M.

J. Langrange's idea of biblical inspiration, Driscoll affirmed

for a third time the importance of respecting tradition. He said:

... the revealed fact of inspiration has come
down to us accompanied by certain traditional
inferences, which though not pertaining to the
substance of the doctrine, nor all of equal
theological or scientific value, are nevertheless worthy of great respect, nor may they be
lightly set aside without endangering belief in
dogma itself. [3]

Here Driscoll called for a respect not only for the sub-

---

[2]
Ibid., 83.

[3]
"Recent Views on Biblical Inspiration II", I, No. 2 (August-
September, 1905, 198.

stantial beliefs of Christian Tradition but also for their accompaniments because of their inter-relationship. Although peripheral, these accompaniments still were intimately connected with the substantial beliefs as vehicles or supports. For this reason, Driscoll believed that they commanded respect throughout scientific investigations so that the substantial beliefs may not be rendered useless or vulnerable.

These references to the indispensability of the respect for tradition in modern scientific investigations of sacred scripture are found at the outset of Driscoll's discussion of the modern view of inspiration. Their introductory position in his articles suggest that the author was laying down the ground rules before he entered the discussion of modern views which, considered in isolation from tradition, could work havoc on the Christian faith. Also, although they were made in the context of an essay on biblical inspiration, it seems that these references could easily have been stated in a consideration of any topic in any branch of theology. They appeared to have had value for the whole of theology's endeavor to reconcile science with faith. This universal and convertible value that these references have for all of theology in this apologetic endeavor becomes more evident upon considering the statements that Francis E. Gigot made concerning respect for tradition in his articles in The Review.

Gigot, as was already indicated, was a prolific and

acclaimed writer in the field of sacred literature. Being a close

colleague of Driscoll's on the Dunwoodie faculty and a firm

believer in The New York Review's objective, he contributed more

than 20 percent of the writings in it. Their caliber seemed

strikingly to be a balance between tradition and science. In them

he always seemed to approach a piece of sacred scripture with

the wisdom of an aged craftsman who had lived and labored long

enough to know that truth resided in both the old and the new.

As convincingly as he wrote about being open to the new scien-

tific methods, Gigot wrote just as convincingly about reverencing

the ancient traditions.

This is evident in a series of articles he wrote for The

Review on the subject of higher criticism of the Bible. Respond-

ing to numerous requests from priests who desired a clear

statement on the meaning and bearings of the then much discussed

method of biblical study, Gigot presented in this series guiding

norms that would help maintain one's respect for tradition and

openness to new methods of biblical investigations.[4] Although

in these articles one would get the impression that his primary

aim was to have the readers accept the new scientific methods,

he did make strong and explicit reference to the importance of

---

[4]
This fact that numerous requests gave rise to this series
of articles by Gigot was mentioned by the editors in I, No. 6
(April-May, 1906), 802.

respecting tradition. He regarded this respect to be the starting

point of the critical venture as well as the beacon in uncharted

theological areas. One statement that expressed Gigot's respect

for tradition was:

> It must be granted that throughout his
> scientific study of the problem of higher
> criticism of the Bible, a Catholic worthy
> of the name will feel in his heart that
> respect due to the teaching authority of
> the Church of God, which should always
> accompany him in the pursuit of any
> branch of knowledge which borders on
> the domain of divine revelation. [5]

Here Gigot spoke of the imporatnce of this respect pervading

all the work of the Catholic scripture scholar. He also extended

this importance to any knowledge which concerned itself with

divine revelation. By so doing he demonstrated the indispens-

ability of respect for tradition in any theological endeavor in

order to safeguard the data of revelation.

In another place Gigot spoke of a double respect for the new

as well as the old because he believed this was the only way one

could come in a scientific way to a fuller possession of the truth.

> Whatever is proved solid and good in
> time-honored positions, he will hold as
> precious gold; and so will he do also
> with whatever amount of truth he per-
> ceives in modern views; for in either
> case nothing short of anti-scientific

5
"The Higher Criticism of the Bible: Nature of Its Problems",
II No. 1 (July-August, 1906), 69.

prejudice would prompt him to act
otherwise. [6]

He then suggested a method for the students of higher

criticism for employing this double respect that would bring

them to this fuller knowledge of sacred scripture.

> State impartially ancient traditions
> bearing on the point at issue, together
> with the chief grounds, in their favor.
> Should they, upon the examination of
> these grounds, think that the traditions
> are but partly true, they carefully re-
> frain from treating the traditional
> position as if altogether worthless.
> Much rather do they endeavor to
> determine the amount of truth contained
> therein and to modify the ancient opinions
> to the extent actually required by newly
> ascertained data. In their striving to
> re-state the traditional views they plainly
> aim at securing more correct positions
> for scriptural science, and indeed posi-
> tions in organic connection with ancient
> biblical knowledge so that in all such
> cases their desire of doing constructive
> work cannot reasonably be questioned. [7]

Gigot was speaking here of a method that would have been

applied to the traditional forms of substantial beliefs and not to

the substantial beliefs themselves. In it respect for tradition

was the starting point and it strongly pervaded throughout. This

---

[6]
"The Higher Criticism of the Bible: Its General Principles",
II, No. 2 (September-October, 1906), 160.

[7]
"The Higher Criticism of the Bible: Its Constructive
Aspect", II, No. 3 (November-December, 1906), 303.

respect would have preserved the total identity of a traditional form and whatever was valuable in it. The respect for the new seemed to rest only in its value to modify and refine the form. It was an important factor in the reparation or improvement of the form so that the form could be a more effective vehicle or support for the substantial belief. In this way, then, the method is constructive; or perhaps re-constructive would be better word.

Gigot utilized this method in four other articles that he wrote in The Review. concerning the authorship of Isaias XL-LXVI, and the literary genre of some Old Testament books. [8] Following his method he first set out the traditional arguments in favor of the time honored view of these scriptural topics. Then considering their value he pointed out how new discussions suggested some flaws in them. His investigations led him not to a blanket dismissal of the traditional views but to their corroboration or refinement. In this way, then, the truths of the history of salvation upon which these traditional views

---

[8]
"The Authorship of Isaias, XL-LXVI:PLI. Arguments in Favor of the Traditional View," I, No. 2 (August-September, 1905), 153-168; and Pt. II: "Arguments Against the Isaianic Authorship", I, No. 3 (October-November, 1905), 227-296; "The Book of Jonas: Arguments For and Against Its Historical Character", I, No. 4 (December, 1905-January, 1906), 411-424; and "Leading Problems Concerning the Book of Job: A Brief Exposition and Discussion", I, No. 5 (February-March, 1906), 579-596.

touched came into bolder relief.

Most often what Gigot meant by tradition in his references to respecting it, was the traditional views and opinions concerning the question of authorship, date, literary genre, method of composition of the sacred books. Like Driscoll, he believed that these could undergo investigation and perhaps even change because they did not belong to the sacred deposit of faith. Also like Driscoll, he believed that revealed doctrine, Tradition par excellence, was not debatable. On this point Gigot's respect for this type of Tradition came out forcefully.

> Of course, if the questions mooted by
> higher criticism of the Bible belong to
> the sacred sphere of revealed doctrine;
> they could not be controverted by anyone
> without making him chargeable with the
> taint of Rationalism. In vain would he
> protest against such an accusation, the
> very fact that he [the student of higher
> criticism] dared to lay an impious hand
> upon what pertains essentially to the
> Catholic faith would stand against him
> as an undeniable proof of his rash audacity.
> But if there be a well ascertained fact, it
> is that the question of author, date, literary
> kind, method of composition, etc. i. e. ,
> the questions discussed by the higher critics
> of the Bible do not belong to the sacred
> deposit of Revelation. [9]

The reason why he held this forceful respect for this type of tradition was because it was essential to the Catholic faith.

---

[9]
"The Higher Criticism of the Bible: Its Relation to Tradition", II, No. 4 (January-February, 1907), 442.

Without this type of tradition or even modifying it, the faith would cease to be Catholic. Therefore, no one, he affirmed, could have a just reason to depart from its authentic teaching. In subsequent Review articles Gigot underlined this dictum when he elucidated the teachings of scripture concerning contemporary issues.

One of these contemporary issues was divorce. It was making headlines at the time not only by the increased number of American marriages that were ending in divorce but also by the increasing liberalizations that its laws were undergoing.[10] Gigot wrote his second series of articles for The Review on divorce in the New Testament.[11] They contained no special pleading pro or con this marital trend in the modern world but presented only a calm objective evaluation of the scriptural texts with the aim of discovering the mind of Christ and of the Church on the permanence of the marriage bond. Evaluating these texts in the light of modern biblical criticism he proved

---

[10]
"Prevalence of Divorce in U. S. Discussed", New York Times, October 22, 1906, sec. 3, p. 4. Cf. also The New York Review, II, No. 4 (January-February, 1907), 528.

[11]
In this series Gigot wrote for The Review under the same title six articles on several New Testament texts concerning the indissolubility of marriage. "Divorce in the New Testament: An Exegetical Study," II, No. 4 (January-February, 1907), 479-494; No. 5 (March-April, 1907), 610-620; No. 6 (May-June, 1907), 749-760; and in Vol. III: No. 1 (July-August, 1907), 56-68; Nos. 4 & 5 (January-February: March-April, 1907), 545-560; and No. 6 (May-June, 1907), 704-721.

that the Catholic teaching on divorce was none other than that
which was ascribed to Christ in the gospels. In fact, his use of
the most recent methods of literary and historical criticism on
these texts simply confirmed that the authentic teaching of the
Church on this subject could not be dismissed.

It is significant that many of the statements regarding
respect for tradition came from Driscoll and Gigot, the editor
and a close associate of The New York Review. In them, both
men disclosed their thoughts on this subject. No doubt, it was
these thoughts that guided the editors to select for their journal
only articles which contained this respect for tradition in order
that The Review would fulfill its apologetic purpose.

In addition to these men's expressions of the importance of
respecting tradition, there were others who made similar ones
in The Review. The Reverend Joseph Turmel headed the list of
these contributors with his nine articles on the teachings of the
early Fathers of the Church.[12] The way he accentuated in them

---

12
"St. Justin Martyr I", I, No. 2 (August-September, 1905),
206-216; "St. Justin Martyr II", I, No. 3 (October-November,
1905), 326-345; "St. Justin Martyr III", I, No. 4 (December-
January, 1905-1906), 466-587; "Tatian: A Patristic Study", I,
No. 6 (April-May, 1906), 782-795; "The Dogma of the Trinity
in St. Augustine", II, No. 1 (July-August, 1906), 86-105;
"Athenagoras: A Patristic Study", II, No. 2 (September-October,
1906), 189-203; "Clement of Alexandria", II, No. 5 (March-
April, 1907), 625-639; "Clement of Alexandria II", II, No. 6
(May-June, 1907) 761-768; and "Clement of Alexandria III, III,
No. 1 (July-August, 1907), 69-73.

this importance was by his method. Without any commentary or
development, he simply presented the various teachings of
these Fathers on such topics as God, the Church, the Eucharist,
and the Trinity.

Although such a method caused his articles to read very
drily and lifelessly like catalogues or manuals, one does get the
idea, as George Tyrrell did, that Turmel's reason for employing
such a method was to let the facts speak for themselves.[13] Then,
in this way, those readers who were unenlightened about patristic
teachings would have drawn their own conclusions that these
teachings, which, in fact, make up Christian tradition had
contributory value for the theological questions of the day. Another writer for The Review also used this same method in his
two unsigned articles on the doctrine of the real presence in the
Church Fathers.[14]

----

[13]
    Letter, George Tyrrell to James F. Driscoll, January 6,
1906. "Turmel's line (in The New York Review) is the safest and
the most telling of all.... He has a wonderful way of making facts
speak for themselves and making readers draw their own conclusions. And thus he is incontrovertible -- for he says nothing'.'
    This letter and one other of Tyrrell's to Driscoll were
given to Rev. Terrence F. X. O'Donnell of the Archdiocese of
New York by the Keogh Family of New Rochelle, New York.
Driscoll resided for a while with this family after he became
pastor emeritus of St. Gabriel's parish, New Rochelle in 1919.
He died July 5, 1922 in St. Joseph's Hospital, Yonkers, New
York. The Keogh Family told Father O'Donnell that these were
the only two letters belonging to Driscoll in their possession.
This writer is grateful to Father O'Donnell for the use of them.

[14]
    Père Pourrat , "The Real Presence in the Fathers I",

In speaking of Turmel in The Review, the editors praised
the use of such a method. They said that if five-hundred
scholars would continue with this method and only a half-dozen
would work on the openness to new knowledge and development
of truth, then some of the theological problems raised by the
use of new scientific methods would be solved. The solutions
resulting from this strong regard for tradition and scholarly
openness to science, the editors confidently believed, would
be in favor of the ancient claims of the Catholic Church.[15] This
editorial commendation of Turmel's method leaned heavily toward the importance of presenting ancient truths. It manifested
once again the favorable regard that the editors had for the
tradition of the Church.

Other articles in The Review also accentuated a respect
for tradition. Addressing themselves to such contemporary topics
as different notions of morality, modern substitutes for the soul,
and philosophical relativism, they considered them in the light
of the tradition of the Church and modern knowledge.[16] Although

---

II, No. 3 (November-December, 1906), 362-378; "Real Presence
in the Father II," II, No. 4 (January-February, 1907), 495-513.

15
   "With Our Contributors", I, No. 2 (August-September,
1905), 257.

16
   John T. Driscoll, "The Notion of Morality", I, No. 6
(April-May, 1906), 714-723; Edward A. Pace, "Some Modern
Substitutes for the Soul", I, No. 5 (February-March, 1906),
541-554; and Giuseppe Calderoni, "Relativism and Logic", III,
Nos. 4, 5 (January-February-March-April), 1907), 457-470.

their aim was to integrate some of the modern teachings on
these topics with the traditional ones, their apparent unbiased
attempts led them to reaffirm only the traditional teaching of
the Church on these subjects.

A quote from one Review article, "The Dawn of Europe"
by Charles Plater, S.J., summed up well the spirit and aim
of all these expressions.

> The nation which endeavors to adopt
> foreign methods without reference to
> its own past is a narrow minded nation.
> And our specific type of Western civil-
> ization as a whole can only realize itself
> by attending to the lines along which it has
> already developed. [17]

Although Plater was speaking of a nation's development he
could have very well been speaking about any organism, in
particular the Church, because of the convertible value of his
statement. He acknowledged respect for tradition as an in-
dispensable condition for progress. All the references in The
Review to the importance of respecting tradition were always in
the context of progress that Plater here articulated so well --
a context which conveyed the idea that progress hinged on the
respect for tradition.

As was said earlier, all The Review articles contained this
respect even though not all articulated it explicitly as the above-

---

[17]
II, No. 5 (March-April, 1907), 545-565.

mentioned ones did. None ever indicated a rejection of tradition, but in one way or another, they all expressed a respect for it. Without this respect, they seemed to indicate, progress would never take place. Like a wheel which only progresses with equilibrium and takes on new ground by tending to its past position, these articles seemed to say that theology too can only move steadily and surely, into new areas by regarding its tradition.

This image of the wheel portrayed verbally in these articles, is very much in line with The Review's editorial policy. It saw no reason to abandon or reject tradition. But, using it as a guide from falling into unbalanced or anti-Christian conclusions, theology could move forward by adopting new scientific methods. Only thinkers, it held, who were steeped in tradition and open to the scientific methods of the day could prevent a rejection of the culture of the times and effectively come to a reconciliation of the new with the old. Respect for tradition then was the first aspect of The Review's approach to theology as its articles demonstrated.

Openness to Scientific Methods of Day

Just as The New York Review's articles portrayed a deep respect for the ancient tradition of the Church, they also displayed a scholarly openness to the scientific methods of the day. This openness constituted The Review's second aspect of its

approach to theology so that it could fulfill its apologetic objective of reconciling science with the tradition of the Church.

As was indicated in chapter one of this dissertation these
conditions of the day were the upshot of the nineteenth century's
remarkable discoveries in the historico-critical method,
archeology, philology, Egyptology, and Assyriology, as well as
philosophy's turn toward "interiority". These intellectual advancements focused a new, unexpected, and occasional dis-
concerting light on the historical bases of religion and the
interpretation of sacred scripture. It was undeniable that the
promoters of such scientific advancements at times treated the
history of Israel and the origin of Christianity exclusively from
a rational point of view without acknowledging the point of view
of faith. This shook the very foundations of the religious edifice
and easily led in some cases to a rejection of the supernatural.
But, it was also undeniable that at times science purified and
strengthened the faith by understanding the work of God here
below in its historical contingencies, by following it in its human
evolution and causation, by discovering the date, character
literary form of the inspired writings concerned with this divine
work, and by estimating the historical form and moral and
religious idea of these books.

In view of this contemporary situation of science and
theology, then, the theological approach that The New York
Review took was an informed progressive one. Consistent

with the editorial policy, its articles remained faithful to the

Church and the established conclusions of theology as well as open

to the contemporary scientific methods. In this way then, it could

have recommended to the Church what was of value to the faith

in these methods and it could have proposed to be rejected what

aspects in them were detrimental to the faith.

Historico-Critical Method

One of the first modern scientific methods that gradually

emerged in the middle of the nineteenth century and found full

acceptance in the scientific world in the twentieth century was

the historico-critical method. This method determined the bare

order and connection of events in time and place which is prior

to all discussion of these events' inward meaning.[18] For the

historian this is an end in itself. When it applied to events in

salvation history, it dispelled or refined such time-honored

theories related to such biblical questions as the number of men

participating in the Exodus event, the incredible longevity of the

patriarchs, and Josua's conquest of Jericho. However, carried

to extremes it, at times, cursorily dismissed some basic truths

of the Christian faith such as the divinity of Christ, the super-

---

[18] This definition is taken from George Tyrrell's article in
The New York Review, "The 'Dogmatic' Reading of History",
I, No. 3 (October-November, 1905), 270.

natural character of his mission, the virginity of Mary, and the historicity of the Resurrection.

Being the scholars that they were, the editors of The New York Review were very much aware of the progress in theological knowledge achieved by this method as well as its limitations. They therefore included in their journal a fair number of articles concerned with it and its relationship to the data of revelation. They also published ones that employed this method in their treatment of theological topics.

One article concerned exclusively with this method of historico-criticism and its relation to religion was George Tyrrell's "The 'Dogmatic' Reading of History." In it he suggested a via media between the historical critical method and the certain reading of history which Christain tradition incorporates. He defined this latter type of history under his own label "Dogmatic" as the idealization of facts effected by specifically Christian faith and hope in the collective mind of the community of the faithful. His via media, he believed, would resolve the conflict between these two readings of history; the "dogmatic" which somewhat misconstrued facts in order to bring into bolder relief their inward religious meaning, and the scientific reading which judged the historical value of these facts. The resolution was that both types of history were important to religion; the former, to furnish inward truth and meaning to the mere sequence and external connection of events;

the latter, to refine continually the correspondence between these events and their meaning.[19]

The significance of Tyrrell's article was that it attempted to incorporate a new scientific method into the traditional way of viewing ancient truths. He demonstrated that the incorporation of such a science which in itself could treat the objects of faith profanely and perhaps even deny them would not conclude to the detriment of the faith but rather to its strengthening. Because Tyrrell indicated that this conclusion could only come about by a positive regard for both science and tradition, his article exemplified well the apologetic objective of The Review.

The editors also published four articles which, using tradition as a guide, employed the historico-critical method. Gigot wrote three of these articles.[20] They concerned themselves with the question whether or not the leading personages in the Books of Jonas, Job, and Genesis XII to XXVI were historical figures or literary fabrications. Gigot first hypothesized, as contemporary proponents of literary criticism also did, that the religious purpose of these writings and their

---

[19]
  Ibid., pp. 269-276, passim.

[20]
  Gigot, "Book of Jonas", op. cit.; "Book of Job", op. cit., and "Abraham: A Historical Study", II, No. 1 (July-August, 1906), 37-48.

literary genre would seem to have mitigated against the historicity of these biblical heroes. Then, with deference to the conclusions of the "dogmatic" understanding of history, as Tyrrell called it, Gigot proceeded to apply the historicocritical method to these writings. His conclusion was that although literary embellishments are present in them nevertheless there is some historical basis to these men which gave rise to these spiritual allegories and religious parables. These conclusions which not only refined the traditional opinions on these questions, but also reaffirmed their bases witnessed the value of such an approach to theology that would respect tradition and utilize the new scientific methods. [21]

Of even greater importance than Gigot's articles concerned with Old Testament personages was the fourth article in The Review which employed the historico-critical method in defense of the ancientFaith. This article written by Cornelius Clifford addressed itself to a critique of a then famous biography of

---

[21]
    Catholic exegetes today are increasingly inclined to conclude that the Books of Job and Jonas were intended by the inspired author to be pieces of didactic fiction. They admit that they cannot be certain as to the historical existence of Job and Jonas. In the case of Job, the modern exegetes hold that the author wrote a didactic dialogue with a view to casting light on the problem of evil; with regard to Jonas, the author intended to each the lesson of religious universalism. The name "Jonas" means "done". -- the Hebrew symbol for universal mission. Cf. Levie, 225.

Jesus Christ. [22] This biography written by Oscar Holzmann was
the result of the author's extreme use of modern historical
criticism. [23] It therefore dismissed the Christ of Christian
tradition and the orthodox interpretations of such substantial
Christian beliefs as the virginity of Mary, the Resurrection, the
miracles, Jesus' Baptism, and the Eucharist.

In his article Clifford pointed out where Holzmann failed in
the use of the scientific method. It was due, he said, to the
paucity of his sources and his misuse of them. [24] This failure,
he stated, rendered the biography false and led it into anti-
Christian conclusions. Then Clifford using the same historical
method dealt with only the main questions of Holzmann's biography, viz., the authentic teaching of Jesus; his reported
miracles; his view of himself; and the counter-view of his
disciples. Because he used more sources and more reliable
ones such as the Synoptic Gospels and the writings of St. Paul,
whereas Holzmann only used the apocryphal Gospel of the

22
"Holtzmann's Life of Christ", I, No. 1 (June-July, 1905),
47-58. Oscar K. Holtzmann (b. 1859 in Stuttgart) was a German
protestant clergyman and professor of New Testament exegesis
at the University of Giessen. His book referred to here was
Leben Jesu, Tubingen: 1901. It was translated into English in
1904 as Life of Jesus and published in Edinburgh.

23
Ibid., 49.

24
Ibid., 54.

Hebrews and St. John's Gospel, he kept intact the substantial
beliefs of the Christian faith as well as elucidated them.

These articles which concerned the use of the historico-
critical method witnessed a careful reverence for tradition but
also a scholarly openness to the application of this method to
tradition. By doing so, they did come to a new and better understanding about questions peripheral to the substantial beliefs of
the Christian faith. They also confirmed rather than weakened
the substantial beliefs. Their value rested in their demonstration to the reader and to the Church-at-large that the historico-
critical method was a great benefit and service to the ancient
faith.

Egyptology

Besides being conversant with the historico-critical
method, The New York Review also included articles addressed
to the specific science of Egyptology. Like historical criticism,
this new science which concerned itself with the literary texts
and monuments of ancient Egypt also emerged during the middle
of the nineteenth century. Because of Egypt's proximity to
Palestine and its role in Israelitic history, this science obviously
began to throw considerable light on the dates and places of
events that touched on salvation history. It elucidated for the
scripture scholar such biblical events as Joseph's sojourn in
Egypt, the establishment of the Jews at Goshen, and the Exodus.

One Review article considered in the light of Egyptology

the date of the Exodus, an important question for salvation

history. [25] In this article the author, Hugh Pope O. P., system-

atically treated this question in order to ascertain whether the

exodus of the Jews from Egypt occured c. 1230 B. C. as Egyp-

tologists said, or c. 1491 B. C. as the chronology of the Bible

would put it. Giving fair treatment to both Egyptology and

the Bible's chronology, Pope thoroughly investigated further

the dates of the pharoahs of the oppression and Exodus. He

hypothesized that it may not have been the Egyptologists'

recently discovered steles, that would have had suggested a

date contrary to the Bible's but rather one Egyptologist's, Mr.

Flinders Petrie, tentative decipherment of those monuments

that brought the date down too low. Pope's scientific reasoning

for a decipherment of the monuments concluded in the article to

a date which coincided with that assigned to the Exodus by the

Bible. [26]

---

[25]
Hugh Pope, O. P., "The Date of the Exodus", II, No. 5
(March-April, 1907), 566-584.

[26]
Later biblical scholarship and archoelogical excavations
discounted Pope's calculations of the date of the Exodus and
confirmed Petrie's. The early part of the reign of Ramses II
(1290-1224) is the probable time of the Exodus. Ex. I, 11 says
that the Israelites built Pithom and Raamses, and we know that
this work was begun under Seti I (ca. 1303-1290) and completed
under Ramses. The accounts of Moses' frequent interviews
with the pharoah (Ex. V - XII) suppose that the royal court was
near Goshen, and this detail too points to the time of Ramses II.
The evidence of Meneptahs stele also situates the Exodus

Another article, "The Jewish Military Colony of Elephantine under the Persians" by the founder of the Biblical School at Jerusalem and then editor of the Revue Biblique, M. F. Langrange, also examplified how Egyptology contributed to an understanding of Jewish history. [27] Although the subject of this article, the religious customs of the exiled Jews in Egypt after 500 B.C., was perhaps not as significant to salvation history as Pope's, nevertheless, its conclusion expressed contemporary theologian's confidence in this new science to augment their knowledge of the Bible.

The fact that The New York Review published two articles concerned specifically with Egyptology shows how much it was open to that science and considered it to be an auxiliary in understanding the ancient faith of the Church as it was revealed through sacred scripture.

Assyriology

Of greater importance for biblical studies was Assyriology, the science which attempted to understand the Assyrian, Babylonian, Accadian, and Sumerian civilizations by means of

---

under Ramses. Cf. Pierre Montet, Tanis. Douze annees de forilles dans une capitale oubliée du Delta égyptien. Paris: Collection Bibliothèque Historique: 1942.

[27] III, No. 2 (September-October, 1907), 129-144.

archeology and the deciphering of cuneiform script. Aware of
this importance The New York Review published several articles
and book reviews on this scientific method.

About Assyriology's contribution to the understanding of the
Bible and its status in the world of sciences at the time, Gabriel
Oussani, professor of oriental theology at Dunwoodie, wrote in
his first of many articles in The Review on this science:

> Assyriology is a comparatively young science
> but very promising. The results already
> attained have reached such gigantic propor-
> tions that we may safely predict a complete
> revolution in our past and present knowledge
> of ancient history and civilization. Even
> many of our religious conceptions and beliefs
> have been deeply affected by this branch of
> Oriental archeology. It has already placed
> biblical exegesis and criticism on a far
> more scientific basis than was possible ten
> or twenty years ago; and the conclusions
> derived from it, arbitrary in some cases,
> doubtful in others, discouraging to certain
> minds, and to some unacceptable, have proved
> to be nevertheless, of a very real benefit to
> the scientific study of the Old Testament,
> history, liturgy, and theology. We are far
> from accepting as proved all the conclusions
> of a certain school of young and enthusiastic
> assyriologists and biblical critics, such as
> Deletrych, Winchter, Gunhert, Jeremias,
> Cheyne, and others; but we are still much
> less disposed to accept as headed by Hammil,
> Sayce, et al, that oriental archeology in
> general and assyriology in particular, have
> dealt the death blow to modern school of
> biblical criticism or that they have even
> demonstrated in any degree the untenability
> of the main conclusion of that science. [28]

---

[28]
"The Code of Hammurabi", I, No. 2 (August-September,
1905), 180.

This quote demonstrated at least Oussani's openness to Assyriology, and its influence on biblical knowledge. It also showed his balance in regard to the science's various schools of thought. However, since Oussani was a member of the Dunwoodie faculty and wrote most of the numerous articles and book reviews on Assyriology that The Review published, one may take this quote here as an indication of a similar openness and regard for this science that the editors had. He corroborated this observation when he revealed in a book review the editors' policy as regards Assyriology.

> ... more than once The New York Review emphasized the importance of these studies (Assyriology) showing how assyriological research is no longer the exclusive property of a few experts and specialists but have become the common property of all cultured laymen and clergymen. [29]

And more than once The New York Review had articles on Assyriology. Besides an ample number of reviews in it on books concerned with this science, Oussani had published in The Review five more articles concerned with Assyriology -- three of which were about the Code of Hammurabi which French archeologists discovered on a stele in 1901 and which disclosed

---

[29]
III, No. 1 (July-August, 1907), 97. The book reviewed was Paul Dhormes' Choix de Textes religieux Assyro - Babyloniens, Paris: Lecoffre, 1907.

a great similarity to the Mosaic Law. [30] He also had an article
in this same journal on Chapter XIV of Genesis from the point
of view of Assyriology because of this Chapter's importance in
helping scholars date Abraham's entrance into Canaan. [31] In a
later article he disclosed to the readers his plans to write in
subsequent issues of The Review more articles that would have
had sketched the principal results achieved in Assyriology,
Egyptology, Palestinian and Syrian archeology. [32] However,
Oussani was unaware that he was making this disclosure in the
next to last issue of The Review and his plans never materialized.

Because of Oussani's contributions, The Review presented in almost every issue at least one article or book review.
concerning Assyriology -- a fact which points to its openness
to this science.

---

[30]
"The Code of Hammurabi and Mosaic Legislation", I,
No. 4 (December-January, 1905-1906), 488-510; "The Code of
Hammurabi and Mosaic Legislation II", I, No. 5 (February-
March, 1906), 616-639; "The Administration of Law and
Justice in Ancient Israel", I, No. 6 (April-May, 1906), 739-
761; "Oriental Archeology and Higher Criticism", II, No. 6
(May-June, 1907), 719-748; "The Story of Assyro-Babylonian
Explorations, III, Nos. 4, 5 (January-February: March-
April, 1908), 516-544.

[31]
"The XIV Chapter of Genesis", II, No. 2 (September-
October, 1906), 204-243.

[32]
"Assyro-Babylonian Explorations", 516.

Archeology and Philology

At the heart of Egyptology's and Assyriology's concern
with deciphering cuneiform scripts and studying ancient monuments of the Middle East were their fundamental sciences of
archeology and philology, the science of biblical languages in
their case. Because it is impossible to speak of Egyptology
and Assyriology as sciences applied to sacred literature without presupposing these two fundamental sciences, very few
articles in theological journals specifically addressed themselves
to them. They would include them in their consideration of
biblical topics. However, in the three years that it was
published, The New York Review had three articles concerned
with philology and three articles on the role of archeology as
an auxiliary science to understanding sacred literature. [33]

The New Apologetics

Concomitant with the revolution in biblical studies
occasioned by the rise of the new sciences of historical criticism, Egyptology, Assyriology, archeology and philology, which

---

[33]
    Leon Gry, "The Idea of Light in the Old Testament", II,
No. 1 (July-August, 1906), 70-85; Hugh Pope, "The Geography
of the Greek Bible", III, No. 6 (May-June, 1908), 686-703;
Gabriel Oussani, "Resources of the Arabic Language and Litera-
ture", III, No. 1 (July-August, 1907), 36-51; Pope, "A Visit to a
Modern Excavation", III, Nos. 4, 5 (January-February: March-
April, 1908), 418-428; Oussani, "Oriental Archeology and Higher

together made up what was called biblical criticism, was also a
revolution in apologetics. This was so because at that time
scholars considered criticism and apologetics to go naturally
together. The relation of the one to the other was the same as
that of the concave and convex sides of a lens. Criticism takes
arguments apart, points out their weakness, is apt to abound
in negative results. Apologetics, on the other hand, puts
arguments together, shows their strength and has a positive
tendency. If criticism of biblical data came to the fore at that
time, it was only natural that apologetics would also do so. Criticism
opened and examined the treasures of revelation; apologetics
prepared and helped men believe in them. [34]

However, it was not only because of its intimate relation
with criticism that apologetics changed, but more significant,
it grew and changed because the trend of philosophy changed to
interiority. This growth and change of apologetics became known
as the "New Apologetics" in contrast to the traditional kind. The
difference between the two was that the traditional type of
apologetics concerned itself only with Christians with the view

Criticism", II, No. 6 (May-June, 1907), 719-748;
"The Bible and the Ancient East", II, No. 3 (November-
December, 1906), 322-334.

[34]
    Anthony M. Mass S. J. , "The New Apologetics", The
Messenger, XLV, No. 1 (January, 1904), 21.

of bringing them to or strengthening them in the Catholic religion; whereas the new apologetics addressed itself to Kantians or agnostics, as the case may be, with the intention of making them Christians or of strengthening them in the Christian faith. [35] From the number of articles in The New York Review which were concerned with this new type of apologetics it was evident that the editors were at least aware of it.

William L. Sullivan, in his article "Catholicity and Some Elements in our National Life", which purported to direct the reader's attention to the influence that democracy had on man's non-speculative side of his personality, summed up well the apologetical situation of the day.   He wrote.

> We are becoming every day more familiar
> with the thesis that the proofs of religion
> must appear not only to man's intellect but
> to his entire personality. A school of
> apologists has risen up and grown strong in
> the Catholic Church, who are calling our
> attention to other human needs over and above
> the need of the pure reason for logical veri-
> fication. We are reminded that men in in-
> vestigating religion do not ascend into some
> third heaven of speculation there to balance
> rival theories and arrive at a conclusion with-
> out having once set foot upon solid ground or
> opened their eyes upon the customary course
> and environment of their lives; but that in
> coming to the practical judgement that such
> and such a religion is true, they are in-
> fluenced by a great number of non-speculative
> elements, such as impulses of will, neces-

35
Ibid.

sities of the moral sense, intimations of
conscience, aspiration of the affections and
many others of a similar scope and tendency. [36]

This school of apologetics about which Sullivan spoke was

the "New Apologetics" whose aim was to establish a defense of

Christianity by addressing itself not only to the intellectual side

of man's nature but also especially to the non-rational elements

in him such as his will, feelings, and instincts which together

with the intellect make up his whole personality. This turn to

the subjective side of man was because the apologist believed

he must present supernatural truth to non-believers on the same

platform that the modern world at that time had chosen; viz.,

Kantian subjectivism. [37] At that time the modern world ruled

out intellectualism and apologetics. If apologetics was to

dialogue seriously and effectively with the world, it had to

adapt itself to the world at that time.

The editors of The New York Review, for whom apologetics

was of top priority, therefore, very gently and gradually in-

troduced their readers to this new school of apologetics. They

published articles that defined it; put it in historical perspective;

pointed out its value and limitations; and demonstrated its

importance for their day.

---

[36]
    I, No. 3 (October-November, 1905), 259.

[37]
    William Turner, "A Contemporary French School of
Pragmation", II, No. 1 (July-August, 1906), 28.

In its first issue James Fox had an article on the new
apologetics under the title "Scotus Redivivus". [38] In it he
showed that this new school of apologetics was by no means
novel but that its roots lay in the thought of Duns Scotus who
asserted the dominance of the will over the intellect. In doing
so, Fox also presented in his article a good definition of the
new apologetics. He said that for Scotus as well as for the
new apologists the apprehension of truth was an act of the
entire moral personality rather than a function of the speculative intellect alone. For both, truth was the harmony between
the objective thing and the entire personality as well as the
intellect. [39] This manner of apprehending truth was the heart
of the new apologetics and the manner was called the "method
of immanence".

He also pointed out the value that the new apologetics had
over mere intellectualism. He said intellectualism, no matter
how rigorously it established the motives for credibility, cannot compel conviction in the unbeliever. Christianity belongs
first to the category of being, and secondarily to that of
thought. Hence, the appropriation of religious truth demands

[38]
I, No. 1 (June-July, 1905), 33-46. The works of Scotus
that Fox based his article were Theoremata and De Creditis.

[39]
Ibid., 42.

something more than a passive attitude of the intellect. Rather

it entails the whole of the person, his will, heart, appetites,

sentiments and conduct. [40] Fox seemed to say that for a world

bent at that time on subjectivism the new school of apologetics

was opportune and feasible for presenting Christianity to it.

But, he wanted to make certain that his readers knew that this

method was employed by such an accepted thinker in the Church

as Duns Scotus.

Besides attributing this new apologetic method to Scotus

there were thinkers at the time who also claimed it was used

by Thomas Aquinas and Newman. The reason for these appeals

to these great thinkers was because the Church suspected the

method as leading to a denial of the supernatural and, if it

could have been shown that the great thinkers of the Christian

faith used it, then it would become acceptable. The New York

Review also published articles of this apologetic movement's

appeals to such authority.

An English priest of the Archdiocese of Westminster,

Thomas Gerrard, wrote three of the four articles for The

Review which discussed the relation of this apologetic move-

ment to Aquinas and Newman. One of his articles concerned

the positive value that sin may have for a person. In referring

---

40
  Ibid.

to St. Thomas' views on this subject he said that Thomas was
one who also affirmed the method of the new apologetics. He
wrote:

> Much has been written lately of the New
> Apologetics and its indebtedness to Scotus.
> Let not this seem to imply that it in any
> way excludes St. Thomas. His "utrum
> conveniens sit" is nothing else but the
> mark of the pre-existing exigency for the
> Christian creed in the present order of
> providence. Thus, by adopting the second
> article of the pars tertia, we can construct
> an apologetic argument for the truth of
> the Christian faith, weighty when taken
> in conjunction with the rest. [41]

Gerrard also said that the opinion of St. Thomas on the subject of sin put forward was potent because it appealed to the
whole man: to his intelligence, his reason, imagination, feelings,
and affections. The elements were the same to which the new
apologetics appealed.

There were several other articles in The Review which
concerned Newman's illative sense by Gerrard and another
English priest, Vincent McNabb, O. P. [42] Although they did not

---

[41]
  Thomas J. Gerrard, "O Felix Culpa", I, No. 4 (December-
January, 1905-1906), 447.

[42]
  Thomas J. Gerrard, "The Dilemma of Epicurus", I, No.
6 (April-May, 1906), 701-713; _____ , "Newman and
Conceptualism", II, No. 4 (January-February, 1907), 430-441;
_____ , "Dichotomy", III, Nos. 4, 5 (January-February:
March-April), 381-390; and Vincent McNabb, "Logic and Faith",
I, No. 4 (December-January, 1905-1906), 393-399.

refer explicity to the new apologetics in them, they did seem
to be expounding on the illative sense in such a way as to show
its similarity, if not identity, to the new apologetic's method
of immanence.

In addition to publishing articles defining the new apologetics
and attributing its use to accepted thinkers in the Church, the
editors of The Review also selected writings for their journal
that considered the limitations of this apologetic and discussed
its weak points. William Turner in an article of this type
pointed out that the new apologetic's method of immanence
bore many similarities with the method and principles of
philosophical progmatism. He scored the new method as
Kantianism even though, he said, its proponents deny this
charge. He went on to denounce the new apologists for suiting
themselves to the conditions imposed by their adversaries and
adopting the Kantian doctrine of the unknowableness of noumenal
reality. He also took them to task for stating that scholasticism
could not discover anything new because it is based on syllogisms.
Finally, although he acknowledged, as the new apologists often
did, that the psychological immanence of something in man
which is attuned to the divine was not new, he did ridicule them
for appealing to the Gospel of John and Newman in order to have
immanence accepted. [43]

---

[43]
    Turner, 27-36, passim.

Turner concluded his article by saying that the new
apologetics had no future as a system. However, he did acknowledge that as a tendency it may be productive of good. [44]

Another Review article which addressed itself to the weak
points of the method of immanence was Giuseppe Calderoni's
"Relativism and Logic". [45] Here he discussed the inherent
destructiveness of philosophical relativism because it denied
metaphysics' attempt to deal with matter which was beyond the
range of our experience and granted validity of knowledge which
is based on our experience. Having said this, Calderoni
jumped to the subject of immanence and pointed out its weak
points too. Like relativism, immanence denied to reason the
capacity of attaining certain truth in the metaphysical order
thus doing away with that body of knowledge which would put
it in possession of the treasurer of religious truth. Its weakness,
he said, was that it had lost all faith in things spiritual and
divine. By so doing it could not prescribe any remedy. His
conclusion was that the school of apologetics which held fast
to the pure teaching of Christian philosophy was the one that
would effect harmony, not discord, between science and faith. [46]

---

[44]
Ibid., 36.

[45]
Calderoni, 457-470.

[46]
Ibid., passim.

Walter MacDonald also had an article in The Review which criticized an essay of Edouard Le Roy on the subject of miracles.[47] He proffered this critique, he said, principally because Le Roy's essay was intended as an illustration and proof of one of the conclusions formulated by those apologists who relied on the method of immanence. MacDonald allowed the readers to see how this method went against the traditional concept of miracles which affirmed the existence of sensible phenomenon which was beyond the reach of nature's powers. For Le Roy, he said, a miracle was a religious fact and that it therefore supposed religious conditions so that it could be produced and perceived. A miracle could only happen, for Le Roy, by and for faith. [48] This would have made one to believe that the faith of the subject produced the miracle and not God's special intervention into nature. MacDonald took Le Roy to task for this.

However, all the articles in The Review were not negative in regard to the New Apologetics. After its method of immanence was condemned by Pope Pius X's encyclical, Pascendi Dominici gregis, William Barry wrote an article

---

[47]
"A New Theory of Miracles", II, No. 6 (May-June, 1907), 675-690. Edouard Le Roy (1870-1955) was a Catholic layman and disciple of Henri Bergson. He held that dogma could not require an absolute intellectual assent.

[48]
Ibid., 687.

for The Review, that aimed to encourage the Church to keep the true value of experience in belief and not dismiss it altogether because the condemned modernists tried to find a sufficient warrant for faith in the experiences and needs of each person; i. e., the method of immanence. [49] He said that error is merely an exaggeration of the truth and the Church must realize this. If not, then, it would disclaim the aid of man's individual experience, not only as an exclusive basis of faith, but even as a valuable auxiliary in confirming man in its profession when he had obtained it through external revelation. Barry then went on to illustrate some cases where it was specifically manifested that the firmness and vividness of belief, though not in its actual inception in a person, were due to experiencing the pleasures and benefits of living the supernatural life. His conclusion was that experience occupied an important place in man's spiritual life and it should not be discarded because some modernists exaggerated its role in an agnostic method of immanence.

These several articles concerned with the new apologetics illustrate the scholarly openness that The Review editors had to it. They published articles by writers who were for it and

---

[49]
"The True Function of Experience in Belief", **III, No. 3** (November-December, 1907), 258-267.

by those against it. If some presented a positive view of the new
apologetics, others presented its limitations. Some demonstrated
how it could not fit into traditional thinking of the Church and others
wrote to salvage its redeemable features after the Church condemned it. This sic et non approach to it was The Review's
policy toward regarding anything new, including the new
apologetics.

Conclusion

By publishing these articles which witnessed to the theological approach that consisted of a respect for tradition and
an openness to science for the purpose of reconciling both, the
editors demonstrated how much they believed in the approach.
But, even more than publishing the articles, they acknowledge
this belief in their editorials. In these statements they
pointed to the recommendation of such an approach by popes
and cardinals, to its venerability in the Church, and to its
indispensability for the conditions of theology and science at
that time.

In one editorial they referred to the approach when they
extolled Pope Leo XIII for turning the Church from logic chopping
scholastic textbooks to the broad-minded philosophy of St.
Thomas Aquinas. They pointed to Leo's recommendation to
the age: "Vetera novis augere et perficere" and said that the
time was ripe for a great synthesis that would amplify and per-

fect the old. To do this, they affirmed, men were needed who
appreciated the spiritual element and had a thorough knowledge
of the whole field of scientific discovery - the two aspects of
their theological approach. [50]

To underline the importance of the two aspects they often
quoted in The Review Pope Pius X's tribute to Bishop Le Camus
of Rochelle, France.

> You deserve a special praise for your
> constant care, in explaining Holy Writ,
> to adhere to that method which, through
> respect for the truth and honor of the
> Catholic doctrine should absolutely be
> adhered to under the guidance of the
> Church. For as we must condemn the
> temerity of those who, having more re-
> gard for novelty than for the teaching
> authority of the Church, do not hesitate to
> adopt a method of criticism altogether too
> free, so we should not approve the attitude
> of those who in no way dare to depart from
> the usual exegesis of Scripture even when,
> faith not being at stake, the real advance-
> ment of learning requires such departure.
> You follow a wise middle course, and by
> your example show that there is nothing
> to be feared for the sacred books from
> true progress of the art of criticism,
> nay that a beneficial light may be
> derived from it, provided its use be
> coupled with a wise and prudent dis-
> cernment. [51]

---

[50]
"Notes", I, No. 2 (August-September, 1905), 239.

[51]
Pope Pius X to Bishop Le Camus, January 11, 1906, cited
in The New York Review, I, No. 6 (April-May, 1906), 796. This
quote also appeared in The Review in another editorial, II, No.
3 (November-December, 1906), 496; in Francis E. Gigot's
articles, "The Higher Criticism of the BibleII", II, No. 1

The reason why the editors often quoted this tribute is evident from its content. The two aspects of respect for tradition and openness to science is very much present in it. But more, the tenor of the tribute reprimands those who refused to advance in learning more than those who hold novelty above tradition. This tenor was very similar to the Review's editorials and articles which attempted to demonstrate that very little was to be feared from science if it was guided by tradition.

Another time the editors referred to Pius X in their editorial attempts to recommend their theological approach. They stated that people who had spoken with the Pope reported that he was anxious to see knowledge and science prosper among Catholics and to have modern heresies met with modern weapons. In view of this the editors therefore encourage Catholic writers to go ahead in their expositions and investigations but to do so within the limits of Catholic tradition. [52]

In addition to appealing to popes' statements to recommend

(July-August, 1906), 69; _____ "The Higher Criticism of Bible III", II, No. 3, (November-December, 1906), 305; and _____ "The Higher Criticism of Bible IV", II, No. 4 (January-February, 1907), 451.

[52] This report came from Monsignor Baudrillart, rector of Catholic Institute of Paris, who during his visit to Rome had an audience with Pope Pius X. Cited in The Review, III, No. 1 (July-August, 1907), 76.

their approach to theology the editors also quoted cardinals in their journal. In one editorial they acknowledged that although those times were a period of transition and many minds were confused by the light of the new scientific discoveries, this was no reason to refrain from the further pursuit of the truth. They reprinted from The Tablet a caution to Church members not to fear or feel that danger was increasing when an adventurous apologist struck out a new line and made concessions and compromises. They should never by themselves, the caution stated, denounce him as a heretic because this is a danger. The editors to prove this point quoted from Cardinal Pietro Pallavicino's History of the Council of Trent which said that possibly Luther's opponents by declaring him a heretic forced him to become one. [53] It is obvious from this editorial that the editors were encouraging the Church to maintain an openness to new science, even in the midst of the then confusing situation.

Another Cardinal they appealed to was Cardinal Antonio Capecelatro of Capua whom they described as a "saintly old prelate whom all the world reveres." They said that he

53

Cited in The New York Review, II, No. 1 (July-August, 1906), 112. Cardinal Pietro Pallavicino (1607-1667) taught theology at the Colleguim Romanum. He was a member of the commission appointed to examine the writings of Jansenius. His book History of the Council of Trent, Rome, 1656 was considered to be the principle work on Trent up until the beginning of the twentieth century.

recently reminded scholars to have at all costs the supernatural
in mind when they utilized biblical criticism and to love it
because the supernatural is Christianity. And also, they quoted
him as saying that Catholics should love what is new, and love
it as springing from respecting and perfecting what is old.
Again the editors presented a quote that supported the two
aspects of their approach to theology. [54]

A third reference in The Review to a cardinal who explicitly
approved of this approach was in Gigot's recommendation of a
book. He said that the book treated biblical questions by means
of the approach that preserved a genuine respect for traditional
positions while at the same time it utilized the ascertained
data of modern science. Gigot said that this approach was
praised by Pius X in his letter to Bishop Le Camus, and had
also been commended by Cardinal Merry del Val, Pius X's
secretary of state, in a letter to Canon A. Cellini. [55]

Finally, Duffy pointed out the venerability of this approach
in one of his book reviews in the Dunwoodie journal. Considering
a book by Ferdinand Brunetière who recently returned to the

54
    "Notes", The New York Review, III, No. 1 (July-
August, 1907), 76.

55
    From a review of E. Jacquiers book, History of the Books
of the New Testament, Vol. I, New York: Benziger Bros., 1907
in III, No. 1 (July-August, 1907), 92. The letter of Merry del
Val's referred to was his October 19, 1906 one to Canon A.
Cellini.

Church at that time, he said:

> Converts, whether to the Faith or to the
> call to a higher life, have most frequently
> brought to the aid of religion the stimulus
> of new ideas and new methods. It was so
> with St. Paul, with Justin Martyr, with
> Jerome and Augustine...with Newman and
> Brunetiere - each has brought with him
> some fresh ideas or method from his secular
> pursuits, or from seemingly antagonistic
> schools of philosophy to give new vitality
> or force to the cause of religion. It is in
> harmony with Catholic principles that this
> should be so. We maintain that whatever
> is good or true in the world is Catholic,
> and accordingly, we have always made
> free use of the principles of pagan
> philosophy, and the methods of heretical
> religions to establish and propagate the
> truths of Catholicity. [56]

Coming from The Review's associate editor, we may take
this statement as another indication of the editors' thinking on
this approach. In speaking of the giants of the Christian faith
who brought new ideas into the ancient tradition, Duffy was
appealing to their authority to underline that the assimilation
of new and fresh ideas which are good and true was not contrary
to Christianity. Rather, it was important so that Christianity
could grow and be propagated.

These articles, editorials, and book reviews all pointed to
respect for tradition and openness to new scientific methods so
that The New York Review's objective of reconciling science with

56
    From a review of Ferdinand Brunetiere's book, Sur les
Chemins de la Croyance; Premiere Etape: L'Utilisation du
Positivisme, Paris: Perrin et cie, 1905 in I, No. 1 (July-August,

faith could be realized. The editors believed that only by this continual reconciliation would Catholic theology be a living and progressive science and not dwindle down to a mere Catechismus pro Rudibus Instruendis. Also, they believed that such a reconciliation would cause theology to utilize the methods of other sciences in order to arrive at a better understanding of the data of revelation. The two aspects of respect for tradition and openness to science which could effect this reconciliation constituted The New York Review's approach to theology.

1905), 123.

CHAPTER IV

THE CONCEPT OF THE CHURCH IN THE NEW YORK REVIEW

As was indicated in the last chapter, the editors of The
New York Review held the opinion that theology should be
approached by simultaneously being open to the new scientific
methods of the day and respecting the ancient tradition of the
Church. Only in this way, they believed, could their journal
fulfill its primary objective of reconciling science with faith.
As we have seen, the articles and editorial statements of The
Review demonstrated this approach.

Such an approach would have certainly influenced how the
editors and their contributors would have viewed the Church,
which is an object of theology. And, the way that one views
theology influences how he views any object of theology.

The principal concern of this chapter, therefore, will be
to determine the ecclesiological vision of The Review's editors
as it would follow from their theological approach. In particular,
the chapter will examine the way they conceived the nature of
the Church, its membership, its mission, and its authority.
The results of examining these different elements which comprise an ecclesiological vision will be important later on for
formulating principles of ecclesial reform.

132

The Nature of the Church

As was already mentioned, one's concept of the Church depends primarily on his approach to theology. If he holds theology to be a fixed, static, and an exclusive body of knowledge of a past age and only the domain of clerics, then, he will likewise view the Church as fixed, static, exclusive, and clerical. He will not admit that the Church develops in order to preach the Gospel more effectively to the world in which it finds itself. Nor will he admit that the Church should associate and collaborate with other Christian denominations; but rather he will consider it the only instrument of God's salvation. And finally, he will not affirm that its members who are not of the hierarchy should take a serious adult role in it. Such a view of the Church dominated in Roman Catholic theology from the Council of Trent in the middle of the sixteenth century to the end of the eighteenth century.

However, in the nineteenth century the view of theology began to change and, with it, the view of the Church.[1] No longer did theologians look upon their science as fixed, static, exclusive, and clerical. But now, they considered it to be

---

[1]
The following summary of this correlation between theology and ecclesiology in the nineteenth century was taken from Marie-Joseph le Guillou's article, "Church", Sacramentum Mundi, Vol. I, New York: Herder and Herder, 1968, 316.

developing, capable of using the methods of science, and no longer a clerical domain.

Likewise, following from this concept of theology, there would be a corresponding view of the Church. No longer did theologians who held this new view of their science consider the Church to be primarily a visible and hierarchial society outside of which there was no salvation. Nor did they hold the notion that the Church was fixed and static and its members who were not of the hierarchy had to assume a passive-dependent role in it. Then, the new view of the Church that was emerging alongside of the new view of theology was the Church as a community of people who take an active part in it and which develops, as any organism does, because being "historical", the Church influences history and is influenced by it.

This radical change in views was due to a number of new trends in science, philosophy, and politics that also had a bearing on theology. As was already mentioned at the outset of this study, the nineteenth century saw theories of evolution and new scientific methods emerging. During this century people were becoming increasingly aware of the political principles of self-determination and subsidiarity. Monarchies were therefore giving way to democracies and the freedom of the individual became just as sacred, if not more, than the divine right of kings. Also, at this time, the principal philosophical trend was Kantianism which emphasized the subject's experience of a reality (phenomenon) rather than the

essence of a reality (noumenon). Thus, relativism and subjec-

tivism threatened absolutism, and objectivity. Finally, theology

itself, in addition to being influenced by these trends of the day,

returned to the study of its patristic and medieval sources.

The editors of The New York Review were very much aware

of the effects that these scientific, political, and philosophical

trends had on theology. Their approach to theology, as was

indicated earlier, attested to this. By believing that a re-

conciliation between these trends and the ancient faith should

be effected, they admitted that theology develops, and it

could include other sciences in its endeavor to understand the

data of revelation. Also, by publishing theological articles

written not only by clerics but also by laymen and laywomen,

they professed that this theological endeavor must be carried

out by the whole Church, and the laity could make just as

significant contribution to theology as the clergy.

The concept of the Church, then, that the editors of The

Review held should have been one that corresponded to their

view of theology. An examination, now, of the articles and

editorial statements in their journal will determine more

precisely how they conceived the nature of the Church.

One article, David Barry's "A Plea for a More Compre-

hensive Definition of the Church," called for a concept of the

Church that would include all the children of God - all those who

worship him in spirit and truth according to their lights, non-
Catholics as well as Catholics. [2] The reason why he prescribed
such a comprehensive concept was because it would have dispelled, he believed, the charge of bigotry that non-Catholics
then made against the Catholic Church. At that time, they
considered Catholics to be theologically snobbish and anti-
ecumenical because of the Catholic opinion that salvation was
only through the visible institutional Church of which they alone
were members. This opinion followed from St. Robert
Bellarmine's concept of the Church which was then still prevalent in the minds of most Catholics. He defined the Church
as:

> The Congregation of men who are
> united by the profession of the
> same Christian faith, by partici-
> pation in the same sacraments and
> by obedience to the Vicar of Christ
> on earth, the Roman Pontiff. [3]

This definition made the Church identified with an external
body whose members are those who maintain the three visible
aspects of Church life mentioned in it. The reason for this was
because this definition was formulated in response to the Re-

---

[2]
II, No. 5 (March-April, 1907), 691-697. David Barry, S.
T. L. was ia parish priest in Limerick, Ireland who contributed
theological articles to the Irish Ecclesiastical Record, The
American Catholic Quarterly as well as The New York Review.

[3]
Cited in Barry's article; Ibid. , 691.

formation which called into question, among many things, these three aspects.

Barry admitted in his article that this definition served its purpose well at a time of difficulty and doubt. But, like most declarations made in times of controversy, it did not have the perspective of the whole economy of salvation, and, therefore, it was incomplete. His main criticism of it was that it mentioned only the three-fold bond; i. e. , the means to the end and never referred to the end itself, sanctity, which is invisible. Barry criticized Bellarmine's definition of the Church in his article by saying:

> The <u>genus proximum</u> [the end] is entirely ignored; in other words, the community of end that the Catholic Church has with every other church of legitimate institution, such as Mosaic and pre-Mosaic, and the National Churches of the New Dispensation.

He identified the common end that he spoke of in this critique as sanctity, or the grace of God. Therefore, the inference of his statement is that, although the external means to the end are not a bond of unity for these different churches, the invisible end is. And a definition, he went on to say, that failed to take cognizance of it caused the soul of the Church, and the people who belong to the soul exclusively, to be lost sight of. In such an incomplete definition membership was made co-existent with the threefold bond that the Catholic possesses. It follows from this critique then, that a person possessing sanctifying grace - even though he did not acquire it through the same means as a Catholic can - has the right to membership in the Church.

In view of this inference, the definition of the Church that Barry proffered was, "The Church consists of those, still in this life, who are in the state of grace, and of those who are trying to obtain it through the ordinary means appointed by Christ." He said he preferred this definition because the note of sanctity was brought out and it gave the invisible element of the Church its true place without compromising the visible element. Also, it demonstrated the vital and organic connection between the body and soul of the Church; it could help dispel the charge of bigotry made about Catholics; and it could remind them that possessing the three-fold bond of union with the external Church would avail them nothing, if they were not joined in a closer union with Christ, the head.

Barry is justified in calling for a more comprehensive definition of the Church that would include all people who possess grace which was won for all by Christ. His concept of the Church was very much in line with such Church Fathers as Irenaeus who claimed that the Church is where the Spirit of God is; and St. Augustine who once said that some who belong to God do not necessarily belong to God; and others who belong to God do not necessarily belong to the Church. [4] Augustine was, of course, speaking of the visible Church here vis à vis the invisible one of belonging to God of which people who possess grace are members. Barry's concept also recognized the ecclesial value of the non-Catholic churches because they strive for the same end as the Catholic Church. It is therefore a good concept for ecumenism. Unlike Belarmine's definition, it did not stress the Church as a visible hierarchial society but as a community of people who are in union with Christ.

However, his definition seems to be too concise. He failed to spell out its components. He never mentioned some of the extraordinary means of grace for non-Catholics or non-Christians. He did not consider their relation to the Catholic Church. But, the significant value of Barry's concept of the Church, especially for this chapter, is that he conceived the Church to be a community of people who are in union with Christ the head.[1] It departed from the view of the Church as primarily hierarchial or clerical, and it followed from the then emerging concept of theology.

Another Review article that treated the notion of the Church was Albert Reynaud's "Collective and Individual

---

4
    Irenaeus, Adversus Haereses, III, 38 cited in W. Wigan Harvey's edition of Sancti Irenaci Libros quinque Adversus Haereses, Cambridge: 1857, II, 132; and Augustine, De Baptismo, V, 38, cited in Yves Congar's l'Eglise de Saint Augustin a l'epoque moderne, Paris: Les Editions du cerf, 1970, 21.

Religion: A Synthesis. "[5] The thesis of this layman's article was

to determine what the relation was between the Catholic's mind

and modern principles. He said that people often had a problem

in this regard of reconciling modern thought with the ancient

Faith because they held religion to be either individualistic or

collective. Those who emphasized religion to be individualistic

because of the modern world's affirmation of the liberty and

dignity of the person encountered obstacles from those who

emphasized the collective aspect of religion. Those of the

individualistic camp acknowledged no collectivism whatsoever

in religion. Because of this tension, both camps concluded

that there could be no reconciliation between the modern view

and the ancient Faith.

But then, he pointed out, that the modern movement of

socialism in the world was also threatening individual liberty.

And it also threw light, he said, on religious activity. It

reflected that people were not detached units but that in some

intrinsic way the lot of human beings was more or less bound

up together; that religion's organic life, prayer, and action was

as necessary as the individual's life, prayer, and action. Reli-

gion as a reality - as a real living Church - was as essential

a fact and a factor as the individual's conduct in morals and

---

5

I, No. 3 (October-November, 1905), 297-302.

the intellectual opinions of the units that compose it. The

Church, that divinely constituted organism, he said, has

happily in itself the full recognition of both factors. For, the

Church is a synthesis of the individual and collective aspects

of religion. In this regard he said:

> ... The Catholic Church unquestionably is
> a strong collective entity or organism,
> as it has been called. There is perhaps
> no more striking presentation of it than
> as one body, whose head is Christ, and
> of whom the individuals are physical
> members; ... And the general purposes
> as well as the methods of salvation,
> through the many instrumentalities of
> the Church, are collective as well as
> individual. [6]

Reynaud's notion of the Church was obviously that of the

mystical body of Christ. In it, there is a synthesis of individual

as well as collective efforts. This was important, he maintained,

if a harmony of ancient truth and modern thought was to be

effected.

The significance of this article is that it was not only in

line with the apologetic objective of The Review by offering

some solution for a reconciliation between modern trends and

ancient faith, but also it was au courant with the new theological

trends of the day. It was cognizant of the Church as Mystical

Body of Christ - a concept that was strongly emerging at that

time from nineteenth century theology. And Reynaud adopted

---

[6]
Ibid., 298.

it as his concept of the Church, However, he spoke of the Body
of Christ as if it were identical with the Roman Catholic Church.
His only allusion to non-Catholics in the article was a derogatory
reference to Protestanism as the epitome of individualistic
religion. In this, his concept of the Church was not as comprehensive as Barry's. Reynaud did not say the Church was
the whole people of God, but that it was made up only of Catholics. On the one hand, this was contrary to the teachings of
the Fathers on the Church; but on the other hand, it was, at
least, an improvement over defining the Church as a
hierarchial society. For Reynaud, the Church was an organic
whole. And, in here lies the value of his article.

Like Reynaud's, most articles in The Review when they
affirmed the Church as a whole people used the word organic to
qualify it. By it they meant a whole wherein all the individual
parts which comprised it were interrelated with one another and
to the whole. This diversity of parts worked together for the
unity and development of the whole. Maude Petre in her article,
"A New Catholic Apology" defined organic in this way. [7] As
also did Charles Plater in his article "The Social Value of
Contemplative Life". He offered a more explicit definition of
the word, organic, than the others.

---

[7]
II, No. 5 (March-April, 1907), 602-609.

> We need only see in St. Paul's epistles
> how suggestive and helpful is the metaphor
> [the Body of Christ] when applied to the
> Church. We are members of Christ,
> drawing life from him, deriving worth
> from him, possessing unity of aim amid
> diversity of function, exhibiting that
> combination of unity and variety - the
> "one and the many" of Plato's elusive
> formula - which is the meaning of an
> organism. [8]

Therefore, by this word "organic" with its intended meaning these writers qualified the concept of the Church as a whole people. It connoted the idea that there was some active relation between the parts and the whole, and it precluded any sense that these parts were passive. In this way it made the Church distinct from just a mere aggregate of people.

But, to speak of the Church as an organic whole is not enough. A city, for example, is an organic whole, and it is not a Church. These writers, of course, further qualified it by adding that Christ was its head, and that it was a fellowship constituted by faith in him. No articles were more explicit on this point that an organic whole does not necessarily constitute a Church than Pierre Batiffol's articles, "Was Judaism a Church?"; "Was Apostolic Christianity a Church?"[9]

---

[8]
    I, No. 5 (February-March, 1906), 570-578.

[9]
    I, No. 6 (April-May, 1906), 687-700; and II, No. 3 (November-December, 1906), 306-321.

The point of his first article was that, to say the Church is a whole people is not sufficient. Judaism was a whole people, he said, and it was incompatible with the idea of a Church because it did not go beyond racial particularism. It excluded from itself other races. What, therefore, constitutes people as a Church? To answer this question he first addressed himself primarily to the refutation of W. Bousset who maintained Judaism was transformed into a Church because of its dis-association of religion from national life; the fact that this dis-association issued in the rise of community forms which were religious without being national; and finally, these community forms or organizations extended beyond national boundaries. [10]

Batiffol said that Bousset's tenets for making Judaism into a Church merely testified to the national and religious unity of the Jewish people and did not imply that it became a Church. To corroborate this he referred to historical experience that teaches that the notion of a Church excludes the consideration of race and no less does it exclude a book, namely, the Bible. Church, he said, rather connotes the idea of a spiritual society and a living tradition. He went on to examine by use of the most recent discoveries in the history of the Middle East the hellenization of Judaism and its proselytism to see if this idea

---

[10]
W. Bousset, Die Religion des Judentums im neutestamentlichen Zeitalter, Berlin: 1903.

of Church was present in them. He concluded that it was not because these movements did not broaden the concept of the people of God but still remained indistinct from Judaism and exclusive.

The value of this first article rests in the question that Batiffol raised. If people alone do not constitute a Church, what is necessary for a Church? His second article "Was Apostolic Christianity a Church?" was the sequel to the first, and in it, he gave the necessary element for a Church.

In this second article Batiffol set out to prove that Apostolic Christianity had within itself the essential character of a Church. He said once Christianity broke from Judaism it still had a principle of unity. A consideration of St. Paul's directives on charisms that they were to be subjected to the received Faith and for the edification of the community (I Cor. 14, 12) as well as a consideration of all the good works and social solidarity of Christians, he said, provided the answer. The charisms, good works, and solidarity were fruits of something basic. Batiffol said this basic element is faith. It was faith in Christ that constituted the people into a Church.

Although his two articles were primarily polemical to answer Bousset and those who denied Apostolic Christianity to be a Church, they do provide his understanding of the Church. According to him, it was not a particularized people like Judaism or a brotherhood of mutual love and support like a

fraternity but a people who had the common faith that Jesus is
Lord.

It is unknown whether Batiffol knew at that time the ramifications of his understanding of the Church. If it was, as he
said, people who believe in Christ, then he would have had to
admit that non-Catholic denominations are churches, or that
all Christians belong to the Church and then affirm an invisible
Church as well as a visible one. Apparently, he did not do this
explicitly, and, therefore, did not go as far as Barry who held
that those who worshiped God in their own way belonged to the
Church. Be that as it may, the primary significance of
Batiffol's treatises on the Church in The New York Review
was that he affirmed a concept of the Church as a people who had
faith in Christ and not as a visible hierarchial society which
was then still prevalent among the average Roman Catholic.

In addition to the articles in The Review holding the concept of the Church as an organic whole with Christ as head,
its editorials and book reviews also disclosed that the editors'
thinking on the Church was similar to that of their contributors'.
Although there were few explicit references to this concept,
nevertheless one senses its spirit throughout all of the Review's
editorials and book reviews.

One editorial printed a summation by Wilfrid Ward on
Newman's attitude towards new intellectual questions. Present
in it, is evidently the idea of Church as an organic whole. It

read:

> Advocates of reform... must remember
> that the Church is an organic structure nec-
> essarily containing intellects on different
> levels. The stability of the body politic and
> of theology must be regarded in all efforts
> at intellectual development. All interests,
> and not merely the intellectual must be
> considered. Consequently discussion must
> neither be burked nor be allowed to lead
> to hasty changes. Minds must be gradually
> accustomed to the points at issue or being
> subjects for debate, before being forced
> in a definite direction. The new question
> must be opened and allowed for a time to
> remain open... The extensive qualification
> which time and criticism will bring must
> come first. Time itself is essential that
> the exaggerated interpretations which
> are ever placed on novelty by unelastic
> minds may be got rid of. "Novelty is
> often error to those who are unprepared
> for it for the refraction with which it
> enters into their conceptions".[11]

These principles of reform stem primarily from the fact
that the Church is made up of different types of people. They
reveal a deep sensitivity not only out of respect and concern
for the people but also for the sake of the reform itself - that
it may not be aborted. Only an organic corporate concept of
the Church would issue forth such principles.

Also, Joseph Bruneau, a close associate of The Review,
referred to the Church, in a book review, as a living organism.[12]

---

[11]
"Notes" I, No. 5 (February-March, 1906), 666.

[12]
Cited from his review of J. Tixeront's book, Histoire des
Dogmes: I. La Theologie Auteniceene, Paris: Lecoffre, 1905, in
I, No. 2, (September-October, 1906), 243.

And, likewise, associate editor, Duffy, in an editorial essay on
Pius X's <u>Syllabus</u> spoke of the "great body of the Church with
its corporate wisdom and patience" moving on in its work.[13]

The first point, then, that one can determine about the concept of the Church as it emerged from <u>The Review's</u> articles
and editorials was that it viewed the Church primarily as an
organic community rather than a hierarchial society. Although
all <u>The Review's</u> articles and editorials read in such a way
that they presupposed this view, the above-mentioned ones were
cited because of their specific references to it. They said that
the Church consisted of people who were interrelated with one
another and who were united with Christ. They often used the
metaphor of the Body of Christ to express this fact of head
and members united with one another in a corporate whole.
They emphasized this invisible union which, they said, was
effected by faith and grace rather than emphasize the visible
elements of Church such as doctrine, sacraments, or hierarchy.
Their distinction between the invisible and visible elements of
the Church no doubt came from the influence of Kantianism at
the time. Its dichotomy between the visible (phenomenon or
emperical sphere) and the invisible (noumenon or spiritual
sphere) when applied to the mystery of the Church led to the

---

[13]
"The Syllabus of Pius X", and editorial, III, No. 3
(November-December, 1907), 342-349.

conclusion that the true Church of Christ was primarily invisible and the visible Church was an external expression of it. Therefore, people could belong to the invisible without belonging to the visible Church and vice-versa.

With the exception of Barry's article, and perhaps Batiffol's, The Review's articles did not hold fast to the ramifications of that Kantian distinction. Although they affirmed it, they made it to be included in the Roman Catholic Church and not apart from it. Therefore, for most of The Review's articles the Mystical Body of Christ was identical with the Roman Church.

The value of these articles, however, is that they did depart from defining the Church primarily as a visible hier- archial society and underlined the point that it was an organic community with Christ as head.

The second point made about the nature of the Church in the pages of The New York Review was that the Church was an organism that develops. This idea of development stemmed from the fact that the editors and writers of The Review viewed theology as developing when it assimilated new discoveries in knowledge into the Church's tradition. Several articles in this journal illustrated the fact that the Church develops so that it could effectively proclaim the gospel to the world in which it found itself.

Maude Petre's article, which was already mentioned, acknowledged this idea of ecclesial development. In praising

William J. Williams' view of the Church pervading all sectors of life and knowledge and bringing them together into a unity under its domain, she said that development was one of the very notes of the Church. Petre wrote:

> So that although the Church be our home, and we look for a certain peace within her walls, it is not a peace of stillness and inaction. Everything that has ceased to grow has begun to perish, and this is true of the individual soul as of the entire Church; finality is death, progress is life.[14]

Petre made her idea of ecclesial development intrinsic to the Church. For according to the context in which the quote is found, the Church, like any organism that performs its function in the world, assimilates, adapts, learns, influences and changes as it performs its function of bringing unity in the world by its pervasive force. By so doing, it cannot help but develop. If it does not develop, it will die. Her statement on development flowing from her view of the Church as an organism is indisputable. With it she dispelled for any thinking man the idea that the Church was static and fixed as some ecclesiological views made it to be.

Plater in his article which was cited above likewise spoke of ecclesial development. He said:

---

[14] Petre, "Apology", 609.

> The metaphor of the Body of Christ has
> been worked upon in modern times by the
> Church's latest apologists - thinkers who
> reconcile for a questioning world the
> elements of permanence and change and
> show how of all the religious bodies the
> Catholic Church alone can develop with
> safety since she alone is permanent.[15]

This acknowledgement of development certainly flowed

again from the concept of the Church as an organism. It was

obviously addressed to the context of the day when many attempts

at reconciliation were taking place. But, in it there was an

added dimension to development. Plater did not admit ecclesial

development in general but only that kind that takes place with-

out any danger to the organism. And he seemed assured that

no danger would come to the Church in its development because

of its "permanence". No doubt, he meant by "permanence"

tradition which is the Church's root and preserves its balance

as well as identity.

William L. Sullivan in his article also affirmed that the

Church develops because in some way it is fashioned by the

spirit of the civilization in which it finds itself.[16] Made up of

people who are likewise members of this civilization, the Church

cannot help but be influenced by it. Sullivan's recourse to the

---

15
    Plater, "Contemplative Life", 570.

16
    "Catholicity and Some Elements in Our National Life",
I, No. 3 (October-November, 1905), 259-268.

Church's history to illustrate his point made his article one of the most effective in The Review from the point of view of its apologetic objective.

Duffy similarly affirmed the fact of development in the Church. In his editorial article praising the then recently promulgated Syllabus of Pius X and scoring those who criticized it, he said that to reconcile the scientific findings of the nineteenth century to a set of divine truths men must venture on solutions and they will make mistakes. He pointed out that this Syllabus did not mean the stifling of intellectual activity in the Church, but, rather, he referred to some of its passages where the pope stated he was in favor of progress and would set up an institution to assure it.[17] To illustrate his confidence in The Syllabus' regard for advancement in learning, Duffy stated at the beginning and at the end of his very positive critique of it that "the great body moves on about its work unashamed and unafraid".

History of course has proven Duffy wrong on many of the points in his critique. However, he still was under the assumption that the Church moves on, develops, and never remains completely still.

These articles all consider ecclesial development in the

17
Duffy, 342-348 passim.

context of the times as the Church endeavored to reconcile the new with the old. This endeavor coupled with the presupposition that the Church is an organic community necessarily led them to affirm the idea of the Church developing. Although these articles failed to offer any substance to their discussion of development by way of principles and direction, they do, however, adequately present the fact that the Church develops. In this their concept of the Church was congruent with their view of theology, and they contributed some insight to the understanding of the Church.

A third point about the nature of the Church that emerged from the Review's articles and editorials was that all the members of this organic community have an active part to play in its life and development. This point follows necessarily from the first two points that were already made about the notion of the Church in The Review and from the view of theology as the endeavor of all and not just the clergy. The fact that articles were written for this journal by laymen and laywomen attests to the latter point. In addition, there are some explicit references in The Review which advert to the fact that all the members of the Church play an active role in it.

Duffy in his review of a book by Judge Frank McGloin, a layman, said:

All these facts show that the defense
of religious truth in this country is not
something which is being left to the
effort of professional clerical supporters
but that the laity are personally interested
in the matter and they are ready to sink
their differences for the time being, to
unite against the common foe. [18]

Duffy did show by this statement that the theological en-

deavor at the time was entered into by all. But, it is difficult

to determine what he meant when he said that the laity were

willing to sink their differences for the time being. If he was

implying that their active participation was only to be tem-

porary, then the force of his statement was directed solely

to the context of his time and was not consistent with his con-

cept of the Church which affirmed a standing active lay-

participation. Since he was reviewing a book of apologetical

lectures written by a judge and not a lay-theologian, he could

very well have meant that "the differences" the laity were

sinking were not those which set them off from the clergy but

those which set them off from professional theologians.

This latter interpretation is corrorabated somewhat by

an editorial in which the editors named the apologists of the

philosophy of religion. They stated that prominent among this

group were also laymen. They singled out George and Wilfrid

---

[18]
Cited in his review of Frank McGloin's, The Light of
Faith, St. Louis: Herder, 1905, in I, No. 3 (October-November,
1905), 389.

Ward, George Mivart, William S. Lilly, Charles Devas, and the then widely known Senator Antonio Fogazzaro of Italy.[19] Here the editors spoke of laymen who were professional theologians and who alongside of clerical theologians participated in the work of the Church. This statement's meaning that theology is very much the work of the laymen would help dismiss the implication of the previous mentioned citation where Duffy seemed to say the laity should only be temporarily involved in it. As has already been indicated, Duffy wrote most of The Review's editorials.

Reynaud in an article that has been already mentioned several times suggested that it was democracy that had impressed upon the people the idea to take their rightful role in the Church and actively participate in its development. He said:

> Democracy (and so modern thought) has done this much: It has increasingly advanced not simply the emancipation of the individual from the collective thralldom of blind authority, but the personal and intelligent ability of the units to participate in the collective energies of the whole. It has made every one of us doubly responsible. It has enlarged and enabled the right and the corresponding duty, of each of us to understand, to be sharers in and to advance the harmony between ancient truth and modern thought, between liberty

[19] "Notes", II, No. 3 (November-December, 1906), 491

and authority, between faith and reason -
to fit the individual freeman for active
value in the collective sense of God's
kingdom. [20]

In the context from which this quote came the author was
speaking of the Church as an organic community. His statement
here demonstrated how much influence the spirit of the age had
on the Church and how active participation was in line with the
concept of the Church that he presented in his article. It was
the only statement that affirmed explicitly that all members of
the Church were to be actively engaged in its endeavors and
not just laity who were professional theologians. In this lies
its great value.

From this consideration of these three ecclesiological
points as they are found in The New York Review we can
arrive at some idea of how the editors and writers conceived
the nature of the Church. Although they did not explicity preclude the visible elements in the Church such as doctrine,
sacraments, and hierarchy, they did however emphasize that
the Church was primarily an organic community of people
constituted by grace or faith in Christ. Implied in this notion
are the ideas that this community develops and that all have an
active part to play in its life and development. These ideas
flow from their understanding of the word "organic"; i. e.

[20]
Reynaud, 302.

individuals living in time who interrelate with one another and to the whole.

There were some limitations to this concept of the Church as it appeared in The New York Review. With very few exceptions its writers spoke of this organic community as exclusively identifiable with the Roman Catholic Church. Thus, they did not follow through completely in their notion of Church by including in it non-Catholics who believed in Christ. Their ideas on ecclesial development are indisputably present, but they failed to offer a fuller treatment of them. And finally, although there are some references to the point of active participation in the Church by non-clerical members, they seem in most cases to limit it to the laity who were professional theologians. Their affirmation of all members engaged in the Church's mission did not come across strong enough.

The way that The Review's editors would have corrected or erased these limitations as their journal developed in time is difficult to say. For, when it ceased publication after only three short years, any refinement or development of these three ecclesiological points was aborted. Nevertheless, in spite of these limitations, the ideas of organic community constituted by faith, development, and active lay participation were central to their notion of Church. And in this The Review's concept of the Church represented a departure from the prevalent Church concept, at the time, that it was primarily a visible hierarchial society. Having determined the way The Review conceived the nature of the Church, we can now proceed from this concept and examine the other elements of its ecclesiology; viz., membership, mission, and authority.

Church Membership and Ecumenism in this Ecclesial Notion

To some extent we have already discovered that the notion of Church membership proceeding from The Review's concept of the Church as an organic whole did not necessarily coincide with it. Large doses from the concept of the Church as a visible hierarchial society still influenced many of the writers' notion of Church membership, even though they maintained that the Church was an organic fellowship with Christ as head. Thus, for these writers only Catholics were members of this fellowship constituted by faith in Christ. The inference from this (whether conscious or unconscious, it is difficult to say), of course, was that only Catholics have faith in Christ. However, because The Review's editors did address themselves to the idea of ecumenism, it is important to give some formal consideration to their notion of Church membership in order to determine their caliber of ecumenism. Let us now consider this notion.

The Review's articles and editorials did stress the invisible element of the mystery of the Church, i.e., the organic fellowship with Christ constituted by faith, rather than the visible elements of sacraments, doctrine, and hierarchy. Therefore, this concept of the Church as it is in itself is not precisely congruent with the Catholic Church as a visible institutional society. In line with this concept, then, people could belong to the invisible organic fellowship without necessarily belonging to the visible Church. They would be members of the wider circle of fellowship because of the essential bond of faith in Christ but no members of the smaller circle of visible Church, the bonds of which, are not only faith, but also communality of sacraments, doctrine and hierarchy. To illustrate this broader concept of the Church, theologians employ the metaphor of the Body of Christ which means all those who were in union with Christ the head are members of his body.

David Barry, Charles Plater, and to some extent, Pierre Batiffol affirmed this broader concept of the Church in their articles for The Review and in them acknowledged non-Catholics to be members of the Church. But others, like Albert Reynaud and Joseph MacSorley who spoke of Catholics who were "inside the Church" and non-Catholics "outside the Church", although they affirmed the broader concept of Church, spoke in a way that made only Catholics members of it. [21] The reason

---

[21]
MacSorley's article was "The Church and the Soul", I, No. 1 (June-July, 1905), 59-68.

for this ambivalence in the notion of Church membership was not because there was any apparent polemic taking place between these two groups of writers, but, most likely, because the latter group admitted intellectually that the Church was an organic fellowship but they had not yet purged themselves completely of the concept of Church as hierarchial society.

However, in spite of this ambivalence of the notion of Church membership in The Review's articles, its editors themselves held the wider concept of the Church as organic fellowship in which Catholics and non-Catholics are members. This is evident because in the editorials in which the editors addressed themselves to ecumenism, this wider notion of Church membership is present.

It was primarily in the editorial statements that one found the editors ecumenical overtures, although they did also publish articles on Buddhism, comparative religions, and the Russian Orthodox Church. [22] In three editorials the editors

---

[22]
Nicola Turchi, "Comparative Study of Religions", II, No. 5 (March-April, 1907), 590-601; Aurelio Palmieri, "Catholic Ideas and Tendencies in Modern Russian Thought", III, No. 1 (July-August, 1907), 3-23; _____, "Monarchism in Russian", III, No. 6 (May-June, 1908), 635-652; Albert Roussel, "A Study in Buddahism", III, No. 3 (November-December, 1907), 292-312; _____, "Studies in Buddhism", III, Nos. 4 and 5 (January-February:March-April, 1908), 429-447; and _____, "The Dhamma of Buddha", No. 6 (May-June, 1908), 653-570. These articles demonstrated the strengths and weaknesses of these religions and denominations. In some cases they seriously considered the possibility of reunion with the Roman Church.

gave extensive treatment to the ecumenical views of Driscoll's friend, Dr. Charles A. Briggs of Union Theological Seminary. In the first editorial they remarked that Briggs intended to devote his efforts during the remaining years of his life to irenics. Their comment on this was that he was sincere in his intention and of good will. [23]

In a second editorial the editors printed Briggs' idea on the papacy. He considered it one of the greatest institutions ever to exist in the world. Also, he pointed out that it had a much firmer basis in the New Testament than Protestants are willing to give it. He chided his fellows for denying all historic rights of the papacy and encouraged them to abandon this false position. And, he went on to express his opinion on the "unessentials" of the papacy; viz., the facts of the pope residing in Rome and being Italian. To this latter point the editors mentioned that this was open to discussion and modification. [24]

In a third editorial the editors mentioned that Briggs read a paper at a meeting of Protestant clergymen in New York in which he proposed a plan for reunion under the headship of the pope. The editors applauded this action and expressed their

[23] "Notes", I, No. 2 (August-September, 1905), 240.

[24] "Notes", II, No. 5 (March-April, 1907), 651.

hope for such a reunion. [25]

This coverage that the editors gave to Briggs' views is an indication of their spirit of ecumenism. No doubt, these views were favorable to the Roman Church but nevertheless the editors first had to be open enough to hear them. One holding exclusively the visible hierarchial concept of the Church would not be open enough to learn how much affinities existed between them and Protestants.

In Duffy's editorial essay on The Syllabus of Pius X he scored the official positions of Protestant opinion on the Syllabus, - positions which he considered critical and destructive. In this blast, he sounded as if he was disappointed by their positions. He wrote:

> One should expect that, as men who in spite of intellectual difficulties (differences) still retain faith in Christ and the Bible, they would welcome a strong pronouncement from the old Church in defense of the common Christian teachings. One should expect that, as members of ecclesiastical organizations, they would have some appreciation of the mind of men who defer to a Church which they have freely accepted as representing divine truth to them. [26]

This statement demonstrates that there is a common link between Catholics and Protestants; viz., faith in Christ, the

---

25
II, No. 4 (January-February, 1907), 518.

26
Duffy, "Syllabus", 344.

Bible, and common Christian teachings. Duffy's use of the
words, "Old Church" implies that Protestants were in some
way related to it. And his call to them to respect Catholics'
obedience to their Church seems to convey the idea of recipro-
city. For, presupposed in this call for respect is that he had
respected them in their actions.

In addition to their openness to Protestanism the editors
also concerned themselves in The Review with the Russian
Orthodox Church. They published two articles on the Church
in Russia, as was already mentioned, and gave a lengthy consideration to it in one of their editorials. In this editorial
they expressed their belief that Catholics should become
acquainted with the Church because it would not have been
long before efforts were made to re-incorporate it into the
general Catholic body. They said that it would be one of the
greatest tragedies of Church history if this re-union failed
because of narrowness and lack of sympathy which are
synonymous with ignorance of facts and feelings.[27]

The caliber of ecumenism that these editorials expressed
was one of irenicism and not one of diviseness or absolutism.
They certainly seemed to indicate that they were the fruit of
friendly dialogue and genuine openness. Also, some editorials,

---

[27]
I, No. 5 (February-March, 1906), 663.

viz., Duffy's essay and the one on the Russian Church presupposed that Catholics and non-Catholics shared membership
in the Church of Christ because of their faith in him and their
possession of the Bible and common Christian teachings. Although these editorials did look forward to the possibility of
a future reunion of Christians who were apart from the visible
Church, never once did they implicate that these Christians
were outside the Church of God. The editors' caliber of
ecumenism stemmed from their concept of the Church as
organic fellowship with Christ as head and therefore from
the notion that non-Catholics as well as Catholics are members of it. Their ecumenism not only affirmed co-existence
with the other Churches but also collaboration with them on
matters pertaining to theology and reunion. The editors also
exhibited a definite sense of co-participation between Catholic
and non-Catholics in the faith and grace of Christ. [28]

The Mission of the Church

The mission that The Review's articles attributed to the
Church was none other than the one that is common to any view

---

[28]
Although the editors did not mention it in their editorials,
they did invite non-Catholics to Dunwoodie "to assist" in some
liturgical celebrations, namely, ordination. Letter, Driscoll
to Briggs, May 9, 1904, Archives of Union Theological
Seminary, New York. Hereinafter this source will be abbreviated U. T. S. A.

that one may hold of the Church. This mission, of course, is Christ-given, and it is to bring all men to salvation. Several articles in The Review explicitly referred to this mission.

MacSorley's article "The Church and the Soul" primarily attempted to assuage the anxiety of people who were confused by the peripheral changes that were taking place in the Church at that time. To accomplish this, he underlined that the Church stood for salvation and that it was the great spiritual teacher that guided man to salvation. People, he said, should never lose sight of this, especially in times of change and intellectual difficulties. The trappings of religion may change because of time but the mission will never.[29]

Likewise, John T. Driscoll's article "Christianity and Human Life" which was also addressed to the context of the day stated that the mission of the Church is to preach salvation to man. In doing so it is preaching what Christ preached. By continuing his mission of preaching it fulfills its mission.[30]

Also, William L. Sullivan in his article attributed the same mission to the Church. The thesis of his article was that the Church favored no political theories or social schemes over the national spirit and institution of any country in the world.

---

[29] MacSorley, 61-65 passim.

[30] I, No. 3 (August-September, 1905), 139-152.

He was pleading the case for the American Church to take into its life the American ideas of democracy and independence. One of his arguments, among others, to prove his thesis was recourse to the Church's mission. Its sole endeavor, he said, is to lead all men to perfect truth and grace of God. [31] His point here was as long as the Church maintains this mission it did not matter if the Church assimilated some aspects of the civilization in which it found itself.

Finally, as we have already seen, Barry in his "Plea for a More Comprehensive Definition of the Church" spoke of the mission of the Church as bringing men to sanctity. [32]

All of these articles attributed no other mission to the Church than that of bringing man to salvation. However, Maude Petre's article "A New Catholic Apology" was the only exception. In this article which was primarily an encomium of William J. William's views on the Catholic Church being the pervasive factor in all areas of life, Petre gave an added dimension to the Church's mission. She wrote:

> And as the Church, even abscinding from
> her divine and supernatural mission, stands
> thus for catholicity of the human mind,
> with its reason, its experience and all
> its other faculties, as against its narrow-
> ness when considered it its purely private

[31] Sullivan, 262.

[32] Barry, 692.

capacity, so likewise does she stand for
its catholicity in regard to time, repre-
senting as she does, neither present nor
past, but past, present and future blended
into one progressive whole. [33]

What Petre was saying here was that just as the Church

unites all areas of life because it pervades all these areas and

thus represents a Catholicity of knowledge for man, so too,

because it pervades time, represents a catholicity of time for

him also. She made the mission of the Church, then in this

regard, to be a mode of continuity, a way for man to have at

his disposal a catholicity of time. This would certainly allow

greater progress for man in his endeavor to know himself

and God. The only drawback with Petre's different dimension

of mission is that like Williams, from whom she received the

idea, she attributed it to the Roman Catholic Church alone.

Both did not affirm that this mode of continuity could exist in

a Church apart from the Roman Catholic one. Other Christian

Churches certainly draw from history and Christian tradition

and, in the present, they anticipate the coming of the Kingdom.

Nevertheless, the value of Petre's different dimension to the

Church's mission is that in it there is a fairly good hint of the

Church's mission to serving the world as well as pointing it to

its final destiny, salvation.

33
  Petre, 607.

Authority

From the concept of the Church as organic fellowship with Christ as head; i. e. , an interrelation of parts to the whole, one may readily draw a concept of authority corresponding to it. An examination of some of the articles and editorial statements that spoke of Church authority in The Review demonstrates that their concept of authority followed from this concept of the Church.

For them authority in such a Church was functional and this function was two-fold. On the one hand, it was at the service of each part of the fellowship. It provided for the individual the richness of the whole fellowship in terms of knowledge, experience, and support. To do this authority coordinated the riches of all the individual parts and put them at the disposal of one or several individuals, as the case may be. It therefore, had to have a sense of the individual which could profit from its function. Insensitivity could lead to his harm.

In such a function of authority the individual is the object of authority. It becomes enriched because of this function, and in turn, enriches the community. In such a function, authority embodies the whole fellowship as in the case of tradition, community spirit or mores. It functions en masse or through its representative.

On the other hand, these articles also conceived authority's function as being at the service of the whole fellowship. It puts the individual at the disposal of the community. It has a sense of the whole which could profit or be damaged by the peculiar gift of the individual. And, it executes this function by integrating the individual into the whole, by adjudicating as to what the whole needs from what the individual offers it, or by safeguarding the whole. Here, the fellowship and the individual are the objects of authority. And, the whole can embody authority or act through its representative.

Review articles by Maude Petre, George Tyrrell, and George Fonsegrieve emphasized and discussed the first function of authority. Petre's article primarily extolled William J. Williams' views of the Church which were a repudiation of the individual existing apart from the whole. In it she spoke of authority's function of putting the whole at the service of the individual. She said that when man realizes what he can become and he has learned through experience that the things that can be tried lie infinitely beyond himself, he should cast himself into the arms of religious authority. This authority, she went on to say, will put at his disposal the riches of the whole, not only of the present, but of the past and future as well.

Petre spoke of authority's function as being embodied in the whole fellowship. She also showed that it proceeded from the concept of Church as fellowship when she said:

> All this conception of authority is, in-
> deed, democratic, but democratic is no
> party sense, rather in the sense in which
> the spirit of man is essentially democratic.
> There is here no suspicion of subserviency
> to mere numbers, no divinizing of the people,
> no setting up of an autocracy of the many
> over the few; such is the democracy of
> party and of passion, and of collective
> egoism. But democracy in its nobler
> sense is based on the conception of
> solidarity; we are at once the governed
> and the governing, the king and the people,
> the rulers and the faithful. To obey, then,
> is no indignity, for it is to bow to the God
> within our souls, as well as above them,
> to be guided by the best lights of our own
> mind as well as those from a higher source. [34]

Petre had the authority stemming from the concept of solidarity and the members govern themselves as a whole. She made no allowance for any outside agent to govern the fellowship. Authority is within it.

The advantage of Petre's discussion of authority's function of putting the whole at the service of the individual is that she showed clearly the merits and value that such a function has for the individual. However, she made no mention whatsoever of representatives of authority who are an inevitable part of the whole and who, in their position, can assume that this function be carried out effectively and continually.

However, George Tyrrell, in his article "Consensus Fidelium" wherein he spoke very eloquently of this function

---

[34]
Ibid., 608.

of authority did single out representatives of authority.[35] He
too adverted to the insufficiency of the separate mind and the
importance of its dependence on collective and communised
experience at its disposal under the label of tradition. But, he
asked how trustworthy tradition is as an instrument of education and a witness and guardian of truth. His answer was
that one must distinguish between controlled tradition and
uncontrolled tradition or the "crowd mind" as he called it.

For him the "crowd mind" or uncontrolled tradition was
the folklore, taboos, myths, and legends of any single group.
No one is responsible for these "traditions". Members of the
group unconsciously had taken them on in the form of the
"mentality" of the group. They never reflect on them for if
they did, they would not allow this "mentality" to influence
their life. In religion, he said, this "crowd-mind" has had
its influence as an instrument of religious tradition and
education in such things as liturgy, art, religious, devotion,
and the moral and ascetical tradition.

In contrast to the "crowd-mind" in Christianity is controlled tradition or Catholic teaching. Unlike the "crowd mind"
it is not made up of legends or folklore that one accepts un-
reflectingly. Instead, it is composed of beliefs that have been

---

35
    I, No. 2 (August-September, 1905), 133-138.

reflected upon and verified by the saints and doctors of the Church. This tradition collects and distributes among the members of the community the assured results of the cooperative labors of these men. It also tries to bring the "crowd mind" under the purifying and elevating influence of these men. The representative of authority, the official hierarchy, exist to gather and dispense this teaching to the members of the community.

George Tyrrell, in his article, described well this function of authority, of putting the whole in the service of the individual. At one point he called the consensus fidelium or tradition an "authority". In this he is very much similar to Petre. But, unlike her he put the representatives of this authority in their proper perspective.

George Fonsegrive's article, "Catholicity and Free Thought" also depicted the function of authority as that of putting the whole at the service of the individual. [36] He defined authority as the source and distributor of the patrimony of the past for the individual. Acknowledging that no man can stand alone, he said that man must always rely on others for knowledge which is impossible for him to acquire. Also, progress would be impossible, if man did not fund their experience in community,

---

[36] I, No. 1 (June-July, 1905), 15-32.

He compared authority to a father who not only gives his child life but also teaches him how to live it. By himself, the child will develop according to his own narrow and selfish instincts. But given the knowledge of accumulated experience, as represented by the father, he will grow to become what he should become. The same, Fonsegrive said, is true of religion.

Although Fonsegrive affirmed the function of authority as the whole in service of the individual, the example he used to translate this concept could be misleading. His comparison of authority to a father and the individual to a child may lead one to think that this function of authority is patronizing and that the individual is completely passive or regarded as a child. However, one must not get these implications from his comparison. For this function of authority, and especially the concept of the Church from which he drew it, have nothing but the highest regard for the individual as an adult active member of the community.

This regard for the individual is also true of the other function of authority which is to put the individual at the service of the whole. This function also presented itself in The Review in articles by Wilfrid Ward, Francis Duffy, as well as some editorial statements. Wilfrid Ward, in "The Function of Intransigeance", observing that most new ideas come from the members of the Church-at-large rather than from the hierarchy, pointed out the function of authority in face of these ideas. [37] He acknowledged that Catholic theology must have an assimilative adaptability that will take in the light of new secular knowledge and intellectual conditions of the day to re-cast the ancient formulas of the Faith. In this way, then, the Faith may be presented to the world in contemporary and familiar expressions.

Authority's function, he said, in regard to this assimila-tion is one of intransigence. It must adjudicate the check what is beneficial and timely as well as harmful and inopportune in the knowledge to be assimilated into the whole community. Sometimes it may reject it completely; other times, it may allow a succeeding partial assimilation of the knowledge. In this way, then, authority is putting individual parts, which are proposing the assimilation of some knowledge, at the service of the whole. It is protecting the whole from being absorbed by a system which on the whole may be false and destructive to the community it is bound to protect.

In this function of authority, Ward made it to have a sense of the whole not only spatially but also temporally. It must not only know what is good for the whole but also know when new knowledge is good for it. He spoke exclusively of the

---

[37]
II, No. 1 (July-August, 1906), 3-26.

representatives of authority, in this case, Rome, which has a
position that affords it to have a sense of the whole. He depicted
it as a safeguard to the life of the whole body.

The one disadvantage to his treatment of authority is that
he treated its function solely from the point of view of authority's representatives. These representatives consciously,
deliberately, and voluntarily carry out this function. But, one
must also remember that the body as authority, apart from its
representatives, likewise execute a function of intransigence,
and of putting individuals at its service. The Arianist controversy is a good example of this. Even though most bishops
affirmed this heretical thought, the body of the faithful
naturally rejected it. However, the value of Ward's treatment
of this function of authority must not be lost. He did present
this function as necessary to a body which respects the individual as well as itself.

Duffy also attributed to authority this same function as
Ward did. In his editorial essay on Pius X's Syllabus he spoke
of the movement of Catholic scholarship proceeding for a
quarter of a century almost unchecked by the central authority
of the Church. [38] Because some results of this movement have
been extreme and seemed out of harmony with orthodox state-

38
Duffy, 343.

ments of belief, authority condemned them. In this action he considered the Church to be merely defending the basic doctrines of Christianity. He also said that the Syllabus did not condemn the whole scholarship movement but only those anti-Christian results of it. In fact, the pope encouraged in his document that progress should continue in scholarship - even to the point of proposing the establishment of an institution to assure this.

Duffy's editorial obviously made The Syllabus a good contemporary example of what Ward was saying about authority's intransigence. He spoke of it as a safeguard to the Church and also as a document which partially assimilated into the Catholic body the good points of the intellectual movement. It is interesting to learn how positively Duffy regarded The Syllabus when from hindsight scholars know that it aborted all scholarly efforts in the Church. The partial assimiliation he was talking about did not take place for another thirty-five years with Pius XII's papacy. Nevertheless, Duffy did hold that the function of authority was to put the individual at the service of the whole.

The Review's editorial statements also spoke of authority from the point of view of this function. They considered it to be more the adjudicator of these scholarly proposals than a check to them.[39] A representative editorial of this consider-

ation was:

> Rome is the depository of tradition
> and the final court of adjudication; and she
> must, if be true to her function, merit the
> reproach (or the condemnation) of being
> old-fashioned and of being slow... Rome
> is at the center of the religious circle,
> and near the center motion is slower
> than at points near the circumference.
> ... "Contemporary thought" makes it
> its proudest boast that it is up-to-date;
> the final decisions of Rome are nothing
> if they are not eternal.[40]

This quote demonstrated the sense of timing that this func-

tion of authority has to have. It must be slow in adjudicating

proposals because its decisions have eternal ramifications.

Even its use of the image of a religious circle implies that the

Church is an organic whole and authority in this case must

bring all the pasts of it into a harmonious relation to the whole.

Also adjudication conveys the idea that those proposals of in-

dividuals have value and are worthy of respect but only some

can be accepted now, others later, and still others not at all

because of their detrimental value to the whole.

Another statement in this editorial likewise expressed this

39
II, No. 3 (November-December, 1906), 492. Other editorials that explicitly spoke of authority in this way are
found in I, No. 6 (April-May, 1906), 797; and II, No. 2
(September-October, 1906), 245.

40
II, No. 3 (November-December, 1906), 492.

sense of timing that this function of authority must have when

it said:

> Rome is generally content to apply the
> brakes whenever she finds the move-
> ment of thought too rapid for the good
> of the faithful or the consistent and
> orderly development of doctrine or
> discipline... When conditions and
> states of mind change, Rome offers
> no objection to theories which its
> officials once condemned. [41]

This statement indicates that Church authority has a two

fold respect; one for the whole which is the higher; and the other

for the individual proposal which may have value but not per-

haps for the contemporary state of the whole. This same edi-

torial continued to discourse further on authority's two-fold

respect. It spoke of the Catholic ideal which

> ... aims, even though it may not
> always succeed, at keeping due
> place for individual initiative and
> organic control. Students of political
> institutions have long since recognized
> that the main task of government is to keep
> the balance true between authority and
> liberty. Excess in either direction is
> destructive... It should be as clearly
> acknowledged that in religious govern-
> ment the same principles hold. The
> individual must possess a measure of
> freedom, but that freedom is limited
> by the needs of the organism of which
> he forms a part; and if it does not
> command him to do or say what his
> conscience forbids, he is bound by

---

[41]
Ibid., 493.

good sense no less than by loyalty to act
in conformity with its decisions. [42]

Here authority is depicted as a moderator between what is
good for the individual and what is good for the organism. But
authority (and even the individual) must have a sense of the
whole, so much so that it curtails the rights of the individual
and the individual himself freely does so because of the good
of the organism. The editorial expresses a very balanced use
of authority in this function of putting the individual in service
of the whole.

Although there are some drawbacks to conceiving authority's
functions as only twofold, there are at the same time many
positive consequences. Some drawbacks of this concept would
be its failure to take into account the function of leadership
which many believed authority should assert. History does
show that many reforms come from the periphery of the
Church but authority could capitalize on its vantage point or
sense of the whole Church and introduce new ideas and reforms
on its own initiative. In this way it would inspire the members
to have more confidence in it. This concept in The Review
conceived authority to be a coordinator or a safeguard of reform and new ideas.

Also it fails to attribute to authority the value of being the

_____

42
 Ibid., 495.

embodiment of an ideal which reminds the members of their raison d'etre and keeps them faithful to it in times of crisis. The same spirit of unity and loyalty that a flag, a king, or a national anthem engenders in the people of a nation could likewise be engendered in a Church by an authority view as the embodiment of its ideal. This is too important not to be considered.

However, the positive consequences of this view of authority's functions are that it causes authority to respect the individual member of the community, to give him freedom and tolerance in his research, proposals, or struggle to grow. It also does not consider the individual to be passive or totally dependent but to be actively at the service of the community. It looks upon him as an adult who has something valuable to contribute in the forms of his gifts. And, by the same token, it forces authority to have at one and the same time a sense of the individual and a sense of the whole. Authority must therefore be in contact with the people of the community to get this double sense. It must never be aloof from them. Also, conceiving authority to be functional dispels all triumphalism that may be granted to authority. It is to serve and not be served. Any privilege that must be given to it is the privilege that would enable it to serve the individual and the community more effectively. And finally, this view of authority fits in with the concept of the Church from which it proceeds and this

makes it authentic which is what authority must be. Its
decisions must be for the community, of the community and
by it.

Conclusion

Having examined how The New York Review editors and
writers viewed the different elements which go to make up an
ecclesiology, we can now present their ecclesiological vision.
They conceived the Church to be primarily an organic fellowship in union with Christ. The metaphor that they frequently
used to express this concept was that of the Body of Christ.
They did not preclude the visible elements of the Church such
as sacraments, doctrine, or hierarchy, but rather considered
them to be secondary in their concept of the Church. These
thinkers also affirmed that the Church developed in time because it existed in history, influencing and being influenced by
the age in which it found itself. And, in this concept of Church,
they acknowledged that membership in the Church belonged to
anyone who possessed the grace of God or faith in Christ. All
these members, they maintained, must actually participate in
the Church's life and development. With such a notion of
Church membership, The Review's editors consequently addressed themselves seriously to ecumenism. They were open
to the ideas of members of different Christian denominations
and spoke several times of irenicism and reunion. The mission,

they attributed to the Church, was the traditional and primary
one of salvation which their writers expressed under several
different labels.   One of the writers added a second mission:
the Church as mode of continuity for man.   Finally, the
function of ecclesiastical authority that these Review writers
held was twofold.   Church authority existed to place the
whole community at the individual's disposal as well as put
the individual at the service of the community.   They contended
that the whole community was this authority and that it could
exercise its authority through representatives from the community.   These views of the basic ecclesiological elements
constituted the ecclesiological vision found in The New York
Review.

From a theological point of view this vision has more
strengths than weaknesses.   First, let us consider its strengths.
It corresponded to its view of theology as any ecclesiology
must do.   The Review's editors considered theology to be an
inclusive body of knowledge rather than exclusive, i. e. , they
affirmed that some new scientific methods which in themselves
do not belong to theology proper may be incorporated into it
because of their relation to theology in terms of its refinement
and development.   Also, The Review's editors considered theology to be a developing science and the endeavor of the laity
as well as the clergy.   In turn, then, they viewed the Church
as a body including not only those who are visibly related to

it but also those who in some way are related to Christ. For them the Church also developed and they believed that the laity should take an active part in it.

Another strength of this ecclesiological vision is that it has its roots in sacred scripture and tradition. The Church as Body of Christ is certainly found in the writings of St. Paul. And, the Church as a fellowship constituted by grace is a predominant ecclesiological view of the early Church Fathers.

Also, it gives a clear identity to the Christian. It underlines what it means to be a Christian: a person who is in relationship to Christ by faith and who is also in relationship with the whole fellowship.

It helps build up the Church as well, by calling all members to take an active part in its life because they are the Church. This fact will motivate people to have a serious concern for the Church's life and not relinquish it to the clergy.

The final strength of this ecclesiological vision is that it is relevant for transitional times. This is particularly true of its view of authority which is open and respectful of proposals of reformers but also respectful of the Church as a whole. Such a vision also allows the Church to reconcile new knowledge with the ancient Faith and consequently move forward in history, adapting itself so that it may effectively fulfill its vital mission in a modern world.

The weaknesses of this ecclesiological vision are fourfold.

First, it makes the Church have a mission only to its members and not to non-members. If it does address itself to non-members, it is only to bring them into the fold. It does not conceive of a mission of service to the world or involvement in it.

Secondly, it does not attribute any sign to the Church. It implies the idea that the Church is dispersed throughout the world through its members. And it is. But, there is a value in signifying to mankind in some concrete way what it stands for, what its mission is, and who its members are. In this way mankind can readily perceive its presence, as well as influence.

Thirdly, it does not attribute any great importance to the Christ-given elements of the Church; viz., sacraments, apostolic faith, and apostolic power. Although grace can come to man in diverse and extraordinary ways, it can come more easily and effectively to man through these elements given by Christ.

Finally, this vision does not convey any real sense of unity other than that effected by faith in Christ. The psychological makeup of man warrants that there be visible unifying factors as well. Visible elements can signify to the members the unity that is theirs because of faith in Christ.

From a journalistic point of view this ecclesiological vision coincided precisely with The Review's editorial policy as it was formally stated in Wilfrid Ward's article, "The Spirit of Newman's Apologetics". [43] In it Ward presented Newman's ideal constitution of the Church with its ecclesiological elements that the Cardinal viewed in the same way as The Review did. For Newman, the Church was an organic whole, a great body of which every baptized Christian is a member. He too affirmed that the Church developed and that this development was accomplished by all its members. The mission he attributed to the Church was the same as The Review's editors and writers considered it to be; i. e., witness to the truth, instrument of salvation. And, he conceived authority's function to be two-fold as well. By it the individual could make his own those elements of sanctity and thought in the organism to which he belonged. And, also authority kept the balance in the organism lest one truth lead to the loss of truths more vital. Newman beli:ved that authority should respect the individual and give freedom to the reformer as well as considering it in the wholistic sense of being the corporate guardian of the faith. And, he maintained that only such an ecclesiological vision would enable theology to take account at once of the ancient Faith and modern science.

The New York Review's editors, as this chapter demon-

---

[43]
I, No. 1 (June-July, 1905), 3-14.

strated, envisioned the Church in the same way so that they could fulfill their apologetic objective of reconciliating modern science with the Faith.

CHAPTER V

MODERNISM AND THE NEW YORK REVIEW

The period of history in which The New York Review appeared was theologically a controversial one. As already has been seen, the new scientific methods of archeology, historical criticism, and philology, and philosophy's turn toward Kantianism emerged at the end of the nineteenth and beginning of the twentieth centuries. When these new methods and philosophical trends were applied to the area of religion, they began to shake the foundations of time honored religious beliefs such as the traditional interpretations of scripture, divine inspiration and inerrancy of scripture, the supernatural character of miracles, the divinity of Christ, and the divine institution of the Church.

During the three years that The New York Review was published its editors addressed themselves to these theological questions. The course that they followed in doing this was a moderate progressive one: opened to the new scientific methods but loyal to the established conclusions of Catholic theology they attempted to reconcile the two. They carefully distinguished between the results of the new scientific methods which could be accepted into the Church's teaching and the anti-Christian

claims of such methods. The former The Review's editors
affirmed; the latter they rejected.

However, contemporary with the New York Review, there
were some progressive thinkers not as discerning or moderate
as The Review. These thinkers were led astray from the
Church's teaching by the new scientific methods. Some scholars
believe that these thinkers approached the scientific methods
with an insufficient theological background; and soured by
excessive attacks or unjustified suspicion on the part of
ecclesiastical conservatives, they gradually accepted some
of these methods' anti-Christian conclusions.[1] Eventually
they broke from the Church or were condemned; abandoned
the faith; and fell under the heresy of modernism. An investigation of the relationship of The New York Review with these
thinkers who eventually were considered modernists reveals
the posture that it had in regard to modernism at that time.

Modernism is difficult to define. Historians give several
different meanings to it depending on the period of history in

---

[1]
Jean Levie, The Bible: Word of God in Words of Men,
London: Geoffrey Chapman, 1961, 43. Cf. also Alec Vidler,
The Modernist Movement in the Roman Church, Cambridge:
University Press, 1934. _____ Twentieth Century
Defenders of the Faith, London: SCM Press, 1965; _____
The Church is an Age of Revolution, Baltimore: Penguin
Books, 1961; _____ A Variety of Catholic Modernists,
Cambridge: University Press, 1970.

which the term is used. [2] Since the sixteenth century the idea

of modernism was used as a characterization of a tendency

which valued modern times more than the ancient ones.   In

the nineteenth century the concept signified the radicalism of

liberal theology and the anti-Christian tendencies in the modern

world.   At the turn of the twentieth century in the Catholic

Church modernism meant a movement toward the reform of

the Church and her teaching in the sense of an assimilation

of modern methods.

Scholars of the movement maintain that any definition of

modernism in its precise sense of the heretical ideology which

sought at the turn of the century a revolutionary transmutation

of Catholic doctrine through the application of naturalistic

evolutionary philosophy and arbitrary historical criticism

must be drawn mainly from the papal encyclical Pascendi

Dominici gregis (1907) which condemned it. [3] This is so be-

cause they believe that Pope Pius X's intention in writing the

encyclical was not to summarize the conceptions of any one

author but rather to abstract a general idea from a multiplicity

---

[2]
    Roger Aubert, "Modernism", Sacramentum Mundi, IV,
99-104; Vidler, The Modernist Movement, 271; and Jean Rivière,
Le Modernisme dans l'Eglise, Paris: 1929, 13-34.

[3]
    John Heaney, "Modernism" The New Catholic Encyclopedia,
994.

of individual cases. [4] In doing so he offered a working definition of modernism which would enable ecclesiastical authority to identify it more readily and deal with it.

Drawing from the encyclical then, modernism becomes an ideological orientation, tendency, or movement within the Catholic Church clearly emerging during the last decade of the nineteenth century and rapidly dying out around 1910 after official condemnation. Loosely and sporadically organized, it was characterized by a antagonism at times to ecclesial authority and by a belief in an adaptation of the Church to what was considered sound in modern thought even at the expense of radically changing what the magisterium considered the Church's essence. At its roots grounded beyond liberal Catholic positions on biblical criticism and theology lay a threefold thesis:

1) A denial of the supernatural as an object of certain knowledge in the totally symbolic non-objective approach to the content of dogma which is also related to a type of agnosticism in natural theology.

4
Alfred Leslie Lilley, a Protestant modernist said concerning Pascendi as the source for modernism's definition: "This supposed Modernist system is but a perverse figment of the imagination of the clever and inveterately scholastic theologian to whom Pius X entrusted the drafting of the Encyclical. ...No one who knows anything of the various movements coordinated by the writer... under the name of Modernism can fail to detect the unfairness or wilful blindness of that lust of system mongering which has impelled him to his task". Cf. Lilley's book, Modernism: A Record and Review, London: Sir Isaac Pitman and Sons, 1908, 258; and also Aubert, "Modernism", 103; and Vidler, The Modernist Movement, 5.

2) An exclusive immanence of the Divine and of revelation ("vital immanence") reducing the Church to a simple social civilizing phenomenon.

3) A total emancipation of scientific research from Church dogma which would allow the continued assertion of faith in dogma with its contradiction on the historical level as understood in certain presentations of the Christ of faith and Christ of history, the Church of faith and the Church of historical distinction.

But modernism in the sense of _Pascendi_ was not the same as what one would describe historically as the modernist movement. Very few modernists subscribed to these three thesis which were the terminal point and not the starting point of their thinking. The few modernists who eventually arrived at these theses in their thought were Loisy, and Turmel, whereas people like Tyrrell, von Hügel, Petre, and Bremond did not. Heretical modernism should not be taken in such a way as to include relatively progressive Catholic opinion.

Historically, then, we can describe modernism as a ideological effort by a number of Roman Catholic intellectuals to reinterpret the Christian faith in terms of contemporary historical, pyschological, and philosophical positions that led to conclusions considered by the Church magisterium at that time as unorthodox and destructive of faith. [5]

---

[5] These definitions of modernism come from John Heaney's book, The Modernist Crisis: von Hugel, Washington: Corpus

Because the editors of The New York Review were open-minded theologians and saw the importance of what was happening theologically in Europe they were in contact with several of these progressive thinkers who were later condemned as modernists. Some of them even contributed articles to The Review since its policy would be amenable to and solicitous of such thinkers who themselves at first desired to reconcile faith with science. In order to consider therefore the posture the Review took in regard to modernism, it is necessary to study its relation with individual modernists who ascribed to these three theses in their thought rather than its relation with modernism per se.

Alfred Loisy

The most prominent of all modernists with whom The New York Review was in contact with was Alfred Loisy (1857-1940). Loisy was a French exegete and professor of biblical criticism at the Institute Catholique in Paris during the 1880's. He believed that the Church's greatest need was that the scientific

---

Books, 1968, pp. 219-234; his article "Modernism", in Corpus Dictionary of Western Churches, ed. by T. C. O'Brien, Washington: Corpus Books, 1970, 504-506; and his article "Modernism" in The New Catholic Encyclopedia, 994-995. For more definitions of modernism confer Chapter 10 of Maisie Ward, Insurrection vs. Resurrection London: Sheed and Ward, 1938; George Tyrrell, Christianity at the Crossroads, London: Longmans, Green, and Co., 1909, p. 5; Rivière, Le Modernisme; and B. M. G. Reardon, Roman Catholic Modernism, Stanford: University Press, 1970, 9-16.

REV. ALFRED LOISY

study of the Bible be in the lines of the modern scientific methods
he possessed brave hopes that his labors would ultimately be
acceptable to the Church. [6]

In 1902 Loisy wrote L'Evangile et L'Eglise to refute Adolph
von Harnack's book Das Wesen des Christentums. [7] Loisy
described Harnack's book as a collection of lectures which
attempted to define Christianity by eliminating from its essence
everything that was regarded ordinarily as Christian belief. [8]
With his book Loisy hoped to present a modernized apology for
Catholicism and to check the tendency of some incipient modernists who were reacting too far from orthodoxy. However,
Rome condemned his book because it called for an essential
reform of the Church's exegesis and ecclesiastical government. [9]

Following his book's condemnation Loisy abandoned its
general position and went on to deny the Incarnation, Christian

---

[6]
Vidler, The Modernist Movement, 78.

[7]
Alfred Firmin Loisy, L'Evangile et L'Eglise, Paris:
Alfonse Picard et fils, 1902; Adolph von Hornack, Das Wesen
des Christentums, Berlin: 1900; translated into English, What
is Christianity? by Thomas B. Saunders, London: Ernest
Benn, 1958.

[8]
Loisy, L'Evangile et L'Eglise, 1.

[9]
Vidler, The Modernist Movement, 134. L'Evangile et
Eglise was put in the Index of Forbidden Books on December
16, 1903.

theism, the divinity of Christ, the Resurrection, and the divine elements of the Church and its sacraments. Eventually, Pius X excommunicated Loisy in 1908 and declared him vitandus. [10]

The editors of The New York Review enjoyed a very warm and close relationship with Loisy. Although Driscoll, Bruneau, and Gigot all attented the Institute Catholique during the 1880's when Loisy taught there, it is not certain that they studied under him. [11] But, available correspondence does indicate that James F. Driscoll, editor of The Review, and Joseph Bruneau, professor at Dunwoodie and contributor to The Review, were in contact with him.

In a letter to Loisy in fluent French, dated 1903, Driscoll introduced himself to Loisy as one who visited him twice at Neuilly and one who came to know him for a long time through

---

10
  After his book's condemnation, Loisy had a stormy relation with Rome until March, 1908 when Pope Pius X excommunicated him, declaring him vitandus. Vitandus is an added qualification to excommunication. It means that the faithful are to avoid him at all costs. It is the severest of excommunications.

11
  John R. Slattery, an American modernist who left the Church in 1906, called Driscoll "a much beloved pupil of Loisy" in his article, "The Workings of Modernism", The American Journal of Theology, XIII, No. 4 (October, 1909), 571. This appellation should not be taken as meaning Driscoll studied under Loisy. As we shall see from his correspondence he only met Loisy twice before 1903.

his works and some of his friends. Because of these encounters,
he said, he felt free to write "intimately" to him. Driscoll
congratulated him for his works concerning St. John's Gospel,
and especially for his response to Harnack which he said
"was welcomed by our pius conservatives with much less
vigilance than the writing of his opponent, Louis Claude
Fillion". Driscoll added that there were some Catholic priests
and even "many" Sulpicions who appreciated his work.

With all this said, Driscoll then asked Loisy if he could
translate L'Evangile et L'Eglise into English, as well as its
supplementary volume, Autour d'un petit livre.[12] The reasons
he proffered for this request were generally to see this work
put into the hands of English readers but more specifically,
and the fact that "many of the Catholic and Protestant English
reviews reproduced only the more 'advanced' and 'radical'
parts of the book"; "the things", as he said, "that they found
to be (or thought to find) of less orthodoxy". It was by these
parts, he wrote, that Loisy's work was judged by the vast
majority of those who cannot read it in the original. But, by
reading the whole book, they would see the context of the
"incriminated" passages.

---

[12] Autour D'un petit livre, Paris: Alphonse Picard et fils,
1903.

Driscoll then revealed a great sense of secrecy as regards this request, for he wrote:

> It goes without saying that I do not put my name on the translation, and although you may agree with my proposition or not, I beg you to hold my name entirely secret - you well understand why - I would publish the translation under a protestant library, v. g., Longmans, and if by chance (for at this moment one hears all kinds of rumors and anything is possible in certain situations) the book came to be condemned, more solemnly that it has been up to now, far from being an obstacle to the sale of the translation, the condemnation would make it sell all the more!![13]

This letter manifests something of Driscoll's regard for orthodoxy. His desire for secrecy to surround his translation of Loisy's book, his plan to use a pseudonym, and his exclamatory glee over the fact that a solemn condemnation would make the book saleable do not exactly portray him as a staunch champion and defender of the then contemporary understanding of orthodoxy. Also, Driscoll knew when he wrote this letter, as this quote somewhat mentions, that Cardinal Richard of Paris and many other French bishops had already condemned this book eleven months before. The French hierarchy also

---

[13]
Letter, James F. Driscoll to Alfred Loisy, December 11, 1903, La Bibliothèque Nationale, Cabinet des Manuscrits, Nouvelles acquisitions francaises, No. 15652, fol. 189-191.

petitioned Pope Leo XIII in February, 1903 to have the book
put on the Index. However, the pope died shortly after this
request was made. But, on December 16, 1903, five days
after Driscoll wrote Loisy requesting permission to translate
L'Evangile et L'Eglise, Pope Pius X had it placed on the Index
of forbidden books. [14]

Evidently, then, the ecclesiastical furor that was surround-
ing this book, and most likely known by Driscoll, did not
prevent him from making plans to translate it into English.
Driscoll seems, then, to have had a strong penchant for
modernist ideas even though the ecclesial authority was condemning these ideas. No doubt, as president of Dunwoodie,
he publicly displayed an allegiance to the Church's teachings
or else he would have been removed from that important position in the seminary. But, as this letter discloses, privately
he was sympathetic to Loisy's ideas which were already being
condemned by ecclesiastical authority, and he was desirous
to propogate them in the English-speaking world. Driscoll,
therefore, seems to have been ambivalent to the official
teachings of the Church at that time. Such a sharp ambivalence as his appears not to be the result of prudence but of a
conscious deliberation to deceive ecclesiastical authorities.

---

[14]
Riviere, 190.

Driscoll ended this long letter by referring Loisy to M. l'Abbé
Klein or M. Mounier who would tell him of Driscoll's competence
to undertake this task of translation. Again, he demonstrated
a great sense of secrecy for he cautioned Loisy not to reveal
to Mounier what he had in mind to do. Driscoll admitted to
Loisy that there was much more he would liked to have written
but because of the length of the letter he simply closed it by
extending M. Bruneau's salutations and mentioned he was sending him a copy of the [seminary's] year book.

This rare letter indicates that the beginning stages of
Driscoll's relation with Loisy were at least professional.
But other correspondence; viz., that of von Hügel's and Tyrrell's,
reveal that this relationship grew as the years went on. A
few years after Driscoll's introduction to Loisy, Baron von
Hügel in a letter to George Tyrrell in which he enclosed a
letter from Loisy referred to Driscoll as "Loisy's good New
York Driscoll" and revealed almost a paternal admiration on
Loisy's part for Driscoll. [15]

Whether or not Driscoll and Loisy maintained this relationship which in its incipient stages seemed to be close, friendly

_____

[15]
Letter, Baron Friedrick von Hügel to George Tyrrell,
January 24, 1905, The British Museum, von Hügel-Tyrrell
Correspondence, Vol. III, British Museum Additional Manu-
scripts 44, 929, p. 8.

and relatively secret is not certain.[16] But, nevertheless,

available correspondence does disclose that they were in con-

tact with one another.

Another close associate of The New York Review, Joseph

Bruneau, was also in contact with Loisy. Bruneau also

studied at the Institute Catholique in Paris in the 1880's but,

from his correspondence his relationship with Loisy seems

to have been much older and closer than that of Driscoll's.

Available correspondence makes Bruneau appear to be a kind

of "literary agent" for Loisy in the United States - at least for

the years before Loisy broke from the Church in 1903. This

fact becomes evident in Bruneau's letter to Herman Heuser,

editor of The Ecclesiastical Review. In it he wrote:

> I take the liberty of sending you an-
> other article of Dr. Loisy which would
> be perhaps well fitting for the August
> number - since the Transfiguration
> of Our Lord is celebrated on August 8th.
>   Did you remark that the last article
> "Vobiscum Sum" - instead of "some
> doubted Mt. 28;17 the printer wrote
> Thomas Doubted?"
>   This instance could be a nice ill-
> ustration for the History of the Sacred
> Books.[17]

16
    Driscoll was removed as President of St. Joseph's Sem-
inary in July, 1909. Slattery in his "Workings of Modernism",
571 said the reason for his removal was that Driscoll was in
touch with a censured priest. The only censured priest that
we are certain Driscoll was in contact with and who was alive
at that time was Loisy.

17
    Letter, Joseph Bruneau to Herman Heuser, June 8, 1897,

The fact that Bruneau acted as Loisy's "literary agent"
comes to the fore again in another letter to Heuser a year
later. Bruneau wrote:

> I received (a copy) of the A. E. Review
> for March. I suppose a copy has been
> sent to the Abbé Loisy, 29 rue du
> Chateau, Neuilly (Seine). If not,
> please cause it to be forwarded.[18]

These two letters indicate that Bruneau did enjoy a close
relationship with Loisy - at least professionally. Their content
also gives some indication that there must have been more
correspondence between the two during these years than just
these letters.[19]

Although the editors of The New York Review enjoyed a
close and professional, if not friendly, relationship with Alfred
Loisy - at least before 1903 as available correspondence indicates - the editorial position that was taken in The Review as
regards this modernist appears to be ambiguous. The editors
most certainly did not publish any of his articles in their
journal. To do so would have caused the ecclesiastical auth-

AAP.

18
    Letter, Bruneau to Heuser, March 14, 1898, BH 168, AAP.

19
    The papers of Joseph Bruneau are located at the Sulpician
Archives in St. Mary's Seminary, Baltimore. Although this is
an extensive and finely organized collection of Bruneau's letters,
there is not a trace of his correspondence with Loisy. The
same is true of Loisy's papers in the Bibliothèque Nationale.
They contain no letters from Bruneau.

orities to suspect them and their review of heterodoxical

thinking. And, they never mentioned in their editorials Loisy's

unstable and precarious status in the Church which at that time

was a cause célèbre and certainly news-worthy.

With one exception, the few references that were made of

Loisy in The Review were of little value. One editorial appealed

to his name as a recommendation for the readers to buy The

Hebrew Bible which was edited by Kittel. [20] Another printed

Paul Sabatier's opinion of Loisy:

> Whatever may be the outward resemblance
> of the exegesis of M. Loisy and the Pro-
> testant exegesis, they are entirely differ-
> ent because their methods are opposed.
> The Protestant exegete starts out with a
> scientific conception, abstract and bare;
> the question with him is to find out the
> meaning of the author. For M. Loisy
> this effort to discover the meaning of the
> author is not secondary, but it is put in
> second place; he sets out with a concrete
> idea, the idea of a fact at once past and
> present, the idea of a Church, of that
> society so difficult to define and yet more
> visible and more fruitful of energy than
> civil society. The sacred books are
> indeed the expression of the life of the
> Church which has gone through a process
> of accepting and rejecting. [21]

The only comment the editors made on this opinion of Loisy

was that it was about a man whose place in the history of Cath-

---

20
   I, No. 5 (February-March, 1906), 668.

21
   II, No. 5 (March-April, 1907), 648.

202

olic theology will not be settled for many years to come. Such a weak comment expresses the non-commital position the editors took in their review in regard to Loisy.

However, there was one reference in the New York journal which was strongly in favor of Loisy. It occurred in S. P. MacPherson's review of Constantin Chauvin's book Les Idées de M. Loisy sur le Quatrième Evangile, (Paris: Gabriel Beauchesne et Cie 1907). [22] Chauvin who was a member of the Biblical Commission considered Loisy's attitude on the fourth gospel to be unorthodox. The reviewer, MacPherson, was blatantly in favor of Loisy's views and wistfully poked fun at M. Chauvin's orothodoxy. For example, when Chauvin stated "that it must surely be embarrassing for a Catholic writer [Loisy] to find himself so entirely at one with rationalistic thought and so much at variance with the stream of Catholic tradition on this subject", MacPherson glibly responded to this by saying "it cannot be said, however that M. Loisy exhibits any signs of such embarrassment. [23]

Although MacPherson praised Chauvin at the end of the

22
Samuel P. MacPherson, review of Constantin Chauvin's book, Les Idées de M. Loisy sur le Quatrième Evangile in The Review, III, No. 1 (July-August, 1907); 106-109.

23
Ibid., 107.

review for his fairness, thoroughness, and especially for a lack
of "odium theologium", in his book, it is unfortunate that the
review seemed to lack these very virtures that it praised Chauvin
for possessing. By lacking these virtues it marred The Review's
policy of openness to thought and loyalty to tradition. [24]

From this discussion we can determine what position the
editors took in their journal in regard to Loisy. Driscoll's
private correspondence certainly manifested that he was close
and friendly with Loisy and in sympathy with his ideas. But,
in their journal, the editors did not exhibit such a strong and
positive regard for him. With the exception of MacPherson's
review which strongly favored Loisy's ideas, all other references to Loisy in The Review were insignificant, weak,
and non-commital. But, as we saw earlier, Driscoll most
likely did not write these editorials. No doubt, Duffy did.
And it is possible that he was unaware of his editor's association with Loisy. However, the position or lack of it, if you
will, that these editorials did take in regard to one of the most
controversial thinkers of the day seems to indicate the editors
desired not to become involved publicly with Loisy - pro or con.

---

[24]
    Loisy's book, La Quatrième Evangile (Paris, Picard et
fils, 1903) that Chauvin refuted in his book and MacPherson
defended in his review was placed on the Index in December,
1903. This review was written in 1907.

George Tyrrell

The second most prominent modernist was the English
Jesuit theologian George Tyrrell (1861-1909). Like Loisy, he
too was in contact with the editors of The New York Review.

Tyrrell was the center of modernism in England. The
thrust of his theology which lay mainly in the field of apologetics was strongly influenced by studying the philosophy of
Maurice Blondel and the criticism of Alfred Loisy. From
these two men's thoughts Tyrrell attempted to formulate an
organic theological system.[25]

The thesis of this system was that Christian truth rested in
the experience of the soul. It was a mystical and intuitive
system rather than an intellectual one. For Tyrrell, then,
faith was not an assent of the intellect to metaphysical and
revealed truths but rather it was a lived experience of God on
the part of man.[26]

Tyrrell whom The Review considered the greatest Catholic
writer since Newman was often in difficulty with his Jesuit

---

[25]
    Aubert, "Modernism", 101.

[26]
    Tyrrell's thesis is principally expressed in his two works:
A Much Abused Letter, London: Longmans, Green, and Co.,
1906; and Through Scylla and Charybdis, London: Longmans,
Green, and Co., 1907.

superiors because of his controversial writings. [27] In 1906 the Society expelled him because of these writings and he was suspended a divinis. For the remaining years of his life he continued to write and live in a stormy relationship with the Church. Even as he laid dying in 1909, he refused to recant his theological positions.

George Tyrrell's relationship with The New York Review was principally due to James F. Driscoll, its editor. As professor of dogma and president of St. Joseph's Seminary, Driscoll first wrote to Tyrrell for fifty copies of his book Oil and Wine, in order to distribute them among his seminarians. [28] This book was a beautiful devotional book for meditation. It concerned the human soul's journey from loneliness and separation to a union with all things and with God. [29] However, it failed in 1901 to receive the Imprimatur

---

[27]
  The New York Review, I, No. 3 (October-November, 1905), 375. Here the editors said of Tyrrell: "Since John Henry Newman laid down his pen, we have had no Catholic writer in English superior to Father Tyrrell in originality of thought, fertility of expression, and an all-pervading sense of religion."

[28]
  This fact is disclosed by Tyrrell in his letter to von Hügel, October 10, 1903, von Hügel-Tyrrell correspondence, Vol. II, BM Addit. Mss., 44928, p. 122.

[29]
  Oil and Wine was circulated privately by Tyrrell until 1906. In that year it was published by Sydney C. Mayle, London.

from Cardinal Herbert Vaughan of the Diocese of Westminster.

After a fight of two years with ecclesiastical authorities

over the censorship of this book and because the book was al-

ready printed, Tyrrell decided to bypass the Imprimatur and

privately circulate some copies of it. [30] Fifty of these copies

Driscoll ordered from Tyrrell for Farley's seminarians.

Tyrrell believed that these copies would stir up controvery

in New York for he wrote to von Hügel:

> I except [expect] squalls from U. S. A.
> where the 50 copies of "Oil and Wine"
> ordered by Driscoll of the N. Y.
> Seminary have done great execution.
> At a public dinner they all set on
> Archbishop Farley for having refused
> the Imprimatur and he had to defend
> himself by lamentable equivocations
> that did him no good. [31]

Most likely Driscoll asked Farley to grant the book an

Imprimatur since Cardinal Vaughan refused to do so. This

request of Driscoll was not unusual. As we have already seen,

when the Sulpicians declined to grant permission to Gigot for

his book on the Old Testament, Driscoll and Gigot petitioned

Farley and he gave it his Imprimatur. However, in the case

30

Maude D. Petre, The Autobiography and Life of George Tyrrell, London: Edward Arnold, 1912, 167-175, passim.

31

Letter, Tyrrell to von Hügel, February 20, 1904, B. M. Add. Mss. 44928, 122.

of Tyrrell's book the reasons why the Archbishop of New York failed to give it an <u>Imprimatur</u> are unknown. [32]

The source of Tyrrell's information about his book's controversy is not certain but most likely it came from Driscoll who would have been at that dinner and probably even participated in the discussion with Farley over his refusal to grant <u>Oil and Wine</u> an <u>Imprimatur</u>. Such a conjecture is possible because available correspondence subsequent to Driscoll's first letter to Tyrrell indicates that Driscoll's relationship with Tyrrell grew stronger and closer as the years went on and also that there must have been extensive correspondence between the two. These indications are evident in two sets of correspondence: the von Hügel-Tyrrell set and the Driscoll-Tyrrell one. Because the von-Hügel-Tyrrell correspondence disclose the early stages of Driscoll's relationship with Tyrrell it would be well to consider this set first.

In a letter a little less than a year after Driscoll first wrote to Tyrrell, von Hügel wrote to the latter that he himself

---

[32]
    Tyrrell mentioned in a letter to von Hugel that "Bishop Spalding told my Paulist friend Joseph MacSorley he would write the preface to it <u>Oil and Wine</u> if I chose to publish it in America of which I am technically free to do any day..." Letter, Tyrrell to von Hügel July 10, 1902, BM, Add. Mss. 44928, 20. Evidently from this letter Tyrrell was considering publishing the book in the United States and need an American bishop's <u>Imprimatur</u>. No reason is given why Spalding did not grant him an <u>Imprimatur</u>.

received a letter from Driscoll. Although he often shared his correspondence with Tyrrell, von Hügel would not do so with this letter of Driscoll for as he said to Tyrrell "You know his mind so much better than I do". [33] However, von Hügel did disclose some content of Driscoll's letter which indicates Driscoll's admiration of Tyrrell. This is the quote:

"He writes of himself as an 'enthusiastic admirer' of Fr. Tyrrell, and shows throughout that he is."

Another letter of von Hügel to Tyrrell disclosed that Driscoll specifically wrote to him about Tyrrell. [34] Von Hügel sent this letter to Tyrrell because, as he said, "he might be saying more to me about you than he would say to you direct. Good man!"

Whatever Driscoll wrote about Tyrrell in this letter could only have been his positive regard for him because in answering this letter of von Hugel's nine days later Tyrrell directed him to extend his gratitude to his daughter, Hildegarde, for sending him a photograph of Father Driscoll. In doing so Tyrrell revealed a similar regard for Driscoll. He wrote:

---

[33]
Letter, von Hügel to Tyrrell, January 24, 1905, BM Add. Mss. 44929, 8.

[34]
Letter, Same to Same, February 10, 1905, BM Add. Mss. 44929, p. 13.

> Will you thank Hildegarde for Fr.
> Driscoll's photograph. How strangely
> fresh and boyish our Yankee brethern
> are. I wish they had more discipline
> and less wisdom. There is something
> of shoddy in. . . . their finest textures.
> Driscoll is perhaps the best of the lot.
> How he stands as a Fosscher [sic] I am
> not competent to say. However he is full
> of youth and enthusiasm and seems to
> inflict his alumni with his spirit. How
> the Archbishop of N. Y. trusts his sem-
> inarians and how I do not know. Probably,
> again, he does not know enough to be
> frightened. [35]

This excerpt from Tyrrell's letter indicates that Tyrrell

at that time was therefore aware of Driscoll's activity at Dun-

woodie. In this regard he seemed also to have indicated that

Driscoll was giving forth to the seminarians views that Farley

would not have approved, if he was aware of what Driscoll was

teaching. He therefore implies that Driscoll was duplicious

and deceptive in regard to his Ordinary. We have already

seen this same attitude of Driscoll to ecclesiastical authority

in his associations with Loisy. Be that as it may, this letter

does, however, reveal that Tyrrell was well aware of what

Driscoll was doing at Dunwoodie.

Tyrrell sent two articles to The New York Review which

the editors published in the first volume. Other letters in this

set of correspondence indicate that he wanted to have it publish

---

[35]
    Letter, Tyrrell to von Hügel, February 19, 1905, BM
Add. Mss., 44929, p. 14.

more of his writings. [36] However, after he was dismissed from the Jesuits in 1906, the editors could not do so out of obedience to Farley. About this censure Tyrrell wrote von Hügel:

"The Archbishop has forbidden them to admit anything from me; and so they published Bremond's eulogy of me instead. "[37]

The editors seem to have had no spirit of obedience to Farley's directive. They seem to have ignored this directive by publishing in Henri Bremond's article which extolled the orthodoxy and balance of Tyrrell's apologetics. By not printing, then, Tyrrell's articles the editors were obedient to their bishop, by publishing Bremond's they were obviously exhibiting their disagreement with Farley's directive. Nevertheless, these letters from von Hügel-Tyrrell correspondence demonstrate how well informed Tyrrell was of what transpired at Dunwoodie and with The Review. [38]

36
    The two articles of Tyrrell that were published in The Review were "Consensus Fidelium", I, No. 2 (August-September, 1905), 133-138; and "The Dogmatic Reading of History", I, No. 3 (October-November, 1905), 269-276. Letter, Tyrrell to von Hugel, June 11, 1905, BM Add. Mss., 44929, p. 29; and von Hugel to Tyrrell, June 12, 1905, BM Add. Mss, 44929, p. 32.

37
    Letter, Tyrrell to von Hügel, June 9, 1906, BM Add. Mss. 44929, p. 109. Henri Bremond's article in The Review was "Father Tyrrell as an Apologist", I, No. 6 (April-May, 1906), 762-770.

38
    Tyrrell mentioned to von Hügel in his letter of June 9, 1906 that The Review was experiencing financial difficulties and Driscoll wrote him asking to have him "beg" for the journal in England.

The second set of correspondence that indicates that Tyrrell and Driscoll were in contact with one another is the Driscoll-Tyrrell correspondence. This demonstrates the later stages of their relationship and how deep the relationship grew within a few short years. Unfortunately, due to strictures on this set of correspondence, as we have seen in chapter three of this study, there are only two letters available to the public, both written by Tyrrell. But, their contents sufficiently prove how friendly he was with Driscoll and point to the fact that there must have been extensive correspondence between the two.

In the first letter Tyrrell mentioned that he wished to congratulate Driscoll in detail on The New York Review but could not do so because his recent dismissal from the Jesuits warranted him to report to Driscoll in detail about his present state of affairs.[39] Having done so he then proceeded to write about The Review and to give his personal appraisal of it.

> I am so far more than satisfied with the
> N. Y. R.; tho I fear it owes its survival
> rather to the naive ignorance of auth-
> orities than to any real sympathy or
> tolerance. Still we may profit by
> simplicity. Turmel's line is certainly
> the safest and most telling of all. He

---

[39] Letter, Tyrrell to Driscoll, January 6, 1906, Keogh Family Papers. These papers are located with Judge Keogh's family, New Rochelle, New York.

woke me up (His series in Original Sin
in "Rev. d'hist. et lit. rel") far more
even than Loisy did. He has a wonderful
way of making facts speak for themselves
and making readers draw their own conclusions. And thus he is incontrovertible -
for he says nothing. As for your own most
helpful articles I am in the position of the
non-expert and can give no criticism that
would not be of any importance. I simply
swallow them down and enjoy them. I
had hoped ere this to send you another
contribution; but you will understand
now why I hesitate lest my name should
bring discredit on your review rather
than credit.

This excerpt indicates that ecclesiastical authority was not

fully aware of what was transpiring in The Review. It makes

Driscoll to appear again as deceptive and not totally open to

authority about his views. It also now implicates his journal.

One conclusion, at least, we may draw from this is not that

Driscoll or The Review were unorthodox but that they most

certainly did not follow the hard intransigeant theological line

of Rome at that time.

This letter in which Tyrrell gives Driscoll a full account

of his status in the Church as well as his friendly appraisal of

The Review gives one a good idea of how deep this relationship

with Driscoll had become in only a few short years. The

letter's conclusion strongly corroborates this depth when he

writes:

Need I say what a solid comfort such a
friendship as yours is to me in these

difficult times.   There are not many
one can count on for foul weather
friends.
                    Ever Yours Most Affectionately in Xt,
                        G. Tyrrell.

Tyrrell's second letter to Driscoll underscores their friend-

ship but even more it discloses the direct influence Tyrrell had

in one of The Review's editorial statements.   Once again he

brought his friend, Driscoll, up to date on what had transpired

in his relationship with the Jesuits.   He wrote that they forbade

him to offer Mass, and suggested that he surrender his private

correspondence as a condition for his non-sunspension from

the Church.   In spite of all this "punishment" he expressed to

Driscoll that he had no intention to break from the Church nor

cease to work for what he believed was the true interpretation

of Catholicism.   He would leave the Church, he said, if it

meant forfeiting his integrity as a man.

Having said all this he then directed Tyrrell to print all

these details in The Review:

> Get as much of this into print as you
> choose - at all events, the fact, if not
> its comment.   Be sure to mention
> Ferrata's name.   He never answered
> my letter from Freiburg, nor a second
> one from London asking that if I might
> not say Mass, I might at least make my
> Easter Communion: which I could not do
> while my irregular ecclesiastical status
> made me absolutionis incapax according
> to my confessor. [40]

---

[40]
    Letter, Same to Same, June 3, 1906,Keogh Family Papers.

And Driscoll did get a good deal into print in compliance with

Tyrrell's wish. In "Notes" for the November-December, 1906

issue the editors presented without comment a summary of the

facts in Tyrrell's case with the Jesuits and the Church. However,

before giving this summary The Review stated that because the

press presented both sides of the case, Cardinal Ferrata's and

George Tyrrell's, there would be "no indiscretion in briefly

summing up the facts of the matter so far as they can be

learned". This statement seemed to identify the press as its

source of information and in no way gave anyone the idea that

the editors were privy to the following facts.

> For some time before his separation
> from the Jesuits, Father Tyrrell's
> liberal views had been looked upon
> with distrust by the central authorities
> of the Society. About a year ago he sub-
> mitted a statement of his views and plans
> to the Master General with an offer of
> resignation from the community; which
> offer he afterwards changed to the
> suggestion that the authorities should
> themselves decide on the question of
> his retention and dismissal, the matter
> even in the latter alternative to be
> settled as amicably as possible, and
> presumably in accordance with due
> forms of law. While a settlement was
> pending there appeared in an Italian
> newspaper a translation of a letter to
> a continental professor of Anthropology
> which had been privately circulated in
> English in pamphlet form. The author-
> ship of this letter was attributed, and it
> seems justly to Father Tyrrell. Upon
> satisfying themselves of this fact, his
> superiors dismissed him peremptorily
> from the Society sine episcope receptore,

the canonical defects of such action
having been supplied by the Congregation
of Bishops and Regulars. [41]

This statement which certainly seemed objective continued

by saying that a certain continental Archbishop wrote to the

Sacred Congregation of Bishops and Regulars offering to

accept Tyrrell as a priest of his diocese. The Congregation,

it said, replied affirmatively but since it required Tyrrell to

submit all his writings, even his personal correspondence, to

a delegate of the Archbishop, he refused to accept the offer on

this condition.

The summary ended with a very hopeful note for Tyrrell,

reporting that his latest book, Lex Credendi, had a reassuring

effect on the minds of many who were suspicious of his

orthodoxy; and, although his letter of protest to Cardinal

Ferrata was written in great stress of mind and some bitter-

ness of spirit, he stated in its conclusion: "I still believe and

go on believing and defending the Roman Church... I accept the

Church and her saints as my guidance in faith and Morals."

The Review's summary, although mostly objective,

seemed to have principally defended Tyrrell's orthodoxy and

---

[41]
    The Review, II, No. 3 (November-December, 1906), 497-
498. An ex-Jesuit without a Bishop is ipso facto suspended a
divinis; i.e., from such rights of his priesthood as offering
Mass. Tyrrell at that time (1906) was not censured by the Pope,
or any Bishop but merely expelled from the Jesuits.

good standing in the Church. The Review continued throughout its issues to present subsequent facts to Tyrrell's case and to defend him.

When Longmans published Tyrrell's A Much Abused Letter which he wrote to a European professor on the occasion of his expulsion from the Jesuits, The Review applauded Tyrrell for allowing those interested in his case to read it. [42] Although it admitted that some parts of the letter were "startling" as regards his attitude towards authority in his case, it did say that the reader would be reassured of Tyrrell's loyalty to the doctrines and authority of the Church when these parts are read in conjunction with the book's preface, explanatory notes, and an understanding of the whole matter. The Review's defense of Tyrrell is very strong and evident here and reads very much as if the editors were impatient with those who misjudged him.

On another occasion when an Italian review attacked Father Salvatore Minocchi, editor of Studi Religiosi, for defending Tyrrell after his expulsion from the Jesuits, The Review commented on his defenders by saying:

> ...as for Father Tyrrell-well, the
> Church has not declared him vitandus.
> Are all who might act as counsel for
> him to be disbarred before his trial?

---

[42]
    The Review, II, No. 4 (January-February, 1907),
520.

The Holy Catholic and Roman Church-
whether considered as the body of the
faithful or as the governing authority -
would never consent to such measures as
that. The Catholic Church is made up of
men who, whatever their individual back-
slidings, are devoted to justice; it is
ruled by men whose concern it is to advance the kingdom of justice, and who
are guided in their decisions by a system
of open and impartial judicial procedure.
In this case as in all others justice will
be done by the Church of Christ in
accordance with the due forms of its
law - to doubt it would be insulting; to
attempt to prevent it, disloyal. [43]

This statement evidently demonstrates their belief and

loyalty in a Church which would assure justice for Tyrrell.

It also discloses very well their corporate concept of the Church

which would make this justice possible.

On the other hand, acknowledging that Tyrrell's friends

attacked Minocchi for stating that in A Much Abused Letter

there were some untenable positions, the same editorial said:

It becomes a fair question for the
theologian to discuss whether positions
tentatively advanced in that letter can
be permanently held. At a time when
so many good souls are puzzled and
led astray, and when every active
minded and earnest priest is looking
about for some means of reconciling
the mind of the age with the ancient
faith, such an inquiry is most natural
and proper. And if an honest inquirer

---

[43]
Idem., II, No. 6 (May-June, 1907), 785.

218

> comes to the conclusion that he cannot
> accept the solution, because it seems
> out of harmony with the faith or facts -
> well, it is exactly through the clash of
> opinion such as this that truth ultimately
> comes into her own. These are mighty
> theological problems to be settled by
> this generation or the next and no one
> man is going to settle them.

Throughout this editorial The Review seemed to be very

fair and objective in Tyrrell's case. It called for a full and

free discussion of the whole matter on all its sides. And it con-

tinued to do so especially when a London Catholic paper report-

ed that Tyrrell severed his ties with the Roman Church.[44] It

lashed out vehemently against the newspaper's report not only

in defense of Tyrrell but, as it said, more importantly for

the wider cause of charity, truth and Christ.

There is no doubt, then, that The Review's editor was in

sympathy with his close friend, Tyrrell, at least in the case of

one of its editorials. Before Tyrrell was expelled from the

Jesuits the editors had published his articles. But after his

expulsion their position in regard to Tyrrell seemed to stem

from their obedience to Farley's directive forbidding them to

publish any more from his pen. In the editorials they seemed

to be noncommital to Tyrrell's cause by merely presenting the

facts of his case without any comment. Any defense the editors

---

[44]
The paper was not identified in the editorial statement.

did take of him seemed to be done, as they said, for the sake of truth, justice, and charity.

The Tyrrell Circle

Besides associating with George Tyrrell <u>The Review's</u> editors were also in contact with his intellectual circle which comprised Baron Friedrich von Hügel, Maude Petre, and Henri Bremond. The Church never condemned these three thinkers precisely for their modernistic thought but it did censure them, as we shall see, because of their friendly relationship with Tyrrell.

Baron von Hügel (1852-1925) whom some scholars consider to be the chief engineer of the modernist movement often stimulated and encouraged modernists and potential modernists in their intellectual pursuits.[45] He acted as liason between them, and was in his own right a theologian, mystic, and guide of souls. Although he never made a literary contribution to <u>The Review</u>, its editors did know him well and originally listed him as one of its prominent contributors.

As was indicated earlier, Driscoll wrote to von Hügel soliciting an article from him for the first number of <u>The Review.</u> He also requested von Hügel to ask Wilfrid Ward to

---

[45]
Vidler, <u>A Variety of Catholic Modernists</u>, 113.

prepare something for the same first number. [46]

In addition to this letter the Von Hugel-Tyrrell correspondence indicates that Driscoll was often in communication with
von Hugel and that the Baron was very much acquainted with
and interested in the success of The New York Review. One
letter in this set of correspondence discloses that von Hugel
wanted to send an article to The Review after several journals
had refused it because of its length and depth. von Hugel wrote
to Tyrrell:

> Lilley might take it into the
> "Independent Review". If they
> will not have it I might try the
> 'Church Quarterly' perhaps. I
> imagine the 'New York Review'
> might fight shy of me for a while
> now. [47]

The reason why von Hügel didn't bother sending it to The
Review at that time was most likely because of the previously
mentioned letter of Tyrrell to him which indicated that Farley
forbade its editors from printing anything of Tyrrell's. [48] Von

---

[46]
Letter, von Hügel to Wilfrid Ward, January 9, 1905,
Wilfrid Ward Family Papers.

[47]
Letter, von Hügel to Tyrrell, July 4, 1907, BM Add.
Mss. 44930, p. 42.

[48]
Letter, Tyrrell to von Hügel, June 9, 1906. Also,
Rome issued Pius X's Syllabus, Lamentabili, the day before
von Hügel wrote his letter of July 4, 1907.

Hügel probably surmised from this that since his material was of the same caliber and vein as Tyrrell's The Review would most likely not be able to accept it due to the suspicious tenor of the times.

Although The Review's editors officially had to "shy" away from his writings, they nevertheless maintained a professional, if not friendly, correspondence with him. This is evident by a letter of Driscoll to Bishop Denis O'Connell of Catholic University of America. In it he enclosed a communication from their mutual friend, Baron von Hügel, regarding the procurement of a teaching position for one of his friends at the Catholic University or anywhere else that O'Connell had influence. Driscoll requested O'Connell to communicate personally with von Hugel as regards the matter and said that he himself would inform von Hügel that he referred the matter to him. [49]

The second avowed modernist of this circle was Miss Maude D. Petre (1863-1942). She had studied theology in Rome with the Jesuits and at one time belonged to a lay institute, the Daughters of Mary.

Miss Petre contributed two articles to The Review The

---

[49] Letter, Driscoll to Msgr. Denis O'Connell, June 21, 1908, ACUA, Rector's Office Correspondence, 1903-1909, Box 2, D-9. In this letter the mutual friend was described as "the Barnabite".

first was "Two of Ibsen's Greatest Works" which concerned the themes of fatality and free will in Ibsen's Brand and Peer Gynt.[50] She noted in her diary that she considered this article so good that she would not send it to any other journal but The Review.[51] This notation indicates again the high esteem these English modernists had for The Review.

Her second article was "A New Catholic Apology" which was an essay on William J. William's book Newman, Pascal, Loisy and the Catholic Church.[52] It underlined the collective aspect of religion, the Church's "Catholicity" and a democratic sense of ecclesial authority. Of this article she said in her diary that it was "so splendid" and "a good apology for Newman" that she read it to her good friend, George Tyrrell, who suggested that she send it to The Review.[53]

No other available correspondence can be found that would indicate her further association with The Review. But her diary

---

[50]
II, No. 3 (November-December, 1906), 282-301.

[51]
Diary, entries for May 17, June 22, and September 20, 1906, British Museum, Petre Papers, Vol. VII, Diary 52373, October, 1903-April 1906.

[52]
II, No. 5 (May-April, 1907), 602-609. William J. William's, Newman, Pascal, Loisy, and The Catholic Church, London: Fernsis Griffiths,

[53]
Diary, entries for January 17th and 24th, 1907, Petre Papers, Idem.

does reveal how much this magazine was held in her esteem as a scholarly theological journal that she would send her better articles to it.

The third member of the circle was Henri Bremond (1865-1933). This French priest who was Loisy's friend and future biographer, seemed to have only one connection with The Review: his article on Tyrrell's orthodox and balanced method of theology. [54]

Two of these three friends of Tyrrell's circle eventually incurred sanction because of the role they played at the time of his death. Bremond heard his final confession, and, despite the fact that Tyrrell was not officially reconciled to the Church, presided at his burial. [55] For this Rome prohibited him from saying Mass. After Tyrrell's death Petre publicized in the press that he did not recant his position and Rome directed the Archbishop of London to refuse her Holy Communion because of her action. [56]

----

[54]
Bremond, "Father Tyrrell as an Apologist", 762-770. Pere Andre Blauchet, S. J. of Paris possesses all of Bremond's papers. He informed me there is nothing in them pertaining to The Review.

[55]
Vidler, A Variety of Catholic Modernists, 125.

[56]
Letter, Archbishop of Westminster to Maude Petre, BM, Petre Papers.

Other Modernists Contributing to The Review

There were two other contributors to The Review who later
were condemned as modernists. These were Joseph Turmel
and Ernesto Buonaiuti.

Turmel (1859-1943) was a former pupil of the famous
theologian, Père Billot, S. J., and a former professor of dogma
at the Seminary in Rennes. Four years after his ordination he
claimed to have lost his faith because of biblical criticism but
remained in the Church writing prolifically under pseudonyms
to deceive the Church because, as he said, she had deceived
him. [57]

Patristics was Turmel's field and he wrote, as we saw,
many articles for The Review on it. On the occasion of
publishing his first article in The Review the editors were
happy to announce that he agreed to become a steady contributor. They said it was an honor to present his Catholic
scholarship to the English-reading public because it was
learned, lucid, honest, and objective. [58]

His articles were merely the presentation of facts about
the thinking of the early Church Fathers. As was indicated

---

[57]
Vidler, A Variety of Catholic Modernists, 58.

[58]
The Review, I, No. 2 (August-September, 1905), 257.

225

earlier, Tyrrell wrote to Driscoll expressing his opinion of
Turmel's presentation of facts. He said that he had a wonderful way of making facts speak for themselves and making
readers draw their own conclusions, thus being incontrovertible -
for he says nothing. [59] The Review's editors had a different
opinion of such a method. They like it because, as they said,
"Turmel is confident that when all the facts are clearly stated
the divine and ever living authority of the Church of Christ
will be shown in the sole power to perpetuate revealed truth and
solve the difficulties of mankind in various ages of human
thought". [60] Unlike Tyrrell's their official opinion affirmed that
Turmel's presentation of these facts would corroborate the
authority of the Church.

The editors expressed their esteem for this future notorious
modernist when they said:

> If we have five hundred men like him
> working at our early literature with
> all the resources of modern scholar-
> ship and half a dozen keen intellects
> engaged in formulating the develop-
> ment theory, we are confident that
> one set of problems which confront
> us today could be solved by this

---

[59]
Letter, Tyrrell to Driscoll, January 6, 1906, Keogh
Family Papers.

[60]
The Review, I, No. 2 (August-September, 1905), 257.

generation in favor of the claim of
the Church Catholic. [61]

During these years when Turmel wrote for The Review

Rome considered him to be in good standing with the Church.

However, during these same years he wrote under pseudonyms

other articles more daring than The Review's for different

journals. [62] In 1930 this was discovered and Rome condemned

him declaring him vitandus. When one reads his articles in

The Review one notices nothing devious or unorthodox about

them. They merely presented without comment a synopsis of

the teaching of the Church Fathers on various subjects of

religion.

Ernesto Buonaiuti (1886-1946) was another future modernist

who wrote for The Review. As a priest of the Diocese of Rome

he taught philosophy and Church history at the Urban College of

the Propaganda. He also was editor of Rivista Storico-Critica

delle Scienze Teologiche, a monthly review.

The Review's association with him was twofold. It

published two articles from his pen. [63] One demonstrated the

---

61
    Ibid.

62
    Vidler, A Variety of Catholic Modernists, 59.

63
    "Lucian of Samosata and the Asiatic and Syrian Christian-
ity of His Times", II, No. 1 (July-August, 1906), 48-65; and
"St. Francis of Assisi in Modern Critical Thought", II, No. 4
(January-February, 1907), 459-478.

similarity between Lucian of Samosata's views and early
Christianity's; the other dealt with St. Francis of Assisi and
his role as a reformer. The Review also gave a favorable review to his own theological journal and a book he wrote on the
history of Gnosticism. [64]

About Buonaiuti's journal the editors said they felt a bond
of sympathy with it because he used the same scriptural slogan
as they did to characterize his magazine's attempt to fulfill
the similar objective of turning minds to vital and important
questions. [65] They praised it also because "Roma" was
written on the cover, a name which The Review said indicates
the source of faith and center of unity in the Church and that
its editor was obedient to the Apostolic See.

Eventually, however, this journal which The Review
praised for its openness to thought and loyalty to Rome went on
the Index of forbidden books in 1910 and its editor was condemned as a modernist. [66]

---

[64]
Lo Gnosticismo: Storia di Antiche Latte Religiose (Rome:
Libreria Editrice Francesco Ferrari, 1907), reviewed by
William F. Hughes, in II, No. 6 (May-June, 1907), 798-799.

[65]
The Review, I, No. 6 (April-May, 1906), 800.

[66]
Michael Ranchetti, The Catholic Modernists, trans. by
Isabel Quigly, London: Oxford University Press, 1969, 223.

American Modernists

Since modernism was primarily a European theological tendency most contributors to The New York Review who were accused of being modernists were European. However, there were two American contributors who later became self-avowed, identifiable modernists: William L. Sullivan and Thomas J. Mulvey.

William L. Sullivan (1872-1935) was the most noteworthy American modernist. A graduate of St. John's Seminary in Brighton and the Catholic University of America, Sullivan was ordained a priest in 1899. Soon after this he joined the Paulists and from 1902-1906 taught theology in St. Thomas College (the Paulist house of studies) in Washington. He worked for the next two years as a campus minister in Chicago. And, from 1908-1909 he was pastor of a parish in Austin, Texas. In 1909, a convinced modernist, he resigned his pastorate in Austin and formally announced his withdrawal from the Paulist community and the Catholic Church. [67]

Sullivan was a prolific writer on religious subjects and a deep believer in the fact that the reconstruction of the Catholic religion for the new age was tied to the American democratic

---

[67]
See his Under Orders: The Autobiography of William Laurence Sullivan, Boston: Beacon Press, 1944, 198-200.

experience. [68] His association with The New York Review was

twofold. He was an enthusiastic supporter of and contributor to

The Review.

As a supporter of The Review, Sullivan, in his autobiography,

spoke of his relationship to its editors as if he were closely

associated with them. He implied that he knew them very well.

As we saw in Chapter one of this dissertation, Sullivan, in

writing about The Review's inception in his autobiography,

seemed to consider himself very instrumental in founding this

journal. He also indicated in his book how well he personally

knew the Dunwoodie editors and how much he considered his

writings and their thinking to be orthodox at the time. About

his opinion of their orthodoxy and his knowledge of them,

Sullivan wrote:

> Certainly at that time I was orthodox in
> every article of defined doctrine and I
> had no reason to think my associates
> were not, despite their radical talk from
> time to time. Gigot, I knew, was troubled
> at the more appalling difficulties in Scripture.
> Driscoll had a nature in which there were
> mingled both a rebel strain and a watchful
> prudence. Duffy would occasionally tell
> us that our torments in scriptural and
> historical study were nothing compared
> with his in the more fundamental
> province of philosophy. [69]

---

[68]
See Sullivan's article "Catholicity and Some Elements in
Our National Life", The New York Review, I, No. 3 (October-
November, 1905), 259-268.

[69]
Sullivan, Under Orders, 106.

Another passage from his book which indicates how close

he was to these editors was when he wrote about Archbishop

Farley's view of The New York Review. He said.

> Cardinal Farley of New York was very
> proud of The Review, and regarded it
> as a fine witness to the scholarship of
> his Seminary. The poor Cardinal had
> not the least idea what these discussions
> in criticism were all about; and once in
> a while he dropped an inept remark con-
> cerning them, which his faculty trans-
> mitted to us with irreverent delights. [70]

From Sullivan's autobiography it is therefore evident that

the editors of The Review were in contact with him. Sullivan,

himself, wrote of this contact as one of close friendship.

Sullivan also contributed three articles to The Review. The

first, "Catholicity and Some Elements in our National Life",

set forth the aim of the Church on dispelling the notion that it

was against liberty and cannot be reconciled with democracy. [71]

His second article, "Judgement Day in Jewish Thought",

was a very scholarly one in which he investigated the

eschotological ideas current in Judaism in our Lord's time,

as they bore on the subject of Judgement Day. He considered

Old Testament texts on this subject and examined non-Jewish

concepts of time which may have influenced Jewish thought as

---

[70]
   Ibid., 107.

[71]
   "Catholicity and Some Elements in Our National Life",
I, No. 3 (October-November, 1905), 259-268.

regards the Judgement Day. [72]

Sullivan's third article, "The Three Heavenly Witnesses",
studied the Johannine Comma; i. e., the text of the three
heavenly witnesses, namely, the Father, the Word, and the Holy
Spirit found in verses 6, 7, and 8 of the fifth chapter of the first
Epistle of St. John. These verses speak of the heavenly and
earthly witnesses that give testimony to Jesus Christ. Sullivan
addressed himself only to the heavenly witnesses. He argued
that they were not mentioned in the genuine Johannine letter but
were interpolated into the original text. [73]

In 1906 Sullivan ended his periodical writing as he became
disillusioned with prospects in the Church for modern thought
and science. He therefore no longer made literary contributions
to The Review. [74] There is no way that one can say how the
editors would have responded to his writings when he vowed himself to be a modernist in 1909, one year after The Review

---

[72]
"Judgement Day in Jewish Thought", I, No. 6 (April-May,
1906), 728-738.

[73]
"The Three Heavenly Witnesses", II, No. 2 (September-
October, 1906), 175-188.

[74]
He did, however, write Letters to His Holiness Pope
Pius X, (Chicago: The Open Court Publishing Co., 1910); The
Priest: A Tale of Modernism in New England, (Boston: Sherman,
French & Co., 1911); and Under Orders: The Autobiography of
William Laurence Sullivan, (Boston: Beacon Press, 1944),
(post-humously).

suspended publication.

Another identifiable American modernist who was in contact with the editors of The Review was Irish born Thomas J. Mulvey (1870-1952). Ordained from the Urban College of the Propaganda in Rome in 1899. Mulvey was a priest of the Diocese of Brooklyn. He served there as assistant pastor in two parishes, St. Francis of Assisi (1899-1904), and St. Edwards (1904-1908). [75] He had considered the Syllabus of Pope Pius X condemning some modernistic errors and came to the conclusion that in conscience he could not accept or agree with it.[76] He therefore resigned from the priesthood in July, 1908.

Cardinal Gibbon's response to Mulvey's resignation was "This is the first defection from the Church on the grounds of modernism since the pope's encyclical letter defining and condemning the heresy". Quite probably Gibbons was correct. But, he and Archbishop Farley tried to dismiss the reason for Mulvey's departure as doctrinal by saying that Mulvey resigned because he was involved with a woman. [77]

---

[75]
See Monsignor John K. Sharp's Priests and Parishes of the Diocese of Brooklyn: 1820 to 1972, (Revised edition by Rev. Herbert P. Redmond, Brooklyn: private circulation, 1973), 170.

[76]
The New York Sun, July 18, 1908, Part I: p. 1.

[77]
The New York Tribune, July 19, 1908, p. 5.

Mulvey contributed two book reviews to The Review. [78] To say that this was the only connection he had with liberal Catholic thought is not very certain. Though he was young and involved in the parochial ministry, some correspondence of Driscoll's does indicate that "a young priest in Brooklyn" was in contact with him on intellectual matters. [79] Whether this young priest was Mulvey is not absolutely certain but from the letter's details of the priest's background, it could very well have been. Be that as it may, Thomas J. Mulvey, contributor to The New York Review, had formed his convictions and was by his own admission a modernist.

Other Modernists

The New York Review's encounter with other modernists who were not associated with it: viz., Reverend Romolo Murri, the Italian Senator, Antonio Fogazzaro, and Reverend Salvatore Minocchi, was one of reporting their status in the Church and commenting on their activities in its editorial "Notes".

78
He reviewed Francis G. Peabody's Jesus Christ and the Social Question (New York: The MacMillan Company, 1906), II, No. 6 (May-June, 1907), 796-798), and H. Delehoyer's The Legend of the Saints (London: Longmans, Green and Co., 1907), III, No. 3 (November-December, 1907), 369-370.

79
Letter, Driscoll to Henri Hyvernat, October 5, 1900, ACUA.

When ecclesiastical authorities suppressed Murri's theological journal, Cultura Sociale, The Review's editors reported this act as well as the rumor that he would publish a reply to the encyclical addressed to the Bishops of Italy. They made it clear to their readers that Murri denied the rumor in La Stampa of Turin because he said he desired to remain faithful to all his obligations as a Catholic and a priest. They commented on his statement by saying:

> [This statement of Murri's] only goes to show how slow many minds are to understand that a Catholic can be virile, enterprising, energetic, and yet be ready to relinquish his most cherished plans at the voice of competent authority. Such a combination of qualities they affect to believe impossible. They have never fathomed the deep good sense of the Catholic ideal, which aims, even though it may not always succeed, at keeping due place for individual initiative and for organic control. Students of political institutions have long since recognized that the main task of government is to keep the balance true between authority and liberty. Excess in either direction is destructive - on the one the knout; on the other, the torch. It should be as clearly acknowledged that in religious government the same principles held. The individual must possess a measure of freedom, but that freedom is limited by the needs of the organism of which he forms a part; and if it does not command him to do or say what his conscience forbids he is bound by good sense no less than by loyalty to act in conformity with its decisions. And yet not infrequently those who guide their actions by these

principles are scorned as insincere or
denounced as traitors to humanity. [80]

This commentary is important as we have already seen because it reveals The Review's attitude toward individual liberty
and Church authority. It also exhibits its belief in the necessity for loyalty to the Church and for viewing the Church as an
organic whole which is responsible for all members and
respectful of an individual.

In regard to Senator Fogazzaro, author of the novel Il Santo
which was condemned by the Congregation of the Index, the
editor of The Review reported that Fogazzaro submitted to the
Index and that a number of his countrymen who were opposed to
Church authority condemned him for his act. [81] Their comment
on this situation was that Fogazzaro was trying to shape his
own conduct in the time of his trial on the model of what his
"Saint" did in similar circumstances - first of all obedience to
authority; then silentium. For this The Review applauded him.

Later, when both Murri and Fogazzaro were under fire by
Rome, the editors reported that the pope was taking severe
measures against them by forbidding priests to attend
Fogazzaro's lectures on religious subjects in Turin. [82]

80
  II, No. 3 (November-December, 1906), 495.

81
  Ibid., Il Santo, Milan: Baldini Castoldi e Co., 1906.

82
  III, No. 1 (July-August, 1907), 74.

Fogazzaro's disrespectful answer to Rome's prohibition drew

from The Review this comment:

> These lectures have been founded with
> the proceeds of a book placed on the
> Index and they are to be managed by a
> committee of Catholics whose Catholicity
> is swallowed up in their liberalism.

The editors continued to emphasize their disagreement

with these "non-Catholic" lectures. But, to do justice to

Fogazzaro they did admit that President Theodore Roosevelt

invited him to lecture in America. They also mentioned that

Fogazzaro said in La Stampa that he was distressed because

of the action that Church authority took in his case. On this

The Review's editors evidently did not believe him because

they said:

> It is to be hoped, indeed, that his sub-
> mission was not merely a matter of form,
> though there have not been wanting signs,
> which make one fear he is not altogether
> sincere in his protestations. [83]

But The Review's editors exhibited objectivity when they

said that Fogazzaro bore firm witness in La Stampa to Don

Murri's firm attachment to the Catholic faith and that he believed

Don Murri would accept the Church's chastisement in the spirit

of a good Catholic. The editors agreed with him on this because

they said that one of Murri's classmates believed that he would

never apostatize for he was at heart a good Catholic, and in his

---

[83]
Ibid., 75.

private life a most holy priest. [84]

As regards Salvatore Minocchi, we have already seen The Review's positive and objective regard towards him when Tyrrell's opponents attacked him for defending Tyrrell after his expulsion for the Jesuits and when Tyrrell's friends scored him for saying that Tyrrell had put forth untenable views. [85] However, because the editors suspended "Notes" in The Review's last five issues they did not report that Minocchi was suspended à divinis for a lecture on Genesis given in Florence in 1908.

Conclusion

From this investigation into the editors' associations with modernists and the position they took as regards them in their journal, we can now draw some conclusions concerning The Review's posture to modernism at that time.

As already has been indicated, the correspondence of its editor, James F. Driscoll, reveals that he was very close and friendly with prominent modernists. He exchanged ideas with them, offered to collaborate with them; invited them to write

---

[84] Murri's works were placed on The Index in 1909 and he ultimately left the Church. However, in 1943, he was received back into the Church.

[85] II, No. 6 (May-June, 1907), 785.

for The Review; published their writings; and accepted their suggestions and criticisms of his journal. When these thinkers were beginning to be suspected and oppressed by Church authorities, his correspondence shows his support for them and his sympathy with their debatable views. Driscoll's associations with the modernists were of such a caliber that one would think that he too was a modernist. It is true that he did want to translate into English two of Loisy's condemned books. We also saw that he procured for his seminarians copies of one of Tyrrell's books that was refused an Imprimatur and which Tyrrell then limited only to private circulation. Von Hügel and Tyrrell in their correspondence with one another and with Driscoll seem to indicate that he was collaborating with them in surreptiously propagating modernist ideas in his journal and in his seminary. These letters mentioned several times that Farley was not really aware of what was transpiring theologically in his seminary and in The Review. But, there is no available evidence that would corrobate the thesis that Driscoll himself was a modernist.

The only evidence we do have that explicitly describes his relation to the modernists is a letter by Driscoll himself which he wrote to Dr. Charles A. Briggs soon after Pius X issued his encyclical, Pascendi Dominici gregis. The purpose of his letter was to express his regret to Briggs that he was unable to lecture at Union Theological. The reason he gave for this was that in the stormy wake of the encyclical, Farley, "out of prudence", directed him to decline. He admitted that Farley was right in this directive. Driscoll then proceeded to write about the turmoil in the Church. In this context he avowed his friendship with the modernists and his sympathy with their views. He wrote:

> Now my sympathy with Modernism is pretty
> well known as well as my intimate friend-
> ship with several of the most noted of its
> promoters and so with all this you can
> readily understand that the Archbishop
> tho very well disposed towards me and some
> of my views is at present anxious lest he
> may be obliged to remove me from my
> present position and suppress the publi-
> cation of The Review. This I am sure
> he would not at all wish to do and he is
> anxious to avoid anything connected with
> me which might easily be misinterpreted
> or even misrepresented in Roman
> ecclesiastical circles. [86]

But, friendship with modernists and sympathy with their views does not necessarily make one a modernist. One could accept their methodology and their orthodox views while still rejecting their anti-Christian conclusions. A modernist, as we said earlier, was one who affirmed anti-Christian con- clusions by the use of the new scientific methods of the day. .

---

[86]
Letter, Driscoll to Briggs, December 8, 1907, UTSA. Briggs was a Protestant scripture scholar of the new school and professor at Union Theological. This former Presbyterian who converted to Episcopolianism enjoyed a very friendly rela- tionship with Driscoll.

The fact that Driscoll mentioned that Farley was still well-disposed to some of his views implies that he did not affirm the anti-Christian conclusions of the modernists nor count himself as one of them. No doubt, if Driscoll had publicly acknowledged unorthodox views, Farley would have removed him from his position in the seminary. As we shall see in the next chapter, Farley did remove Driscoll from his position as president of St. Joseph's Seminary and Rome did suspect that there were eight modernists in New York. Whether Driscoll's removal from the seminary was because he was a modernist or whether he and the other editors were among the eight New York modernists is not certain. All we can conclude with certainty is that Driscoll was friendly with modernists and sympathetic with their views. As for the other editors, Duffy and Brady, there is no evidence that indicates that they were modernists or maintained any friendly or professional associations with these thinkers.

However, in contrast to Driscoll's personal stand as regards the modernists, the official position that his journal took to these thinkers and their views was patently different. This difference is illustrative in several ways.

First, even though The Review's editors were open to the modernists' views, and, in most cases, in sympathy with them. Once these thinkers broke from the Church or became suspect they could not publish any of their articles out of

241

obedience to Archbishop Farley's directive. This was true, as
we saw, with Tyrrell's and von Hügel's articles.

Secondly, at the time Pius X issued Lamentabili and
Pascendi, condemning modernism, The Review's editorials
became more manifestly different from its editor's personal
views towards the modernists. In the cases of Fogazzaro,
Murri, and Minocchi, they reported objectively their status
in the Church and their comments on them plainly exhibited
an agreement with the defense of the Church's stand in regard
to them. They also rejected their views.

Also in another editorial after Pascendi they recommended
to their readers Volume II of The Catholic Encyclopedia mainly
for two reasons.[87] It presented a brief definition of modernism
as it centered around Sacred Scripture, and it offered several
articles by Gabriel Ousanni which dispelled, according to the
editorial, the fear that "Pius X was going to turn off the light
of modern research". This recommendation also called
attention to Ousanni's articles in the encyclopedia because it
said "they witness to the Church's ability to tolerate a proper
freedom of criticism in her exegesis in perfect consistency
with her own inflexible principle. "

Finally, one notices throughout The Review's "Notes" that

___

[87] III, No. 3 (November-December, 1907), 359.

the editors often printed the statements and documents of the
Holy See concerning such issues as the Biblical Commission's
answer to certain debatable scriptural questions, and the pope's
letters regarding seminary reform. [88] However, with one
exception, as we shall see, they always did so without ever
commenting on them.

The absence of comments on The Review's part in such
cases may suggest that the editors refused to commit themselves to what they were reporting. Other cases in which
correspondence is available corroborates such a suggestion.
It is in considering these cases where The Review refused to
comment that the difference between its stand and its editor's
boldly emerges.

As we saw earlier its editorial on Tyrrell's situation in
the Church was just a mere presentation of facts without any
comment. His letters indicate that Driscoll was in sympathy
with and in support of him during times of trial. Although its
editor was fraternally committed to Tyrrell, The Review
exhibited no commitment to his case.

Also, when Pius X issued his encyclical, Pascendi, The
Review dutifully printed it in its entirety but gave no comment

[88]
    I, No. 2 (August-September, 1905), 241; II, No. 1 (July-
August, 1906), 106-109; II, No. 2 (September-October, 1906),
249-250; III, No. 1 (July-August, 1907), 81-83; and III No. 3
(November-December, 1907), 350-354.

on it either by way of introduction, summary, endorsement, or disapproval.[89] However, a letter of Driscoll to Briggs shows how much its editor was in disagreement with it. He wrote:

> To you who know so well the genesis and development of the present crisis in the Catholic Church need hardly say that nothing so violent and drastic as the recent curial document has appeared on the part of the Vatican authorities since the days of the inquisition. I can compare the crisis to nothing but a cyclone during which people must simply make for the cellar; or in other terms it resembles the recent financial panic in N. Y.[90]

Since the letter is dated December 8, 1907 the recent document that Driscoll mentioned was Pascendi. His disagreement with it comes out even greater in the same letter when he wrote, "You must here notice also the absurdly drastic measures imposed upon the bishop toward the end of the Encyclical; how for instance no person having any sympathy with the Modernists can be retained as professor in a seminary."

The only case where The Review did commit itself and openly revealed its sympathy with modernism was, as we saw, in a review of a book by a member of the Biblical Commission who scored Loisy's La Quatrieme Evangile. The reviewer,

---

[89] III, No. 2 (September-October, 1907), 205-241.

[90] Letter, Driscoll to Briggs, December 8, 1907, UTSA.

Samuel P. MacPherson defended Loisy's book which three years
before had been placed on the Index and he dismissed with
absurdity the criticism of a member of the Biblical Commission.

From all this we can see that The Review's posture to
modernism was ambivalent. In private its editor had an unequivocal loyalty to and sympathy with the modernists as the
correspondence of its editor disclosed. But, in print the
editors tried to maintain an appearance of loyalty to the Church.
To accomplish this their editorial was ambiguous. At times,
they were non-committal when they disagreed with the Church's
stand and at other instances they plainly exhibited their loyalty
to the Church.

But, if there is one editorial that can give us an idea of
The Review's official position in regard to modernism, it is
the one that commented on Pius X's Syllabus. [91]

This editorial endorsed the new Syllabus of Pius X and
scored the press for criticizing the pope as well as those who
said the Church was tyranical when all she was doing was defending the basic doctrine of her belief. The reasons for this

---

[91]
    The Review's editors printed it in one issue: III, No. 1
(July-August, 1907), 83-91. Because The Syllabus arrived as
The Review was going to press, the editors promised to give
an editorial on it in a later issue: III, No. 3 (November-
December, 1907), 342-349. Although there is no by-line to
this editorial, the index does indicate Duffy to be its author.

endorsement were that the Syllabus pointed out that the teaching authority of the Church condemned only extreme views and that its spirit was one of moderation. It dispelled the myth that the Syllabus would stifle intellectual activity within the Church and advised "sympathizers not to cry for Catholic scholars' liberty because many are working within lines that the Church laid down." The statement expressed the belief that the Church would be saved by its central authority and that the Syllabus was the beginning of a more glorious period of Catholic intellectual activity. To underline this belief the editorial stated what a fine thing it was to belong to a great wide old Church because of its corporate wisdom and patience as well as its unhurrying confident serenity of things vast and ever-lasting. It also pointed out that the great body of the faithful (Bishops, priests, laity, universities, seminaries, reviews) have accepted the Church's decisions with unanimity and equanimity.

With all this said, the editors then stated that the best refutation to injurious assertions that the Syllabus had rendered Catholic scholarship impossible was to go calmy ahead in union with the Holy See. They set The Review up as an example of this by demonstrating that it would continue to print topics of present day interest by writers well versed in the lore of the moderns. In this way The Review would prove that loyalty to science and to the Holy See a double and not a divided duty.

Then, The Review's editorial gave forth the position it would take to those controversial times and to modernism as it said:

> For our own part, we shall go on about our
> work, devoted to the ancient Faith and to
> its living exponent, the Vicar of Christ;
> meeting what is false in modern thought
> with its own weapons; strengthening our
> souls against "combats without" and "fears
> within." by the reflection with which we
> began this editorial : It is a fine thing
> to belong to a great wide old Church, if
> only for the corporate wisdom and patience
> it acquires. It partakes of the unhurrying
> confident serenity of things vast and ever-
> lasting. Those outside may criticize,
> some within may worry; but the great body
> moves on about its work unashamed and
> unafraid.

Such a statement evidences that The Review intended to relate to the tumultuous tenor of the times by adhering to its approach to theology and its view of the Church. By so doing it would continue its work of reconciling science with faith during unstable times.

However, even though this editorial strongly stated that The Review would continue to maintain its loyalty to the Church and her decisions in the modernist crisis as well as still be open to the questions of the day, the outward appearance of The Review itself began to imply that something radical was taking place in its editorial office. The journal started to take on an erratic form. After the issue in which the editorial on the

Syllabus appeared, subsequent issues no longer contained any more editorials or book reviews. Two issues were combined into one so that The Review would cease publication with the May-June, 1908 issue. The reasons for these erratic changes and suspension of The Review's publication will be the subject of the next chapter.

CHAPTER VI

THE DEMISE OF THE NEW YORK REVIEW

In the last chapter we saw that The Review took an ambivalent stand in the face of modernism. Sometimes its editors rejected the anti-Christian conclusions of modernists' methods and underlined the papal documents condemning them; and at other times, they seemed to have been non-commital to the modernists' actions and thoughts that they were reporting. Upon examining these editorial statements in the light of the editors' correspondence, there were even times when what they said in The Review as regards modernism became the exact opposite of what they privately held and believed.

After Pius X issued his encyclical, Pascendi Dominici gregis, condemning modernism, in September, 1907, The Review's form began to change radically; and within the year, it ceased publication. Some of its articles following the issuance of Pascendi gave some indication that modernism and its spirit were contrary to the teaching of the Roman Catholic Church. But, the most obvious change was in the abrupt cessation of the editorial statements in these remaining issues. No longer did The Review's editors give any reports, observations, commentaries, or recommendations of the progress in

IMPORTANT NOTICE ON NEXT PAGE.

Vol III.   MAY-JUNE, 1908.   No. 6.

THE
NEW YORK
REVIEW.

Published Every Two Months, by John F. Brady

CUM PERMISSU SUPERIORUM

St. Joseph's Seminray, Yonkers,

A Year: 3 Dollars.   NEW YORK.   Single Copy
(Foreign: 12s 6d.)   50 cts.

Registered at Yonkers Post Office as Second Class Matter.

theological scholarship. They gave no reason for this omission which was patently noticeable. Another change was that two issues were combined into one so that The Review would cease publication with its final issue, May-June, 1908.

A consideration of the causes for The Review's termination in 1908 is the object of the present chapter. Such a consideration can add not only to The Review's contribution to a theology of ecclesial reform but also to the history of the Church in America, by presenting an incipient understanding of American Catholic modernism.

I. Official Reason for Demise

The official reason that the editors gave for suspending publication of The Review was that the very small number of Catholics interested in the questions it considered did not justify its continuance.[1] A termination notice, inserted in the final issue, couched the reason in the following terms:

> With this issue which concludes
> Vol. III: The New York Review ceases
> publication.
> At its inception three years ago its
> editors promised to present the best
> work of Catholic scholars at home and
> abroad on theological and other problems
> of the present day. It is the keeping of

---

[1] "Termination Notice", III, No. 6 (May-June, 1908). Cf. Appendix B.

that promise, not the breaking of it,
that is the cause of the suspension of
The Review. For the number of Catholics interested in questions which are
of importance to the thinkers of the
present generation - and which will be
vital to all classes in the next - has been
found to be so small that it does not justify
the continuance of The Review. It would
be possible perhaps to treat the same
topics in a more popular style, but the
editors are strongly of the opinion that
new and difficult problems should be
discussed in a way that will attract the
attention of only trained and scholarly
minds. Or the scope of The Review might
be changed, but this would bring it into
needless competition with other Catholic
periodicals which are doing excellent
work in their chosen departments.

The reason set forth in this statement for The Review's

termination holds true in the light of available correspondence.

Although no subscription list for The Review is extant, it

seemed always to have had a small number of readers due to

its highly scholarly caliber. [2] About this correlation between

---

[2]
N. W. Ayer and Sons, The American Newspaper Annual
which contains a catalogue of American newspapers and gives
a list of monthly and weekly publications of general circulations,
religious and secular, has no circulation figure for The New
York Review (cf. 1907 and 1908 volumes of Ayer). In the
introduction, on page 7, Ayer says: "Circulation is not given
in the following instances - where the paper has been established
during the current year, or is entered for the first time in the
Annual; where the information received is unsatisfactory, or
the reports are conflicting; where publishers have requested
omission, in which case the word 'Decline' is printed in the
circulation column". There is nothing written in the column
of The Review.

scholarship and paucity of subscribers Driscoll once wrote to

Wilfrid Ward that they were endeavoring to maintain a high

standard in The Review even though it would be thereby rendered

dry and unintelligible to many. [3] This resolution expressed by

its editor is the same as that indicated in the termination notice.

It would follow, then, that a small number of subscribers to

The Review would not be sufficient to meet its operational

expenses.

As early as 1906, one year after it first began publishing,

there was indication that The Review was beginning to encounter

financial difficulties. Its editor not only mentioned this

financial situation to Wilfrid Ward, as we have just seen, but

he also wrote to his friend George Tyrrell in England to raise

funds there in order to keep his journal alive. [4]

Raising funds was the only measure, apparently, the

editors would employ to save their review from going under

financially. They hesitated, as the termination notice and

Driscoll's letter to Ward attest, to change the scope of their

---

[3]
Letter, James F. Driscoll to Wilfrid Ward, April 27,
1906, The Wilfrid Ward Family Papers.

[4]
Driscoll's request to Tyrrell is indicated in Tyrrell's
letter to von Hügel, June 9, 1906, Von Hügel-Tyrrell Correspondence, BM Addit. Mss., 44929, p. 109. "The New York Review
is asking for contributions and have asked me to beg for them.
If you think [Charles] Devas would help them, will you ask
him."

magazine so as to appeal to a wider range of readers. To do so, they believed, would not only compete with existing journals with a popular religious trend but also duplicate their efforts. The Review's editors evidently desired to avoid this even to the extent that it would mean its discontinuance. [5]

As was indicated earlier, when The Review was still in its planning stages, its editors made the effort to petition the editors of existing journals inquiring whether its emergence on the American theological scene would threaten their existence. These men's answer to The Review editors was that they would not only not be threatened by it, but they also heartily welcomed such a journal because of its projected scholarly scope which was unique on the American scene. [6] We also saw that one of its contributors at first feared that The Review's emergence would draw readers away from these existing Catholic magazines. [7] However, he soon realized that this would not happen and went on to write five articles

---

[5]
Cf. "Termination Notice"; Chapter One of this dissertation; and Driscoll's letter to the publisher of The Catholic Citizen of Milwaukee, undated, ADR.

[6]
Cf. Chapter One of this dissertation.

[7]
Letter, Edward J. Hanna to Denis O'Connell, January 10, 1905, ADR and ACUA.

in the new journal. [8]

It is true that Archbishop Farley promised to subsidize The New York Review because he believed in its efforts. [9] And most likely he did so, if it lasted for three years on the average subscription rate for most magazines at that time ($3.00 a year) and a small number of subscribers. But, the editors evidently decided that their endeavor was no longer worth their bishop's subsidy. Driscoll admitted this during The Review's final year when he wrote the publisher of The Catholic Citizen of Milwaukee. [10]

The purpose of his letter was to deny an erroneous report that The Review was terminating publication for other reasons than the financial one. In it he referred to the fact that his journal could no longer warrant support when he wrote:

---

[8]
Edward J. Hanna, "The Human Knowledge of Christ", I, No. 2 (August-September, 1905), 303-316; No. 3 (October-November, 1905), 425-436; No. 4 (December-January, 1905-1906), 597-615; and in III, Nos. 4 and 5 (January-February; March-April, 1908), 391-400; and "The Power of the Keys", idem, 561-568.

[9]
Cf. Chapter One of this dissertation.

[10]
Letter, Driscoll to the publisher of The Catholic Citizen of Milwaukee, undated, ADR. Although there is no date on this letter in the Archives of the Diocese of Rochester, its contents reveal that it was most likely written in September, 1908.

It is true that The New York Review
will cease publication with the next
issue which will complete the third
volume. . . .
The reason for suspending publication will be briefly stated in the
forth coming number. It is simply
and solely a lack of support on the part
of the reading public and several months
ago the editors came to the decision of
not trying to maintain the periodical
beyond the close of the present volume.
Three years experience had made it
manifest that the number of Catholic
readers interest in the rather abstruse
and somewhat technical subjects which
we had chosen for our field of work, was
not sufficient to afford a financial support
for the undertaking, even though our
contributors were far from being
adequately compensated.

In addition to Driscoll, Monsignor Michael Lavelle, rector

of St. Patrick's Cathedral in New York, also underlined the

financial reason as being the sole reason for The Review's

termination. In an interview with a New York newspaper soon

after The Review announced its termination, he too dismissed

the rumor that it folded for other reasons than the financial

one. He said:

It is true that The Review will cease
publication at the end of the current
volume. This decision was reached
some months ago on account of lack
of financial support. There is not a
sufficient demand among American
Catholic readers for a periodical
dealing with technical and abstruse
questions to which subjects it was
confined. [11]

---

[11]
Cited in The Rochester Democrat and Chronicle, September

POPE ST. PIUS X

It is interesting to note that these two statements of Lavelle and Driscoll to the press read almost exactly alike. At times they even used the identical words. Such a unanimity of expression cannot help but lead one to believe that there was a prepared statement for expressing to the public that the official and only reason for The Review's demise was financial.

II. Other Probable Reasons for the Demise

Such overstatements to the press on the part of the Driscoll and Lavelle that there was an official and sole reason for terminating The Review could also very well lead one to believe that there were also unofficial reasons for the termination. Investigation into the Review's history seems to affirm this possibility.

A. The Condemnation of Modernism

First, upon considering the historical and theological context in which The Review found itself the financial reason alone cannot account for its demise. A year before it ceased publication, Pope Pius X issued his syllabus of errors, Lamentabili, and his encyclical, Pascendi, which condemned modernism.[12]

19, 1908, p. 6.

[12]
    Lamentabili was issued on July 3, 1907, and Pascendi Dominici gregis, on September 8, 1907.

These papal documents produced a wake of turbulence and suspicion for anyone who taught, read, or wrote theology. The New York Review would therefore be caught up in this wake which would certainly affect its course of direction. Pius's encyclical in condemning the spirit and methods of modernism also presented remedies against this trend of liberal thought. Some remedies were specifically concerned with publications and as such they would have affected The Review. The ones that the editors of The Review would have to weigh in their own case were:

> It is also the duty of the Bishops to
> prevent writings infected with modernism
> or favourable to it from being read when
> they have been published, and to hinder
> their publication, when they have not, No
> book of paper or periodical of this kind
> must ever be presented to seminarists or
> university students... The same decision
> is to be taken concerning the writings of
> some Catholics, who though not badly dis-
> posed themselves but ill-instructed in
> theological studies and imbued with modern
> philosophy, strive to make them harmonize
> with the faith, and, as they say, to turn
> it to the account of the faith. The name
> and reputation of these authors cause them
> to be read without suspicion and they are,
> therefore, all the more dangerous in pre-
> paring the way for modernism. [13]

And again the encyclical stated:

---

[13]
Pascendi Dominici gregis, Part III: Remedies; English Translation, cited in The New York Review, III, No. 2 (September-October, 1907), 237.

257

But it is not enough to hinder the reading
and sale of bad books - it is also necessary to prevent them from being
printed. Hence, let the Bishops use the
utmost severity in granting permission
to print. Under the rules of the constitution Officiorum, many publications
require the authorization of the Ordinary,
and in some dioceses it has been made the
custom to have a suitable number of official
censors for the examination of writings.[14]

The pope gave high praise to the institution of censors and

ordered it to be extended to all dioceses.

The final remedy concerned with publications was:

It is forbidden to secular priests without
the previous consent of the ordinary, to
undertake the direction of papers or
periodicals. This permission shall be
withdrawn from any priest who makes a
wrong use of it after having been ad-
monished. With regard to priests who
are correspondents or collaborators of
periodicals, as it happens not infrequently
that they write matter infected with
modernism for their paper or periodicals,
let the Bishops see to it that this is not
permitted to happen, and should it happen,
let them warn the writer or prevent them
from writing... Let there be as far as
possible a special censor for newspapers
and periodicals written by Catholics. It
shall be his office to read in due time
each number after it has been published,
and if he finds anything dangerous in it
let him order that it be corrected. The
Bishop shall have the same right even
when the censor has seen nothing other
objectionable in a publication.[15]

14
Ibid., 238.

15
Ibid., 239.

The encyclical also stipulated that a diocesan vigilance committee be established to watch most carefully for every trace and sign of modernism both in publications and teaching, and to preserve the clergy and young from it. It was to employ every prudent, prompt and efficacious measure to do this.

There is no wonder, then, that in the light of such remedies The New York Review which was forward looking in theology could easily fall victim to suspicion. Driscoll soon after the promulgation of the encyclical wrote to his friend Briggs testifying that this very calamity came upon his journal. He said:

> Now this institution [St. Joseph's Seminary] has for some time been looked upon by certain invidious heresy hunters in the Catholic Community as a brothel of liberalism or as it is now called Modernism; furthermore The New York Review edited by myself and a couple of confreres is looked upon in the same light and it has been more than once denounced to Roman authorities.[16]

He continued to say that because it was public knowledge that he was friendly and sympathetic with the modernists and their views his position as president and editor was very precarious. Therefore, he told Briggs:

> ... You can readily understand that the Archbishop though very well disposed

---

[16]
Letter, Driscoll to Charles A. Briggs, December 8, 1908, UTSA.

> toward me and some of my views is at
> present anxious that he may be obliged
> to remove me from my present position
> [president] and suppress the publication
> of The Review. This I'm sure he would
> not at all wish to do and he is anxious
> to avoid anything connected with me
> which might easily be misinterpreted or
> even misrepresented in Roman ecclesiastical
> circles.

This letter clearly indicates that in addition to the financial problem The Review was also vulnerable to other problems which could lead to its termination; viz., being suspected of heresy, ecclesiastical authority would suppress it.[17] For some time before Pascendi Driscoll had feared this would happen to his journal. In 1906, without The Review yet completing its first volume, the editor wrote to Wilfrid Ward that "our young periodical has so far escaped censure."[18] Driscoll most likely knew that the caliber and content of his review did not sit well with ecclesiastical authorities during those peak years of

---

[17]
A librarian, Newman Smyth‚expressed well the suppressive tenor of the times for publication when he wrote to Charles A. Briggs of Union Theological Seminary, New York: "Do you know whether the review, Nova et Vetera has continued since the prohibition of it? and what has become of "Il Rinnovimento"? I want to keep track of current literature of modernism for our libraries here; and if any books have come to your notice which we should have. ... If there is any review which authority has not succeeded in suppressing which represents their (modernistic) view, I would like to know that". Letter, Newman Smyth to Briggs, March 2, 1908, UTSA Smyth was writing from Yale, New Haven, Connecticut.

[18]
Letter, Driscoll to Ward, April 27, 1906, op. cit.

modernism and Rome's inquisitional trend.

In light of this correspondence, then, we can see that the suppressive spirit that ensued from Rome's condemnation of modernism had an effect on The New York Review. This spirit would have no doubt discouraged people to read a theological publication such as The Review. It would have caused this journal's small number of subscribers to become smaller and therefore beset The Review with financial problems. Also, this same spirit would have led ecclesiastical authorities to suspect any theological enterprise (in particular, a theological journal) that was open to the new. The encyclical strictures on publications attests to this. We must therefore list among the reasons for The Review's demise the historico-theological context of the day.

B. The Case of Edward J. Hanna

Secondly, further investigation into The Review's history shows also that there could have been still another reason for the Review's termination. In 1908 Rome expressly suspected The New York Review of modernism because of some question-able articles in it.[19] This suspicion by Rome may very well

---

[19] The articles written for The Review by Edward J. Hanna fell under suspicion as this chapter will disclose.

have contributed to the end of The Review because it received

great coverage from the press which considered it Rome's

first great fight in connection with modernism. [20]

The second part of its termination notice denied, however,

that this indictment had anything to do with The Review ceasing

publication when it said:

> A newspaper report which has obtained
> wide circulation renders it necessary
> in justice to our ecclesiastical superiors
> and to ourselves to make a further statement.
> Neither The New York Review nor any issue
> of it has ever been made the object of
> official condemnation or censure by any
> authority, local or general, in the Cath-
> olic Church. It is now suspending
> publication not by command of authority,
> but by the decision of its editors and
> for the reasons set down.

The newspaper report that the notice mentioned was one

which stated that Rome condemned The Review because of

Rev. Edward J. Hanna's unorthodox articles in it. [21] Many

people associated with Hanna and The Review eventually tried

to prove the report false, but, as will be seen later, it did

express well, if not officially, Rome's sentiments about The

Review during its final year of publication. The termination

20
    "Pope Tests Works of Father Hanna", New York Times,
January 5, 1908, Part 3: p. 1.

21
    "A Ban on Catholic Review?", New York Times,
September 17, 1908, p. 9.

notice denied that The Review was ever the object of official condemnation. But,further investigation into the Review's controversy with Rome reveals that although Rome did not "officially" condemn it, it certainly regarded it as modernistic and contrary to the canons of Pascendi concerning publications. Such a regard would no longer favor ecclesiastical subsidy for a journal which the Church suspected of being contrary to her teachings.

The facts of Hanna's life serve as an important background for understanding the controversy.[22] Rev. Edward J. Hanna (1850-1944) was probably the most distinguished churchman produced by the Diocese of Rochester, New York. From his youth he was Archbishop Bernard J. McQuaid's protége and a favorite student of Cardinal Francesco Satolli, professor of theology at the Urban College of the Propaganda in Rome. There Hanna achieved such academic excellence that he once qualified to participate in a public philosophical disputation before Pope Leo XIII and twenty-two cardinals at the papal palace. He made such a fine impression on that occasion that four years later, a student of theology then, his professors invited him again to participate in another disputation before the

---

[22] The following facts of Hanna's life come from Robert F. McNamara, "Archbishop Hanna, Rochesterian", Rochester History, XXV, No. 2, April, 1963, 1-24.

same pontiff. Leo was so pleased with Hanna's brilliance that
he dispensed the young seminarian from the usual doctoral
examinations and awarded him the doctorate in Sacred Theology.

After ordination in 1885, Hanna spent the next year teaching
at the North American College in Rome and assisting Satolli as
lecturer at the Propaganda. Returning home to Rochester in
1887 he awaited the opening of the new major seminary, St.
Bernard's, by serving the diocese in the capacity of classics
teacher at the preparatory seminary and assistant pastor of the
cathedral parish. When the major seminary did open in 1893,
Hanna became a member of its first faculty as professor of
dogmatic theology.

With such a fine academic record behind him it was not
any wonder that in 1901 he was offered the rectorship of North
American College. However, McQuaid directed him to decline
the offer because he had other plans for Hanna. He wanted
him to become his coadjuter bishop with the right of succession.
But, in 1904 McQuaid decided that Rochester was not the diocese
for Hanna and the post went to Thomas F. Hickey, Vicar
General of the diocese.

Three years passed before Hanna again would be considered
for the episcopacy. In the meantime, in response to his bishop's
wish that seminary professors publish, Hanna wrote an article
for The New York Review which later caused Rome to postpone
his appointment as a bishop for reasons of modernism. This

postponement became a cause célèbre in the Catholic world and threw suspicion not only on Hanna but also on The Review.

Although Hanna wrote two other articles which Rome would also investigate, it was his article for The Review that would be his nemisis. [23] This article, "The Human Knowledge of Christ", appeared in three installments in the second, third, and fourth issues of The Review's first volume, 1905-1906. [24]

The first installment opened with a very balanced introduction and should have immediately dispelled any doubt that Hanna would arrive at any conclusion other than an orthodox one. It read as follows:

> Some modern theologians have doubtlessly
> pressed too far the consideration of the
> human element in Christ's life - even to
> the point of losing sight of the divine,
> while others in their eagerness to insist
> upon the divinity, have not mayhaps been
> sufficiently mindful of the human in Christ.
> And what is true of the Incarnation in
> general applies in particular to doctrinal
> theories concerning the human intellect
> and human knowledge of the Saviour. Here,
> likewise, either extreme is dangerous,

---

[23]
    The two other articles by Hanna were "Absolution", The Catholic Encyclopedia, I, 1907, pp. 61-66; and "Some Recent Books on Catholic Theology", The American Journal of Theology, X, 1 (January, 1906), 175-184.

[24]
    I, No. 1 (August-September, 1905), 303-316; No. 2 (October-November, 1905), 425-436; and No. 3 (December-January, 1905-1906), 597-615.

yet the matter is so deeply mysterious
that it is hard to define the happy mean -
perilous even to attempt it. The writer
of these notes believes the time has not
yet come for a perfect synthesis for a
complete and final theological treatise in
the human knowledge of Christ; but he
hopes that the notes may serve as a
contribution to the study of a question
which is interesting in itself, practical
in helping to get a better understanding
of the life of Christ and consequently,
important in its bearing upon New
Testament exegesis. [25]

There is no doubt from this introduction then that Hanna's

purpose was merely to be speculative and certainly not to give

the last word on the subject. With this view in mind, then,

he proceeded to give in the first installment a rapid historical

survey of the problem concerning the human knowledge of

Christ. Then, he raised the question, "Can a man holding the

fullest orthodoxy admit any limitation to Christ's knowledge?"[26]

He answered that the Church has given no definite decision,

and that the question must be settled, so far as may be for the

present, through a careful study of the scriptures, the Fathers,

and the theologians.

In the next two installments Hanna proceeded to investigate

the question in sacred scripture and the Fathers. The second installment exclusively considered the scriptural texts of the question. He pointed out the many texts that demonstrate that Christ had no limit to his knowledge. In contrast to these he then presented the two texts; viz., Lk. 2, 52 and MK. 13, 32, that suggest limits to the knowledge of Christ. He also considered the problem of Christ's inerrancy of scripture, distinguishing it from his infallibility, and the question whether Christ enjoyed the beatific vision from the beginning of his mortal life.

Although throughout most of the article Hanna just raised the question about this problem, his conclusion to the second installment seems to suggest that he would admit limits to Christ's knowledge. It read:

> It seems hard to admit that such is the case since we know that the Man-God was in all points tempted as we are and surely the passages of the Epistle (Hebrews) taken in their obvious sense portray a likeness which would be highly unreal, if Christ had not experience our limitation. [27]

In the final installment Hanna presented the tradition of the Church on the two scriptural texts implying limitation to Christ's knowledge. He showed how the early fathers of the Church up until the time of St. Gregory the Great held some limitation

---

[27] I, No. 2 (October-November, 1905), 436.

to the knowledge of Christ. The article ended with a consideration of Gregory the Great's thoughts on the subject which did not admit any limits to Christ's knowledge.

This study had appeared in The Review a full year before Lamentabili and Pascendi were issued. There was no danger therefore that it would be deliberately contrary to any of the canons set forth by these papal decrees. Moreover, Hanna wrote it for a scholarly theological journal which had a very limited number of subscribers. It really did not say anything new or radical but merely restated the teaching of the Church Fathers on this question. Satolli himself mentioned this to the press.[28]

Although Hanna's article appeared almost without reverberation, it did create a little stir in Rome immediately after publication. In 1906 some American seminarians at the Propaganda received The New York Review's volume containing Hanna's article. They triumphantly exhibited this new American theological journal in the halls of the Urban College. Pere Alexis M. Lepicier O. M. I. (later Cardinal) who at that time held the chair of dogmatic theology there, came upon it. One look, it was reported, into its pages, was sufficient to confiscate it. A few days later he returned to class with it.

---

[28] "Rome Fails to Appoint Dr. Hanna", New York Times, January 14, 1908, p. 11.

Looking very troubled, he began the class by saying that some
of the articles in The Review, the footnotes and authorities, quoted
were in numerous cases people whose works Rome placed on
the Index. He then questioned the correctness of a couple of
sentences from Hanna's article but without mentioning his name.
The matter quickly died then and there in class. [29] But, it
would be a year later when Lepicier would figure prominently
in regard to these writings. The Congregation of the Propaganda
would appoint him to examine them for their orthodoxy. Except
for Lepicier's criticism, Hanna's article passed unnoticed
until 1907.

However, in the springtime of that year, just before
Lamentabili and Pascendi, Archbishop Patrick W. Riordan of
San Francisco was looking for a competent churchman to be
his coadjutor with the right to succession. He asked McQuaid
whether Hanna would make a good choice. [30] Naturally, the
bishop of Rochester highly recommended his protégé, Hanna,
and Riordan placed his name at the tope of the list of possible

---

[29]
This incident of Lepicier's encounter with The Review
and Hanna's articles comes from a letter by Rev. Thomas F.
Coakley to Robert McNamara of St. Bernard's Seminary,
Rochester, New York, June 22, 1946, ADR. In 1906 Father
Coakley was secretary to Msgr. Thomas F. Kennedy, rector
of North American College.

[30]
Letter, Riordan to McQuaid, April 4, 1907, ADR.

candidates.[31] The summer passed. The pope issued

Lamentabili and Pascendi, and Rome's fight against modernism

grew fiercer every day.

By September it was almost common knowledge that Hanna

would be the coadjutor archbishop of San Francisco and Rome

would make this appointment very soon.[32] However, Rome

delayed. It seemed that one of Hanna's colleagues on the

seminary faculty, Reverend Andrew E. Breen, professor of

sacred scripture, upon learning that Hanna was episcopabilis

delated him to Rome on charges of "lacking firmness of

orthodoxy required of the time".[33]

Breen made this delation by means of a letter to his

friend, Monsignor Marini, in Rome, directing him to draw

---

[31]
This is indicated in a letter by Riordan to McQuaid, April 18, 1907, ADR.

[32]
"Candidates for Vacant Mitre". The New York Herald, September 13, 1907, p. 5.

[33]
Letter, Andrew E. Breen to Msgr. Marini, September 18, 1907, General Archives of the Congregation of the Propagation of the Faith, 78658. This source hereinafter will be abbreviated as ACPF.
The materials from this source are written in Italian. For the purpose of this dissertation this writer translated them into English.
The writer is grateful to Rev. George Gaffey of Santa Rosa, California for allowing him to use this material obtained by him from Rome.

the pope's attention to Hanna's writings for the good of the Church. The study Breen referred to was "The Human Knowledge of Christ" which appeared in The New York Review and which according to Breen, should have been entitled the "Ignorance of Christ". He claimed that Hanna's sources for the article were rationalistic, and although the article came to no conclusion, it certainly insinuated a love of liberal thought. Breen concluded his letter with a scathing attack on Hanna's personality stating that he was "ambitious", "spineless", "a courtier" and "changes with the wind". Evidently for Breen more was at stake than just the good of the Church. McQuaid later disclosed to Farley that Breen was insanely jealous of Hanna. [34]

This letter found its way to Cardinal Merry del Val, Secretary of State, who in turn gave it to Cardinal Giovanni Gotti, prefect of the Congregation of the Propaganda. [35] It held up Hanna's appointment to the episcopacy and inaugurated a grave situation on both sides of the Atlantic.

It was reported that upon receipt of Breen's letter, Gotti immediately wrote to Archbishop Diomede Falconio, Apostolic

[34] Letter, McQuaid to Farley, February 2, 1908, AANY, I-11 (M).

[35] Salvatore Brandi to McQuaid, December 28, 1907, ADR.

Delegate to the United States, for a copy of Hanna's article in

The New York Review and for The Review itself. He also

censured Falconio mildly for not notifying Rome of The Review's

existence. [36]

However, Falconio's reply to the Cardinal Prefect seems

not to indicate that Gotti requested Hanna's article nor that he

censured Falconio. Rather, after reporting that Hanna was

certainly the first choice of the American bishops for the post

of coadjutor of San Francisco because of his intelligence and

exemplary life, Falconio seemed to have taken in this report

the initiative to inform Gotti about Hanna's article in The

New York Review. He wrote:

> Finally I must add an observation as
> regards Rev. Hanna. A few days ago
> I have come to learn that he wrote an
> article in The New York Review (Oct. -
> Nov. 1905; Dec. -Jan. 1906), a journal
> which is published in the seminary of
> the Archdiocese of New York by some
> professors there, and which seems a
> little suspect of Modernism, dealing
> with the human knowledge of Jesus
> Christ, an article which it is said
> claimed the attention of Prof. Lepicier
> O. M. I. who teaches at the Propaganda,
> he refuted it somewhat in class. Although
> such writing in America passes un-
> observed, I think I must send them

36
     Letter, George Meehan to John Goggin, December 2,
1907, ADR.

together with a copy of the journal to your
Eminence in order that you come to a
just decision. [37]

Falconio's source of information about Hanna's writings is
unknown. It could very well have come from Breen himself or
from Rome, since he was aware that Lepicier criticized the
article in class. Be that as it may, the significance of
Falconio's letter is that it is the first official mention that
The New York Review was suspected of modernism.

No doubt, then, by November of that year, Rome was
investigating Hanna's article in The Review. Driscoll mentioned this to Briggs when he wrote:

> Dr. Hanna, a professor of dogmatic
> theology in the Seminary of Rochester
> was lately made a candidate for bishop
> of the Archdiocese of San Francisco
> but he has been "held up" in Rome
> chiefly on three articles which he
> wrote for our Review and it is more
> than probable that he never will be
> promoted at least under the present
> papal administration. [38]

Riordan in a letter to McQuaid made a similar observation. [39] He also suggested that Hanna write to Cardinals Sattoli

---

[37]
Letter, Diomede Falconi to Giovanni Gotti, October 15,
1907, ACPF, 78658.

[38]
Letter, Driscoll to Briggs, December 8, 1907, UTSA.

[39]
Letter, Riordan to McQuaid, November 8, 1907, ADR.

and Gotti informing them that he was aware that Rome was examining his article. Riordan even directed that Hanna express his amazement that his orthodoxy be called into question since throughout his entire life he was loyal and devoted to the Holy See. He then encouraged McQuaid to write Gotti, along these same lines. [40]

Hanna took the advice of McQuaid and the suggestion of Riordan and wrote to Gotti. In a very personal letter disclosing his love for orthodoxy Hanna wrote to the Cardinal Prefect about the article in question. He stated that for twenty years as a professor he always taught (conforming to the traditional doctrine of the Roman Church and the mind of St. Thomas) that Our Lord as a man possessed fully the infused knowledge and the beatific vision. The testimony of hundreds of his students, he wrote, would corroborate this. He also mentioned that his bishop granted him permission to write the article for The New York Review and he proceeded to go into detail about that article. He wrote:

---

[40]
Riordan himself wrote two letters to Falconio strongly in favor of Hanna. He even went to Rome to plead for the Rochester priest. Cardinal Gibbons and Archbishops Ryan of Philadelphia and Ireland of St. Paul also wrote to Rome in favor of Hanna; cf. A.C.P.F. Nos. 79419 and 79420, and Gibbons to Gotti, November 19, 1907, Baltimore Cathedral Archives. Ireland in his letter went a little too far in favor of Hanna. He wrote, "For Hanna the Syllabus is the highest law."

If I erred, I erred in method, not in
doctrine. Apart from us the Protestants
held a doctrine called "kenosis" which
truly negates the divinity of Christ; apart
from us the Protestants and some Modernists hold that Our Lord had erred especially
in reference to the day of judgement. I
have written these articles to defend the
divinity of Our Lord against the Protestants
and to affirm him free of every suspicion
of error against some Modernists. This
done I have used the tradition of Sacred
Scripture and of St. Paul up to Gregory
the Great as regards the human knowledge
of Our Lord, citing and commenting on
almost all the passages and explaining all
the difficulties - and as you know better
than I - the difficulties are many. I did
not come to any dangerous conclusion.
Rather, I gave that of St. Gregory the
Great because up to our day, the tradition
is unanimously for full knowledge, etc.
Also, I was only writing an academic
dissertation.

Hanna then mentioned that the editors of The New York
Review wanted him to write the article this way so as to portray
the method used in positive and speculative theology. He also
in the letter disassociated himself from modernism and its
spirit by thanking God that he knows little about it. He
assured Gotti that the method of immanence was not taught in
seminaries nor was it used in the exposition of theological
truth.

Hanna then ended his letter with a very emotional conclusion stating that he detested the same things the Holy Father
condemned and that, ambitious for truth, not honor, he

desired to belong to the Holy Father and Cardinal Gotti. [41]

McQuaid also followed Riordan's suggestion and wrote not only to Gotti but also to Merry del Val. [42] In both letters he underlined Hanna's loyalty and devotion to the Holy See, his fine academic record, and explicitly stated that Hanna had his permission to write the article for The New York Review. He also pointed out to the Cardinals that this article which was purely scientific without arriving at any theological conclusion, was reviewed by some of the learned professors at St. Bernard's Seminary, and given the Imprimatur by Archbishop Farley. McQuaid also made it clear in these letters that Hanna merely gave a resumé of past discussions on the question of the human knowledge of Christ by the Fathers of the Church and all he considered himself responsible for was the accuracy of their quotations. Hanna took great pain, McQuaid wrote, to read in the original all that the Fathers had written and sought to give their ideas concretely.

By this time Roman authorities were gathering all of Hanna's writings together for an investigation. Monsignor

---

[41]
     Letter, Hanna to Gotti, December 16, 1907, ACPF, 79607.

[42]
     Letters, McQuaid to Gotti, November 20, 1907, ACPF; and McQuaid to Merry del Val, November 12, 1907, ACPF.

Thomas F. Kennedy, rector of the North American College,
wrote to his good friend, Archbishop Farley, that Rome was
in "earnest" about obtaining all of Hanna's articles even the
one on "Absolution" which appeared in The Catholic Encyclopedia,
another project sponsored by Farley. [43] Kennedy cautioned
Farley to keep a close watch on all the articles published in the
encyclopedia because it bore his Imprimatur. Then, Kennedy
made reference to Roman circles' opinion of The New York
Review. He wrote;

> Then again I have lately heard some
> very hard criticism of the review published
> at the seminary. First, some of the names
> on your list of contributors are under the
> ban, e.g. I heard it said that Buonajusti
> [sic]was out. I feel I ought as a friend to
> tell you this. Those articles of Dr. Hanna
> in the review are being criticized severely.
> I think Dr. Hanna will be elected coadjuotr
> of S. Francisco. If so, however, it will
> be because of the ardent wish of Abp. Riordan
> and on account of the strong letter from the
> leading Archbishop of the country and in spite
> of his article.

As Kennedy wrote to Farley, Hanna's case did bring about
severe criticism of The New York Review on the part of
ecclesiastical authorities. They began to take a closer look
at this journal.

In the middle of January, 1908 Farley received a letter
from the Apostolic Delegate calling his attention to an

---

[43]
Letter, Thomas F. Kennedy to Farley, December 26,
1907, AANY, I-11 (K).

MOST REV. JOHN M. FARLEY

advertisement in The Review of George Tyrrell's Lex Credendi.[44]

Falconio in pointing out to Farley that such an advertisement was a violation of the "letter and spirit" of Pascendi,
quoted the encyclical:

> It is likewise the task of Bishops to
> guard against the writings of Modernists
> as well as those writings which indicate
> a Modernist tendency lest they be read
> if they are available and to prevent them
> from being published if they have not yet
> been so.

He then advised Farley to see to it that writers who were
modernists should not write for The Review or, at least, the
articles in the journal should be approved by him. He
warned Farley by saying:

> In confidence I tell you it has made no
> favorable impression in Rome to see in
> the Review articles contributed not only
> by Tyrrell, but also Buonaiuti, Nicola
> Turchi, and Abbés Dimnet and Houtin of
> France.

There was no doubt now that Rome was displeased with
The Review which came to its attention because of the Hanna
case. Falconio also expressed to Farley his fear for some
New York priests who were doing graduate studies in Rome

44
Letter, Falconio to Farley, January 15, 1908, AANY,
I-11(K). The advertisement of Tyrrell's book appeared in
The New York Review, III, Nov. 1 (September-October,
1907) and No. 2 (November-December, 1907) issues. The
book Lex Credendi was published by Longmans, Green,
and Co., London, in 1906.

278

because they were meeting with some of the above mentioned

writers. He ended his letter dutifully with the words:

> I have thought it my duty to call your
> attention to these facts in order that
> Your Grace with your well-known
> prudence may avoid future dis-
> pleasures.

Farley no doubt angered by some misinformation in

Falconio's letter immediately wrote him a very crisp and

long letter. [45] He listed the charges Falconio made against

his review and answered each after he first prefaced them with

the insinuation that Falconio himself should read The Review

and not rely on mistaken informers.

> In reply I beg to say that I owe it
> to you as well as to The Review
> that your informant is in error in
> some of the charges against The
> Review.

Farley dismissed the charge that Abbés Dimnet and Houtin

of France wrote for The Review by stating that after a personal

diligent search through it and on inquiry from the editors he

concluded that Dimnet and Houtin never wrote for it. [46] Farley

---

  Letter, Farley to Falconio, January 22, 1908, AANY,
I-11 (K).

  It is not certain whether the name Dimnet refers to
Ernest Dimnet who wrote La Pensée Catholique dans
L'Angleterre contemporaine, (Paris: Victor Lecoffre, 1906)
or one of Joseph Turmel's pseudonyms. Turmel as we saw
wrote ten articles for The Review under his own name. However, he did write under fourteen pseudonyms, one of which
was "Dimnet." In 1929 this pseudonym was attributed to

informed the Apostolic Delegate that the only mention of Houtin

in The Review was in condemning him. [47] Farley then wrote:

> Certainly Your Excellency would admit that it
> must be the very spirit of malevolence which
> promoted the party who complained to you,
> to say that The Review in any way favored
> either Houtin or Dimnet and I feel you will
> not fail to so inform the person whomever
> he be. [48]

In regard to Tyrrell, Buonaiuti, and Turchi writing for

The Review, Farley admitted this to be true but he pointed

out that they wrote at a time when they were still in good

standing in the Church. Farley vowed to Falconio that their

ideas would no longer appear in The Review.

As regards the charge that The Review advertised

Tyrrell's books, Farley replied that it was an accident which

---

Turmel. The question arises, then, that although Farley was
not aware that Dimnet was one of Turmel's pseudonyms, did
Rome or even The Review's editors know this? Further investigation on this point at present is beyond the scope of
this dissertation.

47
    The Houtin mentioned here is Albert Houtin who is noted
for his book, Histoire du Modernisme Catholique, Paris: Chez
L'Auteur, 1913. Driscoll, as we saw in Chapter One of this
dissertation wrote Houtin in 1902 to translate his book, La
Question biblique chez les catholiques de France au XIX siecle,
Paris: Alphonse Picard et Fils, 1902.
    The third person mentioned in Falconio's letter was Nicola
Turchi who was born in Rome in 1882, taught history in
Propaganda Fide School, Rome and founded the review, "Religio".

48
    The Review made three references to Houtin and all in
a condemnatory fashion; cf. I, No. 4 (December-January, 1905-
1906), 51; II, No. 4 (January-February, 1907), 490; and II
No. 5 (March-April, 1907), 645.

280

the managing editor, Father Brady, who was responsible for
it deeply regretted. Farley's support for his priest comes out
in this part of the letter.

> Neither he nor anyone connected with
> The Review would ever think of allowing
> such an advertisement into the magazine,
> if the matter had been adverted to, it
> is needless to say. As explained in
> Fr. Brady's letter which I enclose, he
> was worn out from want of sleep, having
> watched at the deathbed of his father
> for several nights previously. When
> the advertisement came with others and
> not suspecting anything wrong, he did
> not examine it and sent it to the printer.
> No one regrets the blunder more than he
> does, it has filled him with mortification.

Farley then sent his assurance to Falconio that an
explanation would appear in the next issue of The Review show-
ing that The New York Review did not favor the reading or
sale of Tyrrell's books. [49]

Farley then ended his list of replies to the charges that
Falconio had made against The Review with an explanation of
the conduct of his student priests in Rome who associated with
Father Ginnochi, a one-time member of the Biblical Commission and at that time one accused of modernism. Farley
wrote that the reason why his priests associated with

---

[49]
Unless there was an insert in The Review to this effect
and it has been lost, there is absolutely no mention or indication in The Review that Farley followed through on this
promise to Falconio.

Ginnochi was because these young men knew no Italian and wishing to go to confession went to him with whom they were already acquainted and who they knew spoke English. Farley assured Falconio of his confidence in these young priests.

In the final paragraph of his letter he asked Falconio if he should send a duplicate statement to Rome because of the so called unfavorable impression that The Review made there. He then postscripted this long letter with the words:

> Every article which is to appear in
> The Review in the future will pass
> through my hands and that of my
> diocesan censors before going to
> print.

There was nothing in Farley's letter to Falconio that indicated he intended at that time to suppress The Review. In fact, the dismissal of the charges and his determined attitude to read every article himself before it went to print indicate that he intended to continue the journal.

Farley enclosed with this letter to Falconio a letter written by John Brady explaining the situation. [50] Brady's explanation was a little inconsistent with Farley's. He stated that he did not examine the advertisements before they went to the printer because they usually did not go to him but to the "advertising parties." He wrote that he was unaware of

---

[50] Letter, John F. Brady to Falconio, January 17, 1908, AANY, I-11 (K).

Tyrrell's book being advertised in The Review until it appeared in print and that, if he had known this, it would never have gone to print.

However, Farley added a post-script to Brady's letter indicating again to the Apostolic Delegate what he already wrote in his own letter; namely, that the illness of Brady's father caused the managing editor to be too physically exhausted to check the advertisements. It seems from this that Farley obviously wanted Falconio to realize that the advertisement of Tyrrell's book on The Review was not at all deliberate but due to extenuating circumstances, beyond the control of his editors.

A few days after Farley had sent his reply to Falconio, he received another letter from his friend, Kennedy, in Rome. This time again Kennedy put The New York Review in the context of Hanna's case. He wrote to Farley about Hanna being considered for the post of coadjuter archbishop of San Francisco but was delayed appointment because of his writings.[51] One article, Kennedy said, concerned absolution and appeared in The Catholic Encyclopedia and The New York Review: the other, explored the human knowledge of Christ and had been published in The Review. Kennedy closed his letter with these

---

[51]
    Letter, Kennedy to Farley, January 20, 1908, AANY, I-11 (K).

words to Farley about the situation in Rome:

> I assure you I am no alarmist. But
> these writings have made a bad
> impression here and there is no
> telling what might have happened if
> Dr. Hanna's friends had been less
> numerous and less powerful.

This last letter in the Farley collection about the bad
impression The Review and Hanna's article were making in
Rome must have caused the Archbishop of New York to re-
consider whether The Review should continue. Because, the
next issue of The Review was a combination of the January-
February:March-April, 1908 issues so that the May-June,
1908 issue would finish out the third volume and conclude the
journal. Also, after the November-December, 1907 issue
the New York editors no longer gave editorials in their
periodical. Whether these changes in The Review were a
result of Farley's decision is not certain. What is certain,
however, is that these erratic changes in The Review's format
took place at the same time Rome suspected The New York
Review and Hanna's articles. As we shall discover there
was present in this correlation the causation for The Review's
demise.[52]

---

[52]
It is interesting to note that at this time Farley seemed
to be making some efforts to assure Rome of the Archdiocese
of New York's loyalty to the Holy See. He wrote to Rome
seeking permission to translate into English A Catechism of
Modernism, written by J. Lemius. Reports to him from Rome
indicated that Pius X and Merry del Val were pleased at this

The situation in Rome at this time was very fierce against modernism. As one newspaper summed up the scene: "Modernism in Rome was like a red rag to a bull". [53] By January, 1908 everyone knew that it was Breen who had delated Hanna. [54] And by January Hann's writings were being carefully examined by various congregations of the Vatican. All of his articles were translated into Italian so that Cardinal Gotti and the pope could grasp their real meaning. The pope even had several English speaking prelates living in Rome compare in his presence the English and Italian texts in order to be sure that no injustice be done. [55]

The Congregation of the Propaganda now had all of Hanna's writings: "The Human Knowledge of Christ" which

---

effort and commended him for his quick response to Pascendi. However, Farley was unaware at the time that he was seeking this permission that an official English translation was already in process. He, therefore, had to restrict his translation of A Catechism to the private use of his Archdiocese. Cf. Letter, William I. Ring, O.M.I. to Farley, March 28, 1908 AANY, I-11 (R).

Rev. Joseph Lemius (1860-1923) was an Oblate of Mary Immaculate and an able theologian who held various posts in the Curia at Rome.

[53]
The New York Herald, January 26, 1908, p. 2.

[54]
Letter, Meehan to Goggin, January 14, 1908, ADR.

[55]
"Pope Tests Works of Father Hanna", New York Times, January 5, 1908, Part 3:, p. 1.

appeared in The New York Review, "Absolution" published in the

Catholic Encyclopedia, and "Some Recent Books in Catholic

Theology" which he wrote for The Chicago Review. It appointed

Père Lepicier who was its magical consultor, and the pro-

fessor who had criticized Hanna's writings a year before in

class, to give a theological critique of his articles. Lepicier

who was known to have nothing personally against Hanna pre-

sented an objective report of all his writings to the Congrega-

tion. [56]

Lepicier must have given this report to Gotti in November,

1907 because of its chronological position among the official

proceedings of Hanna's case. [57] In this report Lepicier was

apparently very fair and objective to Hanna's article. He

presented, in summary fashion, the main lines of the study

and pointed out its strong points as well as those that, he

believed, ran contrary to the Church's teaching. About the

latter, Lepicier reaffirmed the traditional teaching of the

56
Letter, Meehan to Goggin, December 12, 1907, ADR.

57
Report of Père Alexis M. Lepicier, C. M. I. to the
Congregation of the Propaganda of the Faith, ACPF, No.
79242. For our purpose here I will give only a summary of
Lepicier's report in Hanna's article in The Review, The Human
Knowledge of Christ". His full report on this article can be
found in the appendix of this dissertation. Lepicier also re-
ported to the Congregation on Hanna's other two articles:
"Absolution" in the Catholic Encyclopedia and "Some Recent
Books in Catholic Theology" in The Chicago Review.

Church at that time which did not admit any limitation to Christ's knowledge. He concluded his report by saying that he could not understand how Hanna could admit limitations in Our Lord's knowledge, on the one hand, and attribute, on the other hand, infallibility to Christ.

With this report of Lepecier the Congregation of the Propaganda deliberated on the case. Satolli went to the defense of Hanna's article stating that Hanna said the same things the Father of the Church said about the human knowledge of Christ. [58] The upshot of the Congregation's deliberation was that Gotti refused to appoint Hanna to the episcopcy and requested Hanna to demonstrate publicly that he was not guilty of the charges made against him. [59] The mode of this demonstration was that he had to write another article in The New York Review according to the lines set down for him by the Propaganda. [60] Hanna was also to explain his opinion not only in English but in French, and German as well. [61] If

[58]
"Rome Fails to Appoint Dr. Hanna", The New York Herald, January 14, 1908, p. 11.

[59]
"Hanna to Answer Charges", The New York Herald, January 15, 1908, p. 11.

[60]
Letter, Riordan to McQuaid, February 13, 1908, ADR.

[61]
"Report to Pope on Hanna" New York Times, January 15, 1908, p. 3.

the article was satisfactory then there would be no problem in

raising him to the episcopacy. [62] About this decision of the

Propaganda McQuaid wrote to his friend, Father John Hudson

at Notre Dame:

> Now after all the worry and scandal,
> risking the future of St. Bernard's,
> it turns out that the Holy Office in
> Rome finds nothing in the "Absolution"
> article to strike out and the Congrega-
> tion of Studies only asks that a
> supplementary article in The New York
> Review be added giving the Catholic
> view of the teaching of the Church on
> the question of human knowledge of
> Christ. This will appear in the next
> issue of The Review. . . . in all likeli-
> hood Hanna will be consecrated soon
> after Easter. [63]

Hanna must have written the supplementary article

immediately after they had directed him to do so in January

because there is correspondence from Rome reporting that

Cardinal Satolli expressed his satisfaction with that article in

the middle of February, 1908 and gave it to Lepicier to read. [64]

This article appeared in the January-February: March-April,

62
    Letter, Riordan to McQuaid, February 13, 1908, ADR.

63
    Letter, McQuaid to Hudson, February 18, 1908, copy,
ADR. The original is in the Archives of the University of
Notre Dame.

64
    Letter, Meehan to Goggin, February 19, 1908, ADR.

1908 issue of The Review. [65]   It was radically different in

content and style from the other three articles of Hanna.   Unlike

his preceeding ones it read very cautiously, conservatively,

and most emphatically in assuring the readers about the Roman

Catholic teaching on the human knowledge of Christ.

However, even after Hanna wrote this fourth article along

the lines that the Congregation of the Propaganda dictated,

Rome still delayed in making a decision on his case.   McQuaid,

in an undated letter, but no doubt very close to the summer

of 1908, as the contents suggest, wrote to Gotti protesting the

---

[65]
   "The Human Knowledge of Christ (IV)", III, Nos. 4 and
5 (January-February:March-April, 1908), 391-400.
   This supplementary article seemed strangely out of place
here, appearing two years after the other installments.   No
doubt, the readers would have had to rummage through past
issues of The Review, if Hanna did not provide a summary of
his first three articles.   The summary seemed very defensive
because Hanna clearly pointed out that these earlier articles
could not lead on to think that there was something in sacred
scripture and Tradition that would warrant them holding the
tentative theories of Protestants that affirmed limits to Christ's
knowledge.   He also added in this summary a very clear
rejection of modernism which he never mentioned in the other
articles.   He said that there was nothing in Tradition that
would help the modernist admit possible error in the words
and thoughts of Christ.   For this he cited proposition 33 of
Pius X's Syllabus. He then ended the summary by stating
that he never came to a conclusion in this essay on the
beatific vision of Christ or the limits of his knowledge.
   Having given this summary, Hanna then proceeded to
retrace his steps that he made in the previous articles.   Very
methodically and clearly he qualified these steps so that they
coincided with the Church's teaching at that time.   He ended
this article with fourteen conclusions on the subject which
really amounted to fourteen different ways of stating that
Christ never experienced any limits of knowledge and always
enjoyed the beatific vision.

delay and stating it was tantamount to saying his writings

"smacked" of modernism and blotted his name as well as

St. Bernard's. [66] He then asked Gotti the favor that no action

be taken on a new terna until Gibbons and Farley arrive in

Rome that July and present the merits of Dr. Hanna and the

needs of the Church in San Francisco. [67] Then he wrote:

> I am not asking to shield Dr. Hanna
> from the consequent of heretical
> teaching if of such he has been guilty
> but after extensive inquiry among the
> ablest theologicans we are unable to see
> where the heresy exists.

Farley and Gibbons went to Rome in July of that year and

planned to go to the Eurcharistic Congress in England. Through-

out their stay in Rome and England they complained about how

"severely" Merry del Val treated the American Church in the

modernist question. [68] The only case of modernism up to then

was the one of Hanna's writings in The New York Review. They

kept distinguishing for Roman circles modernism from

Americanism saying that the former is doctrinal and had

never been part of the American theological scene while the

---

[66]
    Letter, McQuaid to Gotti, undated, ADR.

[67]
    Riordan wrote to Farley to endorse Hanna. Cf. Letter, Riordan to Farley, June 25, 1908, AANY, I-11(R).

[68]
    "Merry del Val to Resign", The New York Herald, September 30, 1908, p. 11.

latter was functional. [69]

The summer in Rome for Farley must have been very hot. He went there hoping to receive the "red hat" but from one report about an audience he had with Pius X, he had difficulty hanging on to his episcopal zucchetto. [70] Around August 7, 1908, Farley had an audience with Pius X. The audience seemed to have gone on interminably for those who were waiting for the next audience with the pope. At the end of his meeting, Farley was reported to have rushed out with a look of consternation, his zucchetto was askew, his ferraiulo twisted almost completely around, his hair tousled, his countenance flushed.

When the members of the next audience met with the pope they reported that Pius X walked over to a chair on which was a beautifully bound volume of the Catholic Encyclopedia that Farley just presented. The Holy Father, they said seized the volume with both hands, flung it to the floor of his library saying what an evil thing the Encyclopedia was because it was vitiated by suspected articles. He then said to a member

---

[69]
"Pope Refuses to Make New Cardinal", The New York Herald, August 17, 1908, p. 9.

[70]
The report of Farley's audience with Pius X comes from Rev. Thomas F. Coakley's letter to Robert McNamara, June 22, 1946, ADR.

of the audience that the Cardinals wanted him to make Hanna a

bishop. With clenched fists the pope said that he would never

make Hanna a bishop. [71]

When the Congregation of the Propaganda met again on

September 8, 1908, everyone thought it would appoint Hanna to

the episcopacy. But, still one or two cardinals had their doubts

and the ticket of nominees was dropped. They elected someone

else in his place. Hanna become auxiliary bishop of San

Francisco in 1911. [72]

III. The Demise of The Review

The importance of Hanna's case is that it focused Rome's

attention on The New York Review because of the articles he

had written for it. This case most likely contributed greatly

to its demise. As the final issue of The Review appeared in

September, 1908, with its termination notice, newspaper reports

---

71
Although Coakley reported Pius' adamant opposition to
making Hanna a bishop, John J. Wynne, editor of The Catholic
Encyclopedia had an audience with Pius X on October 23, 1908,
almost three months after Coakley did. Wynne reported that
Pius spoke of Hanna as an "excellent priest" and added. "We
will see him a bishop yet, and you will see him an Archbishop!"
Cf. Letter Wynne to McNamara, July 14, 1946, ADR.

72
McNamara, 17. Monsignor Denis O'Connell, rector of
Catholic University in Washington was appointed auxilary bishop
(not coadjutor) of San Francisco.

implied that Hanna's writings were the center around which The Review's demise revolved.

On September 17th, 1908, The New York Times carried a report of United Press, datelined Washington, that The New York Review suspended publication because it fell under the ban of the pope. [73] It stated that the several articles written by Rev. Dr. Edward J. Hanna of Rochester, N.Y. on the human knowledge of Christ caused the journal's demise. All copies of The Review, it said, containing these objectionable articles were to be immediately cast out of Roman Catholic literature the world over.

The action of the Pontiff, it continued, in condemning the publication was in line with his general crusade against modernism which he believed was growing at an alarming rate especially in America. The Times did admit that Catholic Churchmen in Rochester were not inclined to look upon the Washington dispatch as bonafide. It was regarded in light of a rumor which, however, may be a forerunner of a contemplated action by the papacy Hanna refused to comment except to say that "we have no official knowledge of any such action taken by Rome."[74]

---

[73] "A Ban on Catholic Review?", New York Times, September 17, 1908, p. 11.

[74] The Rochester Union and The Rochester Times also carried the United Press dispatch of September 17, 1908.

Monsignor Lavelle of New York denied in a press interview this report from Washington. The reason, he said, The Review folded was because of financial reasons. [75] As regards Rome censuring the New York journal, Lavelle said:

> With regard to The New York Review, I
> will say that we have no means of know-
> ing what the intentions of the Church
> authorities may be, but we can state
> that up to the present time The Review
> has not yet met with any official
> censure from any authority, local
> or general, in the Catholic Church.
> Nor have we any intimation that such
> a censure is contemplated.

Lavelle's statement implied that the New York Review was vulnerable to Church censure. No doubt because of the Hanna case, he was not sure what Rome would do to The Review. But his use of the word "official" in his interview to qualify the censure leads one to believe that The Review received in an informal way some censure from ecclesiastical authority.

Driscoll, too, absolutely denied in the press the accusation that his journal was suppressed by Rome. In his letter to The Catholic Citizen of Milwaukee in which he stated that the only reason for ceasing The Review was the financial one. He denied the accusation as false:

75
 Cited in the Rochester Democrat and Chronicle,
September 19, 1908, p. 4.

... it is absolutely false that this
action on our part has been determined
by any official censure by Church
authorities either here or in Rome.
Some of our articles have been un-
favorably criticized by a Roman professor of theology of some distinction
but the complete orthodoxy of the same
articles been warmly and ably defended
by a still more eminent theologian,
Cardinal Satolli, and the report that
The Review or any of contributors has
fallen under any official ban is simply
a malicious rumor, one that has been
categorically denied together with a
similar report concerning The Catholic
Encyclopedia by the Archbishop of
New York (who was then in Rome) in
a recent publication published at this
request in The New York Sun. [76]

Driscoll concluded by saying that these denials on his part

were the best possible proof for the necessity of a Catholic

paper to correct the ignorant or malicious misstatements

about our faith and the Church. From what has been seen so

far in the case of Hanna and The New York Review by was of

official proceedings and available correspondence, this part

of Driscoll's letter is half true. He did not admit everything

about Rome's suspicion of The Review.

The communication release of Archbishop Farley that

Driscoll referred to in his letter was a special cable to the

press, datelined Rome, September 21st. It read as follows:

---

[76]
Letter, Driscoll to the Catholic Citizen of Milwaukee,
undated, ADR.

> Farley says that report originating in
> New York to the effect that The New
> York Review had been condemned by
> the Congregation of the Index is
> entirely unfounded. He adds that the
> whole story is false and that the state-
> ments as to the unorthodoxy of some
> articles written by Rev. Edward J.
> Hanna of Rochester for The Review
> were a mere invention. [77]

Farley's absolute statement to the press was the exact

opposite and blatant contradiction of what transpired in the case

of Hanna and The New York Review. It is true that his Review

never received official condemnation but Rome gave it enough

attention to warrant interested Churchmen of the time to have

a foundation to conjecture that it would have been condemned.

Also, Farley's statement that it was a "mere invention" that

Hanna's writings were unorthodox is now, of course, entered

in history as fiction.

On the other side of the Atlantic, in Rome, an Italian

newspaper, Giornale D'Italia was also printing denials about

The Review being suppressed because of modernism. The paper

received an anonymous letter, but evidently, it said, inspired

by the Congregation of the Index. The letter denied statements

recently printed in New York to the effect that The Review

was condemned by papal censure because of modernist

tendencies displayed in the writings of the professors at

---

[77]
   The Rochester Herald, September 22, 1908, p. 11.

Dunwoodie and Hanna. [78]

The letter also stated that The Review was never condemned nor were Hanna's articles which, the writer said, had been inspired by the most rigorous orthodoxy. It concluded by saying that Farley never showed any more partiality toward Dunwoodie than any other bishop would show toward his seminary. The teachers at Dunwoodie, the letter said, were among the most intelligent and clever men in the ranks of the American clergy.

The Giornale D'Italia presented the contents of this letter to a consultor of the Index to be confirmed. He confirmed that the letter came from someone in the Congregation of the Index and even went so far in his confirmation to emphasize that portion of it which referred to Dr. Hanna.

These absolute denials in the press by the hierarchy and people closely associated with The Review stating unequivocally that it ceased publication only because of a lack of funds, would lead one to think that there could very well have been another reason for its demise, and that is, that it was suspected of modernism. The New York Review ceased publication with its May-June, 1908 issue that appeared in September of that year. American Catholics would not see anything of similar caliber for another thirty years.

78
    Cited in Rochester Union, September 21, 1908, p. 5.

IV. The Aftermath

Immediately after The Review's termination there were several events which involved its editors. Investigation into them makes more tenable the thesis that The Review suspended publication because it was suspected of modernism.

Three months after The Review ceased publication, Rev. William F. Hughes, former professor at St. Joseph's Seminary and then the secretary of the Apostolic Delegate in Washington, wrote to Farley to indicate that the cloud of suspicion had not yet passed over New York. He wrote that the Delegate, Bishops Kennedy and Ceretti, were investigating the content of a certain book which Hughes did not identify but which was in some way connected with the New York Archdiocese.[79] As to this he did not reveal much. But, then Hughes reported to Farley what transpired after the three bishops had considered the book. He wrote:

> First of all, the Bishop (Ceretti) told me,
> and the Delegate just reiterated it for his
> own inner consciousness, that the young
> priests together with the Dunwoodie pro-
> fessors (the ex-Sulps.) had done the
> Archdiocese much harm. Despite the

---

[79] Letter, Hughes to Farley, January 4, 1909, AANY, I-11(H). There are no indications in AANY that can identify the book in question.

fact that Msgr. Kennedy warned the
young men, they were repeatedly seen
on the streets with the suspected men
and while in Munich, the doffing of the
Roman collar was merely by-play. The
real offense was attendance at the lectures
of the suspected and - in one case at least,
the condemned professors.

Regarding our professors, the Delegate
went over what he had said so often, and
it is precisely what Msgr. Kennedy said.
If they remain in Dunwoodie, they are a
source of offense and complaint to the
Holy See and a deadly injury to the
prestige of our diocese. I write all this
for what it is worth and only to let Your
Grace know what was said. Msgr.
Ceretti insists that the solution of the
matter has been determined on by Your
Grace and that the gradual renovation of
the seminary will clear things up....

The last point is this. The Delegate
says that it is positively sure that there
is a group of eight modernists in the
Diocese. He does not know their names
for he refused to accept the information.
He has no doubt of the accuracy of his
information and from what I gather, the
Holy See knows of the existence of the
caterie.

This letter certainly corroborates that some professors of
St. Joseph's Seminary were involved in a project that grievously
offended Rome. No doubt the project was The New York Review.
Also the letter's reference that there were eight modernists in
New York could again point to some of the professors at Dunwoodie. Modernism was a scholarly tendency and its first
attraction would be to men on a seminary or university faculty.
As we have seen, Driscoll did admit to his friend Briggs that he
was friendly with the modernists and sympathetic with their
views.

But what is most certain about the letter, is that it
revealed Farley's plan to renovate gradually his seminary
faculty in order to remedy its offenses against Rome. This
renovation, however, was more abrupt than gradual. In the
middle of the summer, 1909, when he was in Rome, Farley
sent a cablegram to his Vicar General in New York directing
him to remove Driscoll from his position as president of St.
Joseph's Seminary and transfer him as pastor to St. Ambrose's
parish in Manhattan. [80] This was certainly an extraordinary
time and manner for an Ordinary to transfer one of his priests.
No doubt Rome's pressure on Farley was so great that it
warranted such a move.

The Catholic News reported this bizarre and mysterious
move believing that it was done on direct orders from Rome. [81]
Some believed Driscoll was removed because of his association
with a modernist. [82] Rome was now serious about tying up the
loose ends of modernism. [83]

80
    Cited in Michael Gannon's "Before and After Modernism",
The Catholic Priest in the United States, ed. by John Tracy
Ellis, Collegeville, St. John's University Press, 1971, 347.

81
    The Catholic News, July 31, 1909, p. 3.

82
    Slattery, "Workings of Modernism", 571.

83
    In Driscoll's place at the seminary, Farley appointed Rev.
John P. Chidwick, the former pastor of St. Ambrose parish, the

As for the other editors of The New York Review their

participation in St. Joseph's renovation was more gradual than

Driscoll's. John Brady, the managing editor, divided his time

between teaching at Dunwoodie and being vice-president of

Mount St. Vincent, a woman's college in New York. He left

Dunwoodie in 1916 to become a pastor but he still retained his

position at Mount St. Vincent's.[84] Eventually he became

president there.

New York Police Chaplain, and an ex-Navy Chaplain. Chidwick
certainly did not possess the educational scholarly credentials
of Driscoll. To compensate for the new president's deficiencies,
Farley conferred the degree of doctor of divinity (honoris
causa) upon Chidwick soon after classes resumed in September,
1909.

The appointment of Chidwick to the presidency of St.
Joseph's seminary was the beginning of Farley's renovation
in Dunwoodie and a harbinger of future policies in American
seminary life and education. Immediately after Chidwick's
arrival, Latin became the language of all classes, the faculty
exchange with Union Theological Seminary and the student
auditing of courses at Columbia University ceased by administration fiat.

This information about Chidwick and Dunwoodie after 1909
comes from Arthur J. Scanlon, St. Joseph's Seminary, Dun-
woodie, New York: The United States Catholic Historical
Society, 1922, p. 119; and from Rev. Terrence F. X. O'Donnell
who gave to this writer a copy of the minutes of Columbia
University's Board of Trustees, January 5, 1925 meeting.
This meeting formally ended Dunwoodie's association with
Columbia because of the many years of non-use.

Msgr. Patrick Skehan of Catholic University of American
and who was once a curate with Chidwick told this writer that
at one of Chidwick's first meetings with the seminary faculty
in the presence of Farley, the new president proposed to
resurrect The Review. Farley's response, Sheehan reported,
was one of an adamant emotional refusal. Farley stated to all
present that he did not wish to hear of the journal ever again.

84
Scanlon, 148.

301

The associate editor of The Review, Francis P. Duffy,
left Dunwoodie in 1912 to become founding pastor of St. Savior's
Church in the Bronx, New York. [85] Americans remember and
honor him for his heroism as an army chaplain with the 69th
Regiment of New York during World War I. After the war
he became pastor of Holy Cross Church in the heart of Time
Square, New York, and served as well there as he did in the
war and in the seminary. He died in July, 1932.

Gigot and Ousanni remained on the faculty of St. Joseph's
Seminary. They no longer engaged themselves in research
but taught from prescribed and approved manuals of theology.[86]
Both ended out their years at Dunwoodie.

Joseph Bruneau who remained a Sulpician but who was
closely associated with The Review when he was at Dunwoodie,
later found himself suspected of modernism. His writing
for The Review did not help his cause. An investigation into
Bruneau's brief encounter with suspicion produces correspondence which reveals that Rome did suppress The New York
Review!

Bruneau fell under Rome's suspicion when he translated
into French, H. E. Oxenham's The Catholic Dogma of the

---

[85]
   Ibid., 128.

[86]
   Gannon, 348.

Atonement. [87] This translation appeared in 1909 and almost immediately The Civiltá Cattolica and Osservatore Romano accused it of containing modernistic tendencies. These accusations sparked Rome's highly volatile sensitivity to modernism and Bruneau was soon suspected of the heresy.

To clarify Bruneau's situation and plead for his cause a fellow Sulpician, X. Herzog, went to Rome. In his letter to Dyer he mentioned that since Cardinals Merry del Val and Gaetano de Lai (Prefect of the Congregation of Consistories) had never before heard of Bruneau nothing serious would come of the suspicion. [88] Nevertheless, he reported, Merry del Val wanted to ask Falconio about Bruneau. After the Cardinal Secretary of State made his inquiry, Falconio directed Cardinal Gibbons to have Bruneau write to Merry del Val giving him the details and circumstances of his translation. [89] Bruneau did so and the matter died quickly.

However, Bruneau did not come off completely unscathed by the incident. Archbishop O'Connell of Boston dismissed

---

87
    Oxenham wrote his book in 1865. Bruneau translated it into French under the title Histoire du dogme de la Redemption, Paris: S. S. Blond, 1909.

88
    Letter, Herzog to Dyer, April 17, 1909, ASMB.

89
    First draft of a letter, Bruneau to Gibbons, undated, ASMB.

him from the faculty of St. John's Seminary, Brighton, because of Rome's suspicion. [90] Bruneau returned to St. Mary's Baltimore, where he taught until his death in 1933.

The relation of Bruneau's case to The New York Review is very significant. It corroborates that Rome suppressed The Review because of modernistic tendencies in it. In his report to Dyer, Herzog stated that throughout all his meetings in Rome to plead for Bruneau's cause, one question was constantly being raised because of Bruneau's assignment at Dunwoodie: "Did he write in the review which came to be suppressed?"[91]

This question suggests unequivocally that Rome suppressed The New York Review. It seems to have been the deciding factor with which Romans would judge on the orthodoxy of American Catholics. It puts into perspective the thesis that The Review suspended publication for another reason than just lack of finances; viz., it was accused of modernism.

Another letter connected with Bruneau's case corroborates that The Review was suppressed by the Church. It also shows that because of this suppression some theologians wanted to disassociate their name from the journal for fear that it would

---

[90] Letter, Dyer to O'Connell, July 19, 1909, ASMB.

[91] Letter, Herzog to Dyer, op. cit.

cast suspicion on them.

A Father Pourrat, professor at the Ecole Superieure de theologie in Lyons, frantically wrote this letter to Bruneau when he heard that he was suspected of modernism. [92] He asked Bruneau to discontinue selling his book in America because he was not under suspicion. Revealing great fear he directed Bruneau to withdraw "totally" from circulation his article on the doctrine of the Fathers on the Eucharist. "This article", Pourrat said, "appeared without signature in The New York Review - it must not circulate any further". [93] He concluded the letter, asking Bruneau to pardon his fear, for if he were attacked, the matter would be very grave.

Pourrat sent a second letter to Bruneau the next day retracting what he wrote in the first one. [94] He said that there was not any reason to go to extremes in the present situation and that Bruneau could continue to sell his book. However,

---

[92]   Letter, Pourrat to Bruneau, March 17, 1910, ASMB. It is not certain what book Bruneau was selling. Pourrat did have at least one; viz., La Theologie Sacramentaire, translated into English, Theology of the Sacraments, St. Louis: Herder, 1910.

[93]   The article was "Real Presence in the Fathers" which appeared unsigned in The Review in two installments: cf. II, No. 3 (November-December, 1906, 362-375; and No. 4 (January-February, 1907), 495-513.

[94]   Letter, Pourrat to Bruneau, March 18, 1910, ASMB.

one thing Pourrat made clear was that Bruneau take from
circulation his article on the Eucharist and the Fathers - the
reason being, he said, "The New York Review, where it first
appeared."

Evidently, this correspondence reveals at least that the
repercussions of The Review's suppression extended for a few
years into the lives of people who were in a small way associated with it. It no doubt instilled fear in some people, like
Pourrat, and cast grave suspicion on others, like Bruneau.
But most important, this correspondence of Bruneau's does
corroborate the thesis that The New York Review was
suppressed by Rome because of modernistic tendencies.

V. Conclusion

From this consideration of the causes of The Review's
demise one may hold as tenable that a paucity of a reading
public was a factor which caused the editors to decide to
terminate publication. However, as has been demonstrated,
it was not the major factor which ended The Review. The
major factor now emerges to be the fact that Rome ordered it to
cease publication, having suspected it of modernism. This
was especially so because of The Review's involvement in the
Hanna case and because of the historico-theological context of
the day; i. e., the widespread suspicion and reckless suppression.
The Review obeyed Rome's order, from all indications faith-

fully, silently, dutifully, but, no doubt, reluctantly. The absence of this journal's scholarly and apologetical spirit from the American theological scene affected the Church in America for several decades.

However, The Review can make some contributions to the Church's understanding of herself today. The first, is that this investigation into The Review's history has dispelled the long-standing myth that Rome never condemned or suspected anyone of modernism in the United States. If any serious work is to be done in the area of American Catholic modernism, it will have to include, if not start, with the demise of The New York Review.

Secondly, since Pope Pius XII's encyclical, Divino Afflante Spiritu (1943) and Vatican Council II (1962-1965) resurrected The Review's spirit, if not vindicated it, theologians and reformers today can learn something from this journal's spirit. The painful repercussions that the American Church is experiencing following Vatican II which has poured new wine into old wine skins can be due precisely because there was no standing institution, like The New York Review, to attempt consistently and progressively a reconcilation between the findings of modern theology and the ancient Faith. In this apologetic attempt lies The New York Review's legacy to the Church. We will consider this claim in the next chapter.

CHAPTER VII

THE REVIEW'S CONCEPT OF REFORM
AND REFORM PRINCIPLES

The final consideration that remains regarding The New
York Review is to determine the significance that this journal
had for its times. We have seen that the historico-theological
context in which The Review published was one of rapid
theological and technological change. It was not without confusion. some theologians went to extremes in the conclusions
of their speculations, discarding a number of indefeasible
truths of Christianity. And, on the other hand, ecclesiastical
authority, in the attempt to check these heretical conclusions,
overreacted and inaugurated an era of integralism which
oppressed and discouraged any serious scholarly endeavors.

The Review's editors, we saw, chose a middle course
between these two extremes of some theologians and Church
authority. Very much open and involved in the scholarly
movements of the day, and yet at the same time believing that
the ancient Faith of the Church demanded respect, they aimed
in their magazine to reconcile faith and science. Their review was known as "A Journal of Ancient Faith and Modern
Knowledge".

This writer believes that the significance of The New York Review for its day lay precisely in this via media which attempted to do justice to both scholarship and tradition. How the editors effected this double responsibility and achieved their objective of reconciliation was by their concept of reform and the principles which followed from this concept. This concept of reform and its principles would have enabled The Review to achieve its objective of reconciling science with faith. Thus, this journal would have contributed theological balance to an era that was being torn apart by extreme theological speculation as well as by ecclesiastical authority's suppression of any speculation.

In this chapter let us re-examine some texts and editorial correspondence that we have already seen when The Review was in its planning stages. It is here that we can perhaps come to some idea of how the editors planned to pursue their objective. This manner of pursuit will disclose their idea or reform. Then, after enumerating more explicitly the principles of reform that followed from this concept of reform and were present in The Review's articles and editorials, we can then evaluate both concept and principles in view of the religious conditions of the day. In this way, we will arrive at the significance that The Review had for its day.

Concept of Reform

We can first catch a glimpse of how The Review's editors
conceived reform on the flyer that announced the journal's
emergence. In part, it read as follows:

> The purpose of The Review is mainly
> apologetic with special reference to
> present day religious and scientific
> conditions. It is intended to be as
> its sub-title indicates "A Jounal of
> the Ancient Faith and Modern Thought".
> In character and method it will be
> positive and constructive. [1]

This description of The Review's character and method
gives us an idea of how the editors thought of reform. In their
private correspondence they explicated what they meant by a
positive and constructive method. Their journal was not intended to be polemical but rather aimed to make a positive
contribution to theology. They said that the word "reconstructive" expressed more precisely what they meant by the word
"constructive". [2] Reconstruction would then have been the

---

[1]
  Cf. Announcement Sheet (Appendix).

[2]
  Letter, James F. Driscoll to Edward R. Dyer, January
11, 1905, ASMB. Driscoll wrote: ".... in tone [it] will be
positive and constructive (better 'reconstructive') rather than
controversial". Cf. also Letter, Francis P. Duffy to Edward
J. Hanna, January 8, 1905, ADR. Duffy said almost the same
thing as Driscoll: "Of course, the sort of apologetics we aim
at is not polemical but of that constructive (or 'reconstructive')
sort that you know is most necessary".

means to achieve The Review's objective of reconciling science with faith.

This writer believes that the word "reconstructive" sums up, for the most part, The New York editors' concept of reform. These editors addressed themselves to an epoch wherein theology and science were making monumental advances and discoveries. These advances and discoveries not only shook the foundation of time-honored beliefs but also exposed the inadequacy and impotence of many of the traditional forms and vehicles of these beliefs vis à vis the modern world. In order to transmit the ancient Faith to the world at that time these forms had to be reconstructed. New forms had to made or found that would allow the modern world to understand the ancient Faith in the light of new scientific discoveries.

The editors said as much in the same announcement sheet when they disclosed the intention of their review. They stated:

> The studies made in scientific and
> historical research during the past
> half century have forced upon us
> consideration of new problems and
> have rendered necessary the restate-
> ment of many theological positions.

The word "restatement" is another way of saying "re-construction". The traditional casing or forms of theological truths, according to this quote, no longer adequately expressed these truths because of the recent scientific and historical advances. It was not the theological position that had to undergo change but their expressions or statements had to be reformulated in order that the modern world could grasp these positions.

In the opinion of this writer this is what the editors of The Review considered, for the most part, reform to be: the reconstruction, reformulation or restatement of the vehicles or form that transmitted the theological truths. As their above-mentioned quote from the announcement sheet indicated, they believed in leaving untouched the substantial and indefeasible truths of the Faith. They maintained that only the forms should be and could be changed. [3]

This belief, therefore, dismissed on the part of The New York Review's editors any idea of revolution. They strongly disassociated themselves and their journal from the concept of revolution in theology and in the Church. Speaking for his journal Driscoll stated:

> In the first place, it is hardly
> necessary to say that there is not
> the least intention on the part of
> the founders and promoters of

---

[3]
The editor, Driscoll, and Francis Gigot, a close associate of The Review, underlined this point in their journal. Cf. James F. Driscoll, "Recent Views on Biblical Inspiration (I)", I, No. 1 (June-July, 1905), 82; "Recent Views on Biblical Inspiration (II)", I, No. 2 (August-September, 1905), 198; Francis E. Gigot, "The Higher Criticism of the Bible: Its Constructive Aspect", II, No. 3 (November-December, 1906), 303; and "The Higher Criticism of the Bible: Its Relation to Tradition", II, No. 4 (January-February, 1907), 442.

312

> The Review to inaugurate a movement
> that could in any sense be termed "a
> new Catholicism". To entertain such
> an idea would be absurd - there could
> be no surer means of defeating the
> real purpose we had in view. The
> purpose as implied in the sub-title:
> "A Journal of Ancient Faith and
> Modern Thought" is not to abandon
> the old in favor of the new but rather
> to interpret with becoming care and
> reverence the old truth in the lite of
> new science. The task as it appears
> to us is not one of involving doctrinal
> change but restatement and re-adjust-
> ment - in other words the preservation
> and not the rupture of continuity. [4]

Revolution implies a complete rupture with the past or a

total denial of the indefeasible, without which the original is

destroyed or discarded, and is replaced by a totally different

reality. In the case of theology, it would mean effecting change

to the point of creating an entirely new religion. But, by this

quote, Driscoll brought out very clearly his journal's respect

for what was indefeasible to Christianity - those truths without

which Christianity would not be Christianity. He also dismissed

the charge that The Review aimed at founding a new religion. All

it intended to do, he said, was to re-state the ancient Faith in

terms that would then have effectively transmitted the Faith to

the modern world. In so doing, The Review would meet the

religious exigencies of the world without incurring a break with

or total rejection of the past.

---

[4] Letter, Driscoll to the editor of The Boston Transcript, February 13, 1906, Copy, ASMB.

Reform conceived as reconstruction also dispels the idea that the editors of The New York Review were involved in the task of renewal. Although the editors only explicitly dis- associated themselves from the idea of revolution, renewal could not have been intended in their concept of reform. It would not bring them to their objective of reconciling science with faith. This is so because renewal, for one thing, means to restore something to its original state. The Review's editors' concept of reform as reconstruction would not have had admitted such a concept of renewal. Reconstruction goes beyond the level of dealing with the original form. It means to build another form that is deemed better, more relevant, or more effective in fulfilling its purpose of transmission.

The religious and scientific conditions of that day were so radically different from those of previous eras that the forms of theological truths warranted reconstruction, not renewal. Renewal would still have rendered the forms in- adequate. It would not have effect in them an appreciable change so that they could have carried out their function in a world which was radically different from the one in which they orig- inated. Revolution, on the other hand, would have caused the rejection of the indefeasible truths that these forms couched. Only reconstruction could have effectively brought The Review to its objective of reconciling science with faith.

And so, from The Review's announcement sheet and the editors' correspondence we can cull some statements that indicate how these editors viewed reform. They saw it as a reconstruction, a reformulation, or restatement of traditional forms of Christian truths because new knowledge rendered these forms antiquated and inadequate. To the editors, reconstruction meant building or finding new forms that would effectively transmit such Christian realities as the divinity of Christ, the Bible, miracles, faith, and the Church to a world that was fast departing from medievalism. [5]

Later on in The Review's articles we find some explicit statements that point to such a concept of reform. Driscoll in his article on "Recent Views on Biblical Inspiration" said that when a scholar's investigation into an area produced results contrary to the traditional opinion (regarding the form, not the substantial truth) then the scholar had to make the adjustment of the form. He said:

> Thoroughly alive to the need of an
> adjustment between these facts and
> certain traditional views they are
> earnestly seeking to establish the
> basis of a more uniform solution of
> biblical difficulties and principles
> in harmony alike with the data of

---

[5]
The New York Review specifically addressed itself to these Christian realities in the context of reconstruction as the titles of many of its articles indicate.

revelation and the scientific progress
in the age. [6]

Gigot said the same thing as Driscoll in one of his articles

on the higher criticism of the Bible. He stated:

> Much rather do they endeavor to
> determine the amount of truth con-
> tained therein and to modify the
> ancient opinions to the extent
> actually required by newly ascertained
> data. In their striving to restate the
> traditional view they [scholars] plainly
> aim at securing more correct positions
> in organic connection with biblical
> knowledge so that in all such cases
> their desire to do constructive work
> cannot be reasonably questioned. [7]

These quotes show that because of new scientific dis-

coveries changes had to be made in the forms so that there be

effected a harmony between science and faith. In their terms

of "adjustment", "modify", and "re-state" the editors expressed

the concept of reform as reconstruction. They manifested that

such a concept of reform was the means by which The Review

could have achieved its objective of reconciling science with

faith.

Throughout The Review's articles we saw this task of

reconstruction being carried out. Articles dealing with the

---

[6]
I, No. 1 (June-July, 1905), 82.

[7]
"The Higher Criticism of the Bible: Its Constructive
Aspect", II, No. 3 (November-December, 1906), 303.

higher criticism of the Bible participated in this task. [8] They

addressed themselves to the replacement of old views regarding

the literary form, authorship, dates, etc. of biblical books with

new ones. Likewise, involved in reconstruction were those

Review articles that presented a more modern way of con-

ceiving the Church, its membership, and its authority. [9] Those

articles that discussed the New Apologetics were also re-

constructive by testing the strengths of the "method of immanence"

8
    Some of these articles were written by Francis E. Gigot
under the same title, "The Higher Criticism of the Bible" and
appeared in The Review in Volume II: No. 1 (July-August, 1906),
66-69; No. 2 (September-October, 1906), 158-161; No. 3 (November-December, 1906), 302-305; No. 4 (January-February,
1907), 442-452; and No. 5 (March-April, 1907), 585-589.
Other articles by Gigot which exemplify this point are "The
Book of Jonas: Arguments For and Against Its Historical
Character", I, No. 4 (December, 1905-January, 1906),
411-424; "Leading Problems Concerning the Book of Job", I,
No. 5 (February-March, 1906), 579-596; "Abraham: A
Historical Study", II, No. 1 (July-August, 1906), 37-48.
Articles in The Review by other authors dealing with this
topic are Cornelius Clifford, "Holtzmann's Life of Christ",
I, No. 1 (June-July, 1905), 47-58; and Hugh Pope, "The Date
of the Exodus", II, No. 5 (March-April, 1907), 566-584.

9
    Some Review articles which fell under this category
were: David Barry, "A Plea for a More Comprehensive
Definition of the Church", II, No. 5 (March-April, 1907),
691-697; Albert Reynaud, "Collective and Individual Religion:
A Synthesis", I, No. 3 (October-November, 1905), 297-302;
Maude Petre, "A New Catholic Apology", II, No. 5 (March-
April, 1907), 602-609; Charles Plater, "The Social Value of
Contemplative Life" I, No. 5 (February-March, 1906), 570-
578; Pierre Batiffol, "Was Judaism a Church?", I, No. 6
(April-May, 1906), 687-700; _____, "Was Apostolic
Christianity a Church?", II, No. 3 (November-December,
1906), 306-321; William L. Sullivan, "Catholicity and Some
Elements in Our National Life", I, No. 3 (October-November,

made against Hanna.[28] Rome unjustifiably condemned The

New York Review which was an innocent victim of ecclesiastical

authority's overreaction to the theological speculation of the

day. This New York journal even with its balanced approach

to theology and reform could not escape the welter of

suppression at that time.

Some may raise the objection that The Review used

orthodox formulas and intended to convey unorthodox meanings

by them. Maisie Ward in her book Insurrection versus

Resurrection mentioned that the modernists did this at that

time.

> The difficulty was that while the
> Modernists were using language so
> nearly orthodox as to be a real
> danger, Catholic orthodoxy was
> easily suspected of a Modernistic
> leaning. There are so many words
> and phrases that mean quite different
> things according to the way they are
> employed, and when they have been
> read in an unorthodox context, suspicion
> is liable to hang about them in an
> utterly different context.[29]

However, throughout the Review's years of publication its

editors always intended that their journal be orthodox and

consistent with the teaching of the Roman Catholic Church.

---

[28]
   Cf. Chapter VI of this dissertation.

[29]
   Insurrection versus Resurrection, New York: Sheed and
Ward, 1937, 177.

Even though its editor, James Driscoll, was very friendly with
prominent modernists and at times expressed in his private
correspondence disagreement with Rome's reactions, not
its teachings, The Review always publicly acknowledged
respect for the Church's teaching. [30] This respect was the
result, as we saw of the journal's editorial policy and
approach to theology. In its pages The Review made numerous
references to obedience and loyalty to Church authority as
well as patience in those times of reform. [31] Also we saw
that the editorial correspondence in the initial stages of
The Review underlined this respect for orthodoxy. [32]

In the end, we can say that The New York Review was not
modernistic nor was it integrist. It was moderately progressive; i. e., open to the new but respectful of tradition.
In this lies The Review's significance for its day. This
theological journal attempted to bring to the then present
theological scene balance, patience, loyalty, a love for the

---

[30]
    Cf. Chapter V of this dissertation.

[31]
    I, No. 4 (December, 1905-January, 1906), 511; I, No. 6
(April-May, 1906), 798-800; II, No. 2 (September-October,
1906), 245; II, No. 4 (January-February, 1907), 495,498, 519,
520, 524; II, No. 5 (March-April, 1907), 645, 646; II, No. 6
(May-June, 1907), 784; III, No. 1 (July-August, 1907), 75, 76;
and III, No. 3 (November-December, 1907), 359.

[32]
    Cf. Chapter II of this dissertation.

new, and a respect for tradition by means of its editorial policy, approach to theology, ecclesiological vision, and its concept and principles of reform. Although these means which The New York Review employed are not new for us today, sixty-five years later, they were advanced for their day and hailed as a contribution to theological endeavors. [33] The significance that The New York Review can have for our times lies in its short-lived history. This history can teach us the need for balance, openness and guidance in our theological speculation and reforms. It can warn us of the dangerous effects that can result from misinformation on the part of authority and the irreparable damage that can ensue because of authority's overreaction to unorthodox speculation. But most important, The Review's history can teach us the value of always having such institutions as theological journals or groups of scholars in the Church to insure the continual reconciliation between science and faith and the continual reform of the Church. Only then will the Church effectively proclaim the Gospel to contemporary man.

------

[33] "Editorial", The Catholic Weekly, November 15, 1905, p. 8.

APPENDIX A

Notice

The New York Review: A
Journal of the Ancient Faith and
Modern Thought

Arrangements have been made to issue in the beginning

of June next, the first number of a periodical to be called

The New York Review.

The new publication has the approval of His Grace,

Archbishop Farley of New York. It will be issued every

two months and will be edited by the professors of the

diocesan seminary at Yonkers.

The Purpose of the Review

is mainly apologetic, with specific reference to present day

religious and scientific conditions. It is intended to be, as

its sub-title indicates "A Journal of the Ancient Faith and

Modern Thought". In character and method it will be

positive and constructive.

The objects in view in founding it are:

(1) To treat in a scholarly fashion, yet in a manner intelligible to the ordinary cultured mind, topics of interest bearing on Theology, Scripture, Philosophy, and the cognate Sciences.

(2) To draw attention to the reader of the present intellectual situation on matters of religious belief.

(3) To secure the united efforts of the most eminent Catholic Scholars, lay and clerical, throughout the world, for the discussion and solution of problems and difficulties connected with Religion.

(4) To treat by means of shorter studies, minor topics in Sacred Scripture and Archeology, etc.

(5) To keep the readers informed on the most recent developments of religious questions, by careful reviews or summaries of important books and publications.

The present need of such a publication in English will doubtless be readily granted by all thoughtful and well in- formed persons. The studies made by scientific and historical research during the past half century have forced upon us consideration of new problems and have rendered necessary the restatement of many theological positions.

The new issues thus raised cannot without every in- creasing harm continue to be ignored by Catholics as has too generally been the case in the past. They are currently discussed in reviews and newspapers by writers of every shade of religious opinions and only too often the solution proposed is irreconcilable with any sane interpretation of historic Christianity.

It is true that many Catholic scholars, especially in Europe are doing excellent work along the lines above indicated. But as their productions are, for the most part scattered through various reviews many of which are not available for the average English speaking public, there will be a manifest advantage in bringing together in one special periodical the combined results of their scientific labors.

Contributors

The efforts made by the editors to secure the cooperation of there able Catholic Writers have met with very gratifying success.

Below is given a partial list of those contributors who are expected to furnish articles in the coming year:

Wilfrid Ward	Gordan Zahm	Anthony Maas
George Tyrrell, S. J.	Thomas Shanahan	Edward Hanna
Freidrick Von Hugel	Edward Pace	Walter McDonald
M. J. Langrange	James Fox	Joseph McSorley
Ernesto Buonaiuti	Francis Gigot	John Driscoll
Giovanni Ginnochi	Henry Poels	Gabriel Oussani

To Catholics and non-Catholics subscriptions went out.

Annual subscription is $3.00

Checks made payable to John F. Brady, managing editor.

James F. Driscoll, D. D. , editor
Francis P. Duffy, associate editor
John F. Brady, managing editor

Dunwoodie Press.

APPEXDIX B

Notice

With this issue, which concludes Vol. III, THE NEW YORK REVIEW ceases publication.

At its inception three years ago its editors promised to present the best work of Catholic scholars at home and abroad on theological and other problems of the present day. It is the keeping of that promise, not the breaking of it, that is the cause of the suspension of the REVIEW. For the number of Catholics interested in questions which are of importance to the thinkers of the present generation - and which will be vital to all classes in the next - has been found to be so small that it does not justify the continuance of the REVIEW. It would be possible perhaps to treat the same topics in a more popular style, but the editors are strongly of opinion that new and difficult problems should be discussed in a way that will attract the attention of only trained and scholarly minds. Or the scope of the REVIEW might be changed, but this would bring it into needless competition with other Catholic periodicals which are doing excellent work in their chosen departments.

A newspaper report which has obtained wide circulation renders it necessary in justice to our ecclesiastical superiors and to ourselves to make a further statement. Neither THE

NEW YORK REVIEW nor any issues of it, nor any article

published in it has ever been made the object of official con-

demnation or censure by any authority, local or general, in

the Catholic Church. It is now suspending publication, not

by command of authority, but by the decision of its editors

and for the reasons set down.

It only remains to return sincere thanks to the sub-

scribers who have given their loyal support to the enterprise;

and especially to the contributors, who have given of their

best so generously with little or no recompense save

the consciousness of doing their duty in the course of religion

and learning.

BIBLIOGRAPHY

PART ONE: ARCHIVES AND MANUSCRIPT COLLECTIONS

Archives of the Archiocese of Boston

Archives of the Archdiocese of New York

Archives of the Archdiocese of Philadelphia

Archives of the Archdiocese of Westminster, England

Archives of the Baltimore Cathedral

Archives of Catholic University of America

Archives of the Company of St. Sulpice, Paris

Archives of the Congregation of the Propaganda of the Faith, Rome

Archives of the Congregation of St. Paul (Paulists), New York, N. Y.

Archives of the Diocese of Birmingham, England

Archives of the Diocese of Rochester, New York

Archives of the English Province of Society of Jesus

Archives of Harvard Divinity School

Archives of St. Mary's Seminary, Baltimore

Archives of Union Theological Seminary, New York

Bibliothèque Nationale, Paris (Loisy Papers)

Bremond Papers, Paris

British Museum

Keogh Family Papers, New Rochelle, N. Y. (Driscoll Papers)

Wilfrid Ward Family Papers, London, England

PART TWO: PRINTED PRIMARY SOURCES

Dyer, Edward T. Letters on the New York Seminary
    Secession. Baltimore: Private Circulation, 1906.

The New York Review, Yonkers, New York, vols., I, II, III,
    1905-1908.

PART THREE: SELECTED WORKS

Acta Sanctae Sedis, vols. XVI-XXVII, 1883-1895, Romae:
    Typis Polyslottae Officinae S. C. de Propaganda Fide.

American Catholic Who's Who. St. Louis: B. Herder, 1911.

Aubert, Roger. "Modernism". Sacramentum Mundi vol. IV,
    New York: Herder and Herder, 1968, pp. 99-104.

Boston Transcript, The. Boston. January-February, 1906.

Catholic Directory, The. New York: Benziger Brothers: 1896-
    1940.

Catholic Encyclopedia and Its Makers, The. New York:
    Encyclopedia Press, 1917.

Catholic News, The. New York. 1900-1910.

Catholic World, The. New York. vols. , LXXX-LXXXV,
    1904-1909.

Catholic Weekly, The. London. 1907.

Cooley, Charles H. Human Nature and The Social Order.
    New York: Charles Scribners and Sons, 1902.

Congar, Yves. l'Eglise de Saint Augustin à l epoch moderne.
    Paris: Les Editions du cerf, 1970.

Documents of American Catholic History. vol. II. ed. by John
    Tracy Ellis. Chicago: Regnery Co. , 1961.

Dolphin, The. Philadelphia. vols. VIII-IX, 1905-1906.

Ecclesiastical Review, The. Philadelphia. vols. III-VI, 1905-1908.

Gannon, Michael V. "Before and After Modernism: The Intellectual Isolation of the American Priest". The Catholic Priest in the United States. ed. by John Tracy Ellis. Collegeville: St. John's University Press, 1971.

Golden Jubilee Bulletin of Church of Our Saviour, Bronx, New York, 1962.

Heaney, John. "Modernism". The New Catholic Encyclopedia. vol. XII.

_____. The Modernist Crisis: von Hügel. Washington: Corpus Books, 1968.

_____. "Modernism". Corpus Dictionary of the Western Churches. ed. by T. C. O'Brien. Washington: Corpus Publications, 1970. pp. 504-506.

Ireland, John. The Church and Modern Society. New York: D. H. McBride and Co., 1896.

Irenaeus. Sancti Irenaci Libros quinque Adversus Haereses, ed. by W. Wigan Harvey, Cambridge: 1857.

le Guillou, Marie-Joseph. "Church" Sacramentum Mundi, vol. I. New York: Herder and Herder, 1968, pp. 313-327.

Levie, Albert. Word of God in the Words of Men. London: Geoffrey Chapman, 1961.

Loisy, Alfred Firmin. Autour d'un petit Liore. Paris: Picard et Fils, 1903.

_____. The Gospel and the Church. Translated by Christopher Home. London: Charles Scribner and Sons, 1904.

Maas, Anthony J. "The New Apologetics". The Messenger. XLV, (January, 1904). pp. 20-26.

McAvoy, Thomas. The Americanist Heresy in Roman Catholicism. Collegeville: St. John's University Press, 1971.

McNamara, Robert F. "Archbishop Hanna, Rochesterian". Rochester History, XXV, April, 1963. pp. 1-24.

New York Herald, The. New York: 1900-1912.

New York Sun, The. New York: 1900-1912.

New York Times, The. New York: 1900-1912.

New York Tribune, The. New York: 1900-1912.

Noble, David W. The Progressive Mind. Chicago: Rand McNally and Company, 1970.

Petre, Maude. The Autobiography and Life of George Tyrrell. London: Edward Arnold, 1912.

Ranchetti, Michael. The Catholic Modernists. Translated by Isabel Quigly. London: Oxford University Press, 1969.

Reardon, B. M. C. Roman Catholic Modernism. Stanford: University Press. 1970.

Rivière, Jean. Le Modernism dans l'Eglise. Paris: Librairie Letouzey et Ave, 1929.

Rochester Democrat and Chronicle, The. Rochester, New York, 1908.

Rochester Herald, The. Rochester, New York, 1908.

Rochester Union, The. Rochester, New York, 1908.

Scanell, T. B. The Priests' Studies. London: Longmans, Green, and Company, 1908.

Scanlon, Arthur J. St. Joseph's Seminary, Dunwoodie, N. Y. 1896-1921. The United States Catholic Historical Society, Monograph Series, 1922, vol. VII.

Sexton, John E. and Riley, Arthur J. History of St. John's Seminary, Brighton. Boston: Roman Catholic Archdiocese of Boston, 1945.

Sharp, John K. Priests and Parishes of the Diocese of Brooklyn: 1820-1972. Revised edition by Herbert P. Redmond. Brooklyn: private circulation, 1973.

Slattery, John. "The Workings of Modernism". The American Journal of Theology. XIII, October, 1909, pp. 569-578.

Sullivan, William L. Under Orders: The Autobiography of William Laurence Sullivan. Boston: Beacon Press, 1944.

Tyrrell, George. Oil and Wine. London: Sydney C. Mayle, 1906.

_____. A Much Abused Letter. London: Longmans, Green, and Company, 1906.

_____. Through Scylla and Charybdis. London: Longmans, Green, and Company, 1907.

_____. Christianity at the Crossroads. London: Longmans, Greene, and Company, 1909.

Vidler, Alec. The Modernist Movement in the Roman Church. Cambridge: University Press, 1934.

_____. The Church in the Age of Revolution. Baltimore: Penguin Books, 1961.

_____. Twentieth Century Defenders of the Faith. London: SCM Press, 1965.

_____. A Variety of Catholic Modernists. Cambridge: University Press, 1970.

Ward, Maisie. Insurrection versus Resurrection. London: Sheed and Ward, 1938.

Weigel, Gustave, "Americanism". Sacramentum Mundi, vol. I, New York: Herder and Herder, 1968. pp. 19-20.

UNITED STATES CATHOLIC HISTORICAL SOCIETY

MONOGRAPH SERIES
XXXIV

THE NEW YORK REVIEW
(1905-1908)

by

The Reverend Michael J. DeVito, Ph.D.

INDEX

NEW YORK
UNITED STATES CATHOLIC
HISTORICAL SOCIETY
1977

VITA

Reverend Michael J. DeVito is a priest of the Diocese of Brooklyn and associate professor of theology at Cathedral College-Seminary, Douglaston, New York.

Born and raised in New York, Father DeVito attended Cathedral College, Immaculate Conception Seminary, Huntington, N.Y., and the University of Louvain, Belgium where he was ordained a priest in 1966 and granted a Master of Arts degree in theology. He also holds a Master of Science degree in education from Saint John's University, N.Y. and a doctorate in theology from Fordham University. He is a member of the American Academy of Religion and the College-Theology Society.